JAMES RUSSELL LOWELL

A BIOGRAPHY

BY

HORACE ELISHA SCUDDER

IN TWO VOLUMES

VOL. I

J M Lowell

Mr. Lowell in 1889

JAMES RUSSELL LOWELL

A Biography

BY

HORACE ELISHA SCUDDER

IN TWO VOLUMES

VOL. I.

BOSTON AND NEW YORK
HOUGHTON, MIFFLIN AND COMPANY
The Riverside Press, Cambridge
1901

GREENVILLE COLLEGE
LIBRARY
GREENVILLE, ILLINOIS

COPYRIGHT, 1901, BY HORACE E. SCUDDER

ALL RIGHTS RESERVED

PUBLISHED NOVEMBER, 1901

GREENVILLE COLLEGE
LIBRARY
GREENVILLE, ILLINOIS

TO

G · O · S ·

"NAUGHT CAN BE UNWORTHY, DONE FOR YOU."

18256

PREFACE

THE existence of the two volumes of *Letters of James Russell Lowell, edited by Charles Eliot Norton,* has determined the character of this biography. If they had not been published, I might have made a *Life and Letters* which would have been in the main Lowell's own account of himself, in his voluminous correspondence, annotated only by such further account of him as his letters failed to supply. As it is, though I have had access to a great many letters not contained in Mr. Norton's work, I have thought it desirable not so much to supplement the *Letters* with other letters, as to complement those volumes with a more formal biography, using such letters or portions of letters as I print for illustration of my subject, rather than as the basis of the narrative.

I have kept the *Letters* always by my side as my main book of reference; by the courtesy of their editor and by arrangement with their publishers, Messrs. Harper & Brothers, I have now and then drawn upon them where it seemed especially desirable that Lowell should speak for himself, but their greatest use to me has been in their disclosure of Lowell's personality, for they undoubtedly contain the cream of his correspondence. I have, however, had other important material for my use. First of all, Lowell's collected writings in verse and prose, and some uncollected writings, both in print and manuscript. After all that a biographer can do, after all that Lowell himself can do through his letters, the substantial and enduring revelation of the man is in that free converse which he had with the world in the many forms which his literary activity took.

After this I must again thank Mr. Norton for his generosity in placing in my hands a large body of letters and papers, which he holds as Lowell's literary executor; perhaps even more for the wise counsel with which he has freely aided me in the course of the work. Without his coöperation the biography could not have been written in its fulness.

My thanks are due, also, to the friends and the children of the friends of Lowell who have sent me letters and other material; to Miss Charlotte P. Briggs, daughter of the late Charles F. Briggs, the warm friend of Lowell in his early literary life; to Mrs. Sydney Howard Gay, who sent me not only letters, but the original manuscript of

Lowell's contributions to the *National Anti-Slavery Standard ;* to Mrs. Richard Grant White; to Dr. Edward Everett Hale, whose *James Russell Lowell and his Friends* has been a pleasant accompaniment to my labors; to General James Lowell Carter for the use of his father's letters; to Col. T. W. Higginson ; to Mrs. S. B. Herrick; to Mrs. Mark H. Liddell for Lowell's letters to Mr. John W. Field ; to Mr. R. R. Bowker; to Mr. R. W. Gilder ; to Mr. Edwin L. Godkin ; to Mr. Howells, Mr. Aldrich, Mr. De Witt Miller, Mr. J. Spenser Trask, and others.

CAMBRIDGE, MASS., 27 September, 1901.

CONTENTS

LIST OF ILLUSTRATIONS

JAMES RUSSELL LOWELL

CHAPTER I

ELMWOOD AND THE LOWELLS

JAMES RUSSELL LOWELL was born at Elmwood
in Cambridge, New England, Monday, 22 February, 1819. When he was about to leave England
at the close of his term as American minister, he
was begged by a friend to make Washington his
home, for there he would find the world in which
lately he had been living; but he answered: " I
have but one home in America, and that is the
house where I was born, and where, if it shall
please God, I hope to die. I should n't be happy
anywhere else; " and at Elmwood he died, Wednesday, 12 August, 1891.

The place was endeared to him by a thousand
memories, and he liked it none the less for the historic associations, which lent it a flavor whimsically
suggestive to him of his own lurking sympathy.
" It will make a frightful Conservative of you before you know it," he wrote in 1873 to Mr. Aldrich,
then living at Elmwood; " it was born a Tory and
will die so. Don't get too used to it. I often wish
I had not grown into it so."

The house was one of a succession of spacious

dwellings set in broad fields, bordering on the
Charles River, built in the eighteenth century, and
occupied for the most part, before the War for Independence, by loyal merchants and officers of the
Crown. They were generous country places, pleasantly remote from Boston, which was then reached
only by a long détour through Brookline and Rox-
bury, and the owners of these estates left them, one
by one, as they were forced out by the revolt of
the province : but the name of Tory Row lingered
about the group, and there had been no great
change in the outward appearance of the neighborhood when Lowell was born in one of these old
houses.

From the colleges, past the unenclosed common,
a road ran in the direction of Watertown. It
skirted the graveyard, next to which was Christ
Church, the ecclesiastical home of the occupants
of Tory Row, and shortly turned again by an
elm already old when Washington took command,
under its shade, of the first American army.
Along the line of what is now known as Mason
Street, it passed into the thoroughfare upon which
were strung the houses of Tory Row; a lane entered it at this point, down which one could have
walked to the house of the vacillating Thomas
Brattle, occupied during the siege of Boston by
Quartermaster-General Mifflin ; the main road, now
known as Brattle Street, but in Lowell's youth still
called the Old Road, keeping on toward Watertown, passed between the estates of the two Vas-
salls, Henry and John, Colonel John Vassall's

house becoming in the siege of Boston the head-quarters of Washington, and wreathing its sword later in the myrtle boughs of Longfellow. Then, at what is now the corner of Brattle and Sparks streets, stood the Lechmere house, afterward Jonathan Sewall's, and occupied for a while by the Baron Riedesel, when he was a prisoner of war after the defeat of Burgoyne, in whose army he commanded the Hessian forces.

The Baroness Riedesel, in her lively letters, re-hearses the situation as it existed just before she and her husband were quartered in Cambridge: " Seven families, who were connected with each other, partly by the ties of relationship and partly by affection, had here farms, gardens, and magnifi-cent houses, and not far off plantations of fruit. The owners of these were in the habit of daily meeting each other in the afternoon, now at the house of one, and now at another, and making themselves merry with music and the dance — liv-ing in prosperity, united and happy, until, alas ! this ruinous war severed them, and left all their houses desolate, except two, the proprietors of which were also soon obliged to flee." Beyond the Lechmere-Sewall estate was that of Judge Joseph Lee, where in Lowell's middle day lived his friend and " corrector of the press " George Nichols, and then, just before the road made another bend, came the Fayerweather house, occupied in Lowell's youth by William Wells, the schoolmaster. Here the road turned to the south, and passed the last of the Row, known in later years as Elmwood.

The house, square in form, was built in 1767 on the simple model which translated the English brick manor house of the Georgian period into the terms of New England wood; it was well proportioned, roomy, with a hall dividing it midway; and such features as abundant use of wood in the interior finish, and quaintly twisted banisters to its staircase, preserve the style of the best of domestic colonial buildings. Heavy oaken beams give the structure solidity and the spaces between them in the four outer walls are filled in with brick, while great chimneys are the poles which fasten to the earth the tent which seems likely still to shelter many generations.

The house was built for Thomas Oliver, the son of a West India merchant, and a man of fortune, who came from the town of Dorchester, not far off, to live in Cambridge, probably because of his marriage to a daughter of Colonel John Vassall. He was lieutenant-governor of the Province, and had been appointed by George III. President of the Council, a position which rendered him especially obnoxious to the freemen of Massachusetts. In that contention for strict construction of the charter, which was one of the marks of the allegiance to law characteristic of the king's American subjects, it was held that councillors were to be elected, not appointed. On the morning of 2 September, 1774, a large number of the freeholders of Middlesex County assembled at Cambridge and surrounded Oliver's house. He had previously conferred with these zealous people and represented that as his office of president was really the result of his being lieutenant-governor he would incur his Majesty's displeasure if he resigned the one office and retained the other. The explanation seemed satisfactory for a while, but on the appearance of some signs of activity among his Majesty's soldiers, the committee in charge renewed their demands, and drew up a paper containing a resignation of his office as president, which they called on the lieutenant-governor to sign. He did so, adding the significant clause: "my house at Cambridge being surrounded by about four thousand people, in compliance with their command I sign my name."

Oliver left Cambridge immediately, never to return. He succeeded to the civil government of Boston, and Sir William Howe to the military command, when Governor Gage returned to England, but when Boston was evacuated Oliver retired with the British forces. The estate, with others in the neighborhood, was seized for public use. When the American army was posted in Cambridge it was used as a hospital for soldiers. Afterwards it was leased by the Committee of Correspondence. A credit of £69 for rent was recorded in 1776. Subsequently the estate was confiscated and sold by the Commonwealth, the land contained in it then consisting of ninety-six acres. The purchaser was Arthur Cabot, of Salem, who later sold it to Elbridge Gerry, Governor of Massachusetts from 1810 to 1812, and Vice-President of the United States under Madison, from 4 March,

1813, until his sudden death, 23 November, 1814, a man personally liked, but politically detested by his neighbors. In 1818 the estate, or rather the homestead and some ten acres of land, was sold by Gerry's heirs to the Rev. Charles Lowell, minister of the West Church in Boston, who now made it his home, establishing himself there with his wife and five children. In the next year his youngest child, James Russell Lowell, was born in this house of many memories.

The Rev. Charles Lowell was the seventh in descent from Percival Lowell, or Lowle, as the name sometimes was written, a well-to-do merchant of Bristol, who, with children and grandchildren, a goodly company, came from England in 1639, and settled in Newbury, Mass.[1] Charles Lowell's father, the Hon. John Lowell, had led a distinguished career as a lawyer and publicist; and as a member of the corporation of Harvard College, and of learned societies having their headquarters in Boston, had been a conspicuous figure in the community. One of his sons, Francis Cabot Lowell, was the organizer of the industries on the banks of the Merrimac which resulted in the building of the city of Lowell. A son of Francis Cabot Lowell was the originator of the Lowell Institute, a centre of diffusing light in Boston. Charles Lowell himself, springing from a stock which, by inheritance and accumulation of intellectual forces, was a leading family in the compact community of Boston, was endowed with a singu-

[1] See Appendix A, The Lowell Ancestry.

larly pure and gracious spirit, and enjoyed an
unusual training for the life of rich service he was
to lead.

Graduated at Harvard in 1800, his bent was
toward the ministry; but yielding to the wishes of
his father, he entered the law office of his elder
brother, and spent a year or more in the study of
the profession of law. His inclination, however,
was not changed, and his father withdrew his opposition and consented to a plan by which the
young man was to pursue his theological studies
in Edinburgh. He had three years of study and
travel abroad. He was a pupil of Sir David Brewster and of Dugald Stewart, and kept up a friendly
acquaintance for many years with Stewart's later
colleague, Dr. Brown. He met Wilberforce, heard
Pitt, Fox, and Sheridan in the House of Com-
mons, and, as his letters show, made eager incursions into the world of art.

He carried through all his experience a nature
of great simplicity and of unquestioning faith. His
son once wrote of him : " Nothing could shake my
beloved and honored father's trust in God and his
sincere piety ; " and his work as pastor of the
West Church in Boston, to which he was called
shortly after his return to America, was characterized by a single-minded devotion which made him,
in the truest sense, a minister. All who have
recorded their recollections of him agree in their
impression of great distinction of manner and a
singularly musical voice. He had a way, it was
said, of uttering very familiar sentences, such as a

quotation from the Bible, with singular effectiveness, — a manner which was peculiarly his own.
After infirmities of sight and hearing had made
his appearance in the pulpit rare, he would still,
now and then, take part in the service by reciting
in his melodious voice one or more of the hymns
— he knew by heart all in the book. Emerson
said of him that he was the most eloquent extem-
poraneous speaker he had ever heard. He had
the natural gift of speech, but until one read by
himself some sermon to which he had listened
with delight, he would scarcely be aware that the
spell lay in the pure tones of the voice that uttered
it.[1]

Above all, he was the parson, making his powers
tell less in preaching than in the incessant care
and cure of souls. In Edinburgh he had studied
medicine as well as theology, and, as his church
stood on the border of a district which was forlorn
and unwholesome, Dr. Lowell was constantly ex-
tending the jurisdiction of his parochial authority,
carrying the gospel in one hand and bread and
pills in the other. He knew every child in his

[1] In 1853 Dr. Lowell contemplated the publication of a volume
of sermons, and his then associate, Dr. Bartol, wrote privately to
the son, discouraging the venture. He had not the heart openly
to oppose Dr. Lowell. " I know," he writes, " I can trust you to
understand me fully when I say it is my persuasion and that of
true and strong friends of your father in the parish, that a volume
could never overtake his actual reputation, that what is best in
him, his voice, his look, his manner, *himself*, cannot be printed,
and that his peculiar glory is one that should scarcely be touched
with ink." There did appear, however, in 1855 a volume by Dr.
Lowell, entitled *Sermons ; chiefly Occasional.*

parish, and if, as he said, his ministry was an unclouded one, it was because he was too busy with the needs of others ever to perplex himself greatly over his own cares. Indeed, it was the unremitting performance of his pastoral duties which impaired his health and led to the necessity of his removal from the city to the outskirts of the country village of Cambridge, four miles away, though doubtless he was largely influenced also by the needs of the growing family that surrounded him.

Dr. Lowell had seen something of the great world abroad, and he stood in an amiable relation to that self-centred, comfortable world of New England which held to the established order, even though there had begun within it already the agitation which was to shake the nation. Like many thus poised, he hated slavery in the abstract, but shrank back when it became a question of meddling with it: the instinct for the preservation of an established order was strong. The "abolitionism" which he saw rising was to him "harsh, dogmatic, uncharitable, unchristian," and it disturbed his gentle, orderly nature. From the sheltered nook of Elmwood, he looked out on a restless, questioning world, but his own part seemed to be marked out for him. He had his parish, with a thousand petty disorders to rectify; he had his books, which he loved and read; he drove to town in his chaise to attend the meetings of the Historical Society, of which he was long secretary, and he watched the chickens and growing things in his green domain of Elmwood. The tall pines which murmur about the old house were planted by him. He brought to the solution of the new problems which were vexing men the calm religious philosophy which had solved any doubts he may have had, and if his equanimity was disturbed he righted himself always with a cheerful optimistic piety. One of his parish who had grown to womanhood under his eye, and had married, made up her mind to take a stand in some reform as a public speaker, and from his chamber at Elmwood — for this was late in his life, when he was in retirement — he sent for her to come to him.

"I shall never forget his greeting," she wrote long after. "As I opened the chamber door he rose from the old easy-chair, and standing erect, cried out: 'Child! my child! what is this I hear? Why are you talking to the whole world?' He was clothed in a long white flannel dressing-gown, with a short shoulder cape hardly reaching to his belt. His was no longer the piercing expression, aggressive to a degree, that Harding has portrayed. The curling locks that gave individuality to his forehead had been cut away, the gentle influence of a submissive spirit had impressed itself upon his features. In a moment I was seated at his feet, and then came a long and intimate talk of why and when and wherefore, which ended in a short prayer with his hand upon my head, and the words, 'Now promise me that you will never enter the desk without first seeking God's blessing!' I answered only by a look." [1]

[1] *Alongside*, by Mrs. Caroline H. Dall. Privately printed.

Rev. Charles Lowell

This Dr. Primrose, as his son once affectionately called him, had for a companion one who was the farthest possibly removed from the fussy, ambitious wife of the Vicar of Wakefield. When he once made a journey to Europe with Mrs. Lowell and their eldest daughter, the little party took especial delight in a trip to the Orkney Islands, and in the enjoyment of friendly intercourse with the Traills from that region; for it was but a step that Mrs. Lowell needed to take to bring her into close kinship with the Orkney folk. Her grandfather, Robert Traill, whose name, together with her own name of Spence, she gave to one of her boys, had come from Orkney to America, had married there, and left a daughter, Mrs. Lowell's mother,[1] when he went back to Great Britain at the revolt of the colonies. Thus, when Robert Traill's granddaughter visited Orkney, she was returning to her own kin. Not only so, but her father, Keith Spence, came of Highland ancestry, and it was easy to find a forbear in the Sir Patrick Spens of the old ballad, as it was also to claim kinship with Minna Troil, whom the Wizard of the North had lifted out of the shadowy forms of life into the enduring reality of "The Pirate."

This close affiliation with the North disclosed itself in Mrs. Lowell in a rare beauty of person

---

[1] " My grandmother," Lowell once said, "was a loyalist to her death, and whenever Independence Day came round, instead of joining in the general rejoicing, she would dress in deep black, fast all day, and loudly lament ' our late unhappy differences with his most gracious Majesty.' "

and temperament, together with a suggestion of
that occult power which haunts the people of the
Orkney Isles. Whether or no Mrs. Lowell had, as
was sometimes said, the faculty of second sight,
she certainly had that love of ballads and delight
in singing and reciting them which imparts a wild
flower fragrance to the mind; [1] and her romantic
nature may easily be reckoned as the brooding
place of fancies which lived again in the poetic
genius of her son. She had been bred in the Episcopal Church, and that may possibly have had its
influence in the determination of her son Robert's
vocation, but in marrying Dr. Lowell she must
have found much common ground with one who
always resolutely refused to be identified with a
sect almost local in its bounds. " I have adopted,"
he wrote in 1855, "no other religious creed than
the Bible, and no other name than Christian as
denoting my religious faith." The few letters from
Mrs. Lowell's pen which remain contain messages
of endearment that flutter about the head of her
" Babie Jammie," as she called him, and betray
a tremulous nature, anxious with pride and fond
perplexity.

The companionship of the elder Lowells began
in a happy manner in their childhood. The grandfather of Charles Lowell was the Rev. John Lowell,
of Newburyport, who was twice married. His

[1] In a review of the *Book of British Ballads* in *The Pioneer*,
Lowell says: " And the dear 'Annie of Lochroyan,' too, made
thrice dear to us by the often hearing it from lips that gave an
original beauty of their own to whatever they recited."

widow continued to make her home in Newburyport after her husband's death, but when her husband's son, John Lowell, the lawyer and jurist,
left the place and established himself in Boston,
she also left the town and went to live in Portsmouth near her niece, Mrs. Brackett. Mrs. Lowell
had been John Lowell's mother since his boyhood, and after the manner so common in New
England households the titular grandmother ruled
serenely without being subjected to nice distinctions. Charles Lowell, thus, when a boy, was a
frequent visitor at his grandmother's Portsmouth
home, and his playmate was his grandmother's
great-niece, Harriet Brackett Spence. The intimacy deepened and before Charles Lowell sailed
for Europe a betrothal had taken place.

There were three sons and two daughters when
James Russell,[1] the youngest in this family, was
born. Charles was between eleven and twelve,
Rebecca ten, Mary a little over eight, William between five and six, and Robert [2] between two and

[1] He was named after his father's maternal grandfather, Judge
James Russell, of Charlestown.

[2] Robert Traill Spence Lowell was graduated at Harvard College in 1833. He became an Episcopal clergyman in 1842, went
shortly after as a missionary to Newfoundland, had a parish later
in New Jersey, then took the headmastership of S. Mark's School,
Southborough, Mass., and finally was called to the chair of Latin
language and literature in Union College. He remained in Schenectady till his death, 12 September, 1891, just a month after the
death of his younger brother. He had a distinct literary gift, and
published several books, which were the outcome of his life in its
varied scenes. *The New Priest in Conception Bay* has vivid pictures of Newfoundland, and contains one character, Elnathan

three. All these lived to maturity, excepting William, who died when James was four years old. Charles by his seniority was the mentor and guide of his younger brother during his adolescence, especially when their father was absent, as he was once for a journey in Europe, but Mary [1] was the sister to whom he was especially committed in his childhood. She was his little nurse, and as her own love of poetry came early, she was wont to read him to sleep, when he took his daily nap, from Spenser,[2] and she used to relate in after years how

Bangs, who is as racy a Yankee in his own way as Hosea Biglow himself. The book unfortunately was published by Phillips & Sampson just as Mr. Phillips died and the firm went into bankruptcy, and lost thus the advantage of a good start. It was revived a good many years later, but never enjoyed the vogue it might have had. Mr. Lowell's experiences at S. Mark's lay behind a story for schoolboys, *Antony Brade*, and his life in Schenectady suggested *A Story or Two from an Old Dutch Town*. He published also *Fresh Hearts that Failed Three Thousand Years Ago, and Other Poems*, a book which his brother had the pleasure of reviewing in the *Atlantic*. His best known poem, " The Relief of Lucknow," appeared also in the *Atlantic*, under his brother's editorship.

[1] Mary Traill Spence Lowell was born 3 December, 1810, was married to Samuel Raymond Putnam, 25 April, 1832, and died in Boston, 1 June, 1898. She was a woman of intellectual power and literary accomplishment. She chose to write anonymously, but the books she wrote, *Records of an Obscure Man*, *The Tragedy of Errors*, *Fifteen Days*, and *The Tragedy of Success*, though remote from the current of popular taste in her day, not only disclose a most thoughtful nature, and one profoundly interested in great subjects of racial and philosophical moment, but not infrequently are exceedingly felicitous in expression.

[2] In a lecture on Spenser, given in 1856, Lowell said, " *The Faery Queene* was the first poem I ever read, and I had no suspicion of any double meaning in it."

hard the little boy found it to go to sleep under
the charm of the stories, yet how firmly nature
closed his eyes at last.

His own recorded recollections of childhood are
not many, yet as far back as he could remember
he was visited by visions night and day. An oft-
recurring dream was of having the earth put into
his hand like an orange. Dr. Weir Mitchell notes
that Lowell told him he had since boyhood been
subject to visions, which appeared usually in the
evening. Commonly he saw a figure in mediæval
costume which kept on one side of him, — perhaps
an outcome of his early familiarity with Spenser
and Shakespeare. Most of all in his memories of
childhood he recalled vividly the contact with nature in the enchanted realm of Elmwood, and the
free country into which it passed easily. With
the eye of a hawk he spied all the movements in
that wide domain, and brooded over the lightest
stir with an unconscious delight which was the
presage of the poet in him. " The balancing of a
yellow butterfly over a thistle broom was spiritual
food and lodging for a whole forenoon."

Indeed, there could scarcely have been a better
nesting-place for one who was all his life long to
love the animation of nature and to portray in
verse and prose its homely and friendly aspects
rather than its large, solemn, or expansive scenes.
In after life, especially when away from home, he
recurred to his childish experiences in a tone which
had the plaint of homesickness. From the upper
windows of the house — that tower of enchantment

for many a child — he could see a long curve of
the Charles, the wide marshes beyond the river,
and the fields which lay between Elmwood and the
village of Cambridge. Within the place itself were
the rosebushes and asters, the heavy headed goat's-
beard, the lilac bushes and syringas which bordered
the path from the door to what his father, in New
England phrase, called the avenue, and which later
became formally Elmwood Avenue; but chiefest
were the shag-bark trees, the pines, the horse-chest-
nuts, and the elms, a young growth in part in his
childhood, for his father took delight in giving
this permanence to the home; and the boy himself
caught the fancy, for when he was fifty-six years
old he rejoiced in the huge stack of shade cast for
him by a horse-chestnut, whose seed he had planted
more than fifty years before. And in trees and
bushes sang the birds that were to be his companions through life. Over the buttercups whistled
the orioles; and bobolinks, catbirds, linnets, and
robins were to teach him notes, —

> The Aladdin's trap-door of the past to lift."

In those days bank swallows frequented the cliff
of the gravel pit by the river, and Lowell remembered how his father would lead him out to see the
barn swallows, which had been flying in and out of
the mows, gather on the roof before their yearly
migration. "I learned," he wrote long after, —

> "I learned all weather-signs of day or night;
> No bird but I could name him by his flight,
> No distant tree but by his shape was known,
> Or, near at hand, by leaf or bark alone.

This learning won by loving looks I hived
As sweeter lore than all from books derived." [1]

When he was not far away from his childhood,
and in a time of great sensitiveness, he wrote: " I
never shall forget the blind despair of a poor little
humming-bird which flew through the open window of the nursery where I was playing when a
child. I knew him at once, for the same gay-
vested messenger from Fairy-land, whom I had
often watched disputing with the elvish bees the
treasures of the honeysuckle by the doorstep. His
imprisoned agony scarce equalled my own; and
the slender streaks of blood, which his innocent,
frenzied suicide left upon the ceiling, were more
terrible to me than the red witness which Rizzio
left on the stair at Holyrood to cry out against his
murderers." [2]

If we may trust the confession in " The Cathedral " as personal and not dramatic, Lowell was
singularly sensitive in childhood to those subtle
stirrings of nature which give eternity to single
moments, and create impressions which are indeli-
ble but never repeated.

" The fleeting relish at sensation's brim
Had in it the best ferment of the wine."

A spring morning which witnessed the sudden
miracle of regeneration; an hour of summer, when
he sat dappled with sunshine, in a cherry-tree; a
day in autumn, when the falling leaves moved as
an accompaniment to his thought; the creaking of

[1] " An Epistle to George William Curtis," 1874.
[2] *Conversations on Some of the Old Poets*, pp. 170, 171.

the snow beneath his feet, when the familiar world
was transformed as in a vision to a polar solitude : —

> " Instant the candid chambers of my brain
> Were painted with these sovran images;
> And later visions seem but copies pale
> From those unfading frescos of the past,
> Which I, young savage, in my age of flint,
> Gazed at, and dimly felt a power in me
> Parted from Nature by the joy in her
> That doubtfully revealed me to myself."

CHAPTER II

SCHOOL AND COLLEGE

1826–1838

THE outer world came early to the notice of Lowell in his garden enclosure. " I remember," he writes on the fourth of July, 1876, " how, fifty years ago to-day, I, perched in a great ox-heart cherry-tree, long ago turned to mould, saw my father come home with the news of John Adams's death." Two or three journeys also carried him out into the world in his early boyhood. He remembered going to Portsmouth in his seventh year, for the visit was impressed on his memory by the startling effect produced by a skeleton which he confronted when he opened a long red chest in Dr. Brackett's house ; and it was the next year that his father took him to Washington and carried him out to Alexandria, where he spent some days with the Carroll family, who were connections on his mother's side, and whence he made an excursion to Mount Vernon. It all came back to him fifty-nine years later when he took his grandson to the same shrine ; he went straight to the key of the Bastile and to the honey-locusts in the garden.

The rambles, too, to Beaver Brook and the Waverley Oaks, in the country within easy stroll

of Elmwood, were extended when he climbed into
the chaise with his father and drove off to neigh-
boring parishes at such times as Dr. Lowell exchanged with his brother ministers.   In those little
journeys he had an opportunity to see the lingering
reverence still paid to the minister, when boys
doffed their hats and girls dropped a curtsy by
the roadside as his father passed by.   These ex-
changes drew Dr. Lowell and his little son as
far as Portsmouth on the east and Northampton
on the west.   " I can conceive," says Lowell, " of
nothing more delightful than those slow summer
journeys through leafy lanes and over the stony
hills, where we always got out and walked.   In
that way I think I gained a more intimate relation
with what we may call pristine New England than
has fallen to the fortune of most men of my age." [1]
Thirty years after these experiences he could give
this graphic report of the contests he was wont
to witness in the village choir : —

> " Sometimes two ancient men, through glasses dim,
>   In age's treble deaconed off the hymn,
>   Paused o'er long words and then with breathless pace
>   Went down a slope of short ones at a race,
>   While who could sing and who could not, but would,
>   Rushed helter-skelter after as they could.
>   Well I remember how their faces shone,
>   Safe through some snare like *Re-sig-na-ti-on*,
>   And how some graceless youth would mock the tones
>   Of Deacon Jarvis or of Deacon Jones :
>   In towns ambitious of more cultured strains,
>   The gruff bass-viol told its inward pains
>   As some enthusiast, deaf to catgut's woe,

[1] Said at the commemoration of the one hundred and fiftieth
anniversary of the foundation of the West Church, Boston, 1887.

> Rasped its bare nerves with torture-resined bow ;
> Hard-by another, with strained eyeballs set,
> Blew devious discord through his clarinet,
> And the one fiddle, that was wont to seek
> In secular tunes its living all the week,
> Blind to the leader's oft-repeated glance
> Mixed up the psalm-tune with a country dance." [1]

More frequent journeys were those which he and his brothers and sisters invented for themselves by naming different parts of Elmwood after cities of the world and spending thus with their imagination the small geographical earnings of the schoolroom.

The first school which the boy attended was a dame school, which appears to have been somewhere not far from the river in the neighborhood of what is now Brattle Square. Once in verse and once in prose Lowell recorded his childish experience in and out of this primary school. In his introduction to " The Biglow Papers," first series, is a fragment beginning —

> " Propped on the marsh, a dwelling now, I see
> The humble school-house of my A, B, C ; "

and in his " New England Two Centuries Ago " there is a passage often read and quoted, which is a faithful picture of the author's life within and without one of the " martello towers that protect our coast," but he does not add the personal touch of his own return from school, whistling as he came in sight of his home as a signal to the mother watching for him. A bit of childish sport may be added from an omitted extract from the same fragmentary poem, since it brings to view two of Lowell's boy companions : —

[1] *The Power of Sound : a rhymed lecture*, pp. 22, 23.

" Where Felton puns in English or in Greek,
   And shakes with laughter till the timbers creak,
   The ' Idle Man ' once lived ; the man I knew,
   The author dwelt beyond my boyish view.
   There once, the college butler aided, too,
   My pony through his own front door he drew,
   I on her back, and strove with winning airs
   To coax my shaggy Shetlander upstairs ;
   Rejected hospitality ! the more
   He tugged in front, she backed toward the door.
   Had oats been offered, she had climbed at least
   Up to the garret, canny Scottish beast.
   Across the way, where once an Indian stood
   O'er Winthrop's door, carved horribly in wood,
   On the green duck-pond's sea, where water fails
   In droughty times, replenished then with pails,
   Richard the Second from their moorings cast
   His shingle fleets, and served before the mast,
   While Ned and I consigned a well-culled store
   Of choicest pebbles for the other shore.
   Then walked at leisure to the antipodes,
   Changing *en route* to Chinese consignees."

Both Richard and Edmund Dana were his
neighbors and friends, and with these early play-
mates should be named William Story. To him,
as to one who had journeyed with him " through
the green secluded valley of boyhood," he addressed
his " Cambridge Thirty Years Ago." Story and
the two Higginsons, Thatcher and Thomas Went-
worth, were the only day scholars with Lowell at
the boarding-school, kept by Mr. William Wells, to
which Lowell was sent to be prepared for entrance
to college. Mr. Wells was an Englishman, who
brought with him to this country attainments in
scholarship which were disclosed in the making of a
simple Latin grammar and in an edition of Tacitus.

He engaged in publishing under the firm name of Wells & Lilly, but meeting with reverses, he opened a classical school in the old Fayerweather house in Cambridge. He was a man of robust and masterful habit, who kept up the English tradition of the rattan in school and manly sport out of doors. The school had its gentler side in the person of Mrs. Wells, to whom Lowell sent a copy of "The Vision of Sir Launfal" in 1866, with the words: "Will you please me by accepting this little book in memory of your constant kindness to a naughty little cub of a schoolboy more than thirty years ago? I hope you will forget his ill deserts as faithfully as he remembers how much he owes you."

It was at the hands of Mr. Wells that Lowell received that severe drilling in Latin which was one of the traditions of English scholarship transported to New England by the early clergy, and reënforced from time to time by newcomers from England like Mr. Wells, elegant scholars like Mr. Dixwell, and stern disciplinarians like Dr. Francis Gardner, the latter two long holding the Boston Latin School fast bound to the old ways. Mr. George Ticknor Curtis, who was sixteen years old when Lowell was ten, at Mr. Wells's school, in a reminiscence of that period says: "Mr. Wells always heard a recitation with the book in his left hand and a rattan in his right, and if the boy made a false quantity or did not know the meaning of a word, down came the rattan on his head. But this chastisement was never ministered to me or to 'Jemmy Lowell.' Not to me, because I was too old

for it, and not to him because he was too young."
With his quickness of mind and linguistic agility,
Lowell evidently acquired in school rather than in
college a familiarity with Latin forms, to judge by
the ease with which he handled the language later
in mock heroics ; his early letters, too, are sprinkled with Latin phrases, the well worn coin of the
realm, it is true, but always jingling in his pocket.

The schoolroom to an imaginative boy is a starting point for mental rambles.   Lowell studied the
rime on the window panes as well as his Latin
verses.   From his readings with his elder sister,
and out of his own fertile imagination, he told or
made up stories for his young comrades.   T. W.
Higginson, recalling Lowell and Story, remembers
" treading close behind them once, as they discussed Spenser's ' Faerie Queene,' which they had
been reading, and which led us younger boys to
christen a favorite play-place ' the Bower of Bliss.' "
Dr. Samuel Eliot, who was one of Mr. Wells's
pupils, was also one of the small boys who listened
to Lowell's imaginative tales.   " I remember nothing of them," he told Dr. Hale, " except one,
which rejoiced in the central interest of a trap in
the playground, which opened to subterranean mar-
vels of various kinds."

" I can conceive of no healthier reading for a
boy, or girl either, than Scott's novels," says
Lowell, and he had the good fortune to be introduced early to Scott, and to read him as a contemporary.   When he was nine his mother gave him,
one can guess with what Scottish eagerness, the

" Tales of a Grandfather," which had just been
published ; and the then great event of American
history was not so remote but that the freckle-faced
boy who lived in a house once a Tory's, then a soldier's hospital, and then the home of a governor of
the commonwealth and vice-president of the United
States, would have lively reminders of it in the
veterans who turned out at muster, and in the rude
village drama of the " Cornwallis." [1]

Yet, as Lowell himself reminds us, the Cambridge of his boyhood, besides possessing the common characteristics of New England towns, had its
special flavor from the presence there of the oldest
college of New England. Like the Cambridge
boys of to-day, he hovered about the skirts of Alma
Mater, took in, year by year, the entertainment
offered by the college at its annual Commencement
festival, — a greater raree-show then than now, —
and made the acquaintance of the queer misshapen
minds that by some occult law of nature always
seem to be found in the shade of a college town, as
if the " Muses' factories " must necessarily have
their refuse heaps not far away. A boy who grows
up in a college town, especially when the community and the town are somewhat isolated, hardly
knows the wonder and gravity which assail one who
comes up to college from a distant home. In Low-

[1] " 'T is near midnight, and I hear a bass-drum, kettle-drum
and fife in the distance, playing the dear old *boongalang* tune of
my earliest days, the very one to which General Gage marched out
of Boston. It is delightful. I think it is the noise Wagner is
always trying to make and failing." — J. R. L. to C. E. Norton,
16 April, 1889.

ell's youth Harvard College and Cambridge town were singularly isolated in spite of their geographical nearness to Boston. Once an hour a long omnibus, and twice an hour a short one, jogged back and forth between the village and the city, picking up passengers in a leisurely fashion, and going longer or shorter distances from the college yard, according to the importunity of the passenger or the good-nature of the driver. An hourly stage to the city meant much deliberation in making the journey, and Cambridge was by no means the bed-chamber for city merchants and professional men which it has since become.

When Lowell entered Harvard from Mr. Wells's school in 1834, the college was surrounded by houses and gardens which marked almost the bounds of the town as one went toward Boston. The college itself was within a straggling enclosure still known by the homely name of the Yard, and occupied seven buildings therein; the library was in Harvard Hall, for Gore Hall was not begun till just as Lowell was graduating. The chapel was a dignified apartment of University Hall, designed by the architect Charles Bulfinch, who left his mark in Boston and its neighborhood upon buildings which stand in serene reproof of much later architecture. In the chapel also were held the academic functions, one of which, Exhibition Day, was observed three times a year; on two of these occasions the Governor of the Commonwealth attended, and on all of them the President of the college in his academic dress, the Fellows, the Overseers, and the Faculty marched to the chapel with ceremony, there to listen, along with an indulgent crowd of parents and friends, to the youthful speakers, who discoursed in Latin or in English, but were always introduced in Latin.

During Lowell's college course there were only about two hundred and twenty undergraduates, his own class entering with sixty-eight members and graduating with sixty-five ; the whole list of the faculty, including the schools of law, divinity, and medicine, did not exceed thirty-four, and not half of these constituted the college faculty proper. But among them were names known then and later beyond the college enclosure. Felton was professor of Greek, Peirce of mathematics, and Ticknor of modern languages, to be succeeded, when Lowell was nearly through his college course, by Longfellow. Francis Sales, graphically set off by Lowell in his " Cambridge Thirty Years Ago," was instructor [sic] in French and Spanish, and Pietro Bachi in Italian, Spanish, and Portuguese. The president of the college was Josiah Quincy, and when thirty years later Lowell reviewed his friend Edmund Quincy's life of his father, in the article entitled " A Great Public Character," he referred with a fine note of sincere feeling to the association with him which he bore away from his college days, in a passage which reflects a little of Lowell as well as pictures the figure of the president.

" Mr. Quincy had many qualities calculated to win him favor with the young, — that one above all which is sure to do it, indomitable pluck. With

him the dignity was in the man, not in the office.
He had some of those little oddities, too, which
afford amusement without contempt, and which
rather tend to heighten than diminish personal attachment to superiors in station. His punctuality
at prayers, and in dropping asleep there, his for-
getfulness of names, his singular inability to make
even the shortest off-hand speech to the students,
— all the more singular in a practised orator, —
his occasional absorption of mind, leading him to
hand you his sand-box instead of the leave of absence he had just dried with it, — the old-fashioned
courtesy of his ' Sir, your servant,' as he bowed you
out of his study, — all tended to make him popular.
He had also a little of what is somewhat contradic-
torily called dry humor, not without influence in
his relations with the students. In taking leave of
the graduating class, he was in the habit of paying
them whatever honest compliment he could. Who,
of a certain year which shall be nameless, will ever
forget the gravity with which he assured them that
they were ' the *best-dressed* class that had passed
through college during his administration '? How
sincerely kind he was, how considerate of youthful
levity, will always be gratefully remembered by
whoever had occasion to experience it."

The change from school to college, as I have intimated, was not such as to strike very deeply into
the boy's consciousness. He continued for a while
to live at his father's house, a mile away from the
Yard, though he had a room of his own nearer,
at Mr. Hancock's in Church Street, and in the

latter part of his course lived there altogether. Going to college, thus, was very much like going to school as he had always done. The college methods were not markedly different from those of a preparatory school. There were lessons to learn and recite; the text-book was the rule, and the fixed curriculum suggested no break from the ordinary course of formal instruction. Except in the senior year, there was a steady attention to Greek, Latin, and mathematics. In the first year Tytler's History was studied; in the second year English grammar and modern languages were added; in the third year, besides Greek and Latin and modern languages, Paley's Evidences, Butler's Analogy, and chemistry appeared on the list, and themes and forensics were introduced. In the senior year the ancient languages were dropped, and natural philosophy, intellectual philosophy, astronomy, and political economy took their place, with lectures on rhetoric, criticism, theology, Story on the Constitution of the United States, mineralogy, and anatomy — a somewhat confused jumble on paper in the catalogue of the time, which it is to be hoped was reduced to some sort of order, though it looks as if the senior were suddenly released from too monotonous a course and bidden take a rapid survey of a wide range of intellectual pursuits.

In his school days Lowell had been under the close surveillance given to boys, and the partial freedom of college life brought with it a little more sense of personal rights, but throughout the four

years he was boyish, frolicsome, very immature in
expression, and disposed, in a fitful fashion, to as-
sert an independence of authority. He won a " detur " in his sophomore year, and in a public exhibition in the first term of his senior year he took part
in a conference bearing the labored title : " Ancient
Epics, considered as Pictures of Manners, as Proofs
of Genius, or as Sources of Entertainment," but
both in his sophomore and senior years he was at
first privately and then publicly admonished for
excessive absence from recitations and for general
negligence in themes, forensics, and recitations.
There was enough of the boy left in him at the
beginning of his senior year to require the fine of a
dollar for cutting seats in the recitation room ; and
the college discipline of the day frowned on Lowell
as on others for wearing a brown coat on Sunday.
It is difficult for one scanning the records of the
faculty at that time to avoid a feeling of commiseration for these excellent gentlemen and scholars
sitting, as if they were boarding-school masters,
in serious consultation over the pranks and petty
insubordination of a parcel of boys.

Meanwhile in his own fashion Lowell was stum-
bling on his way, gradually finding himself. He
was a reader, as we have seen, before he went to
college, and he continued to find his delight in
books. " A college training," he once said, " is an
excellent thing ; but after all, the better part of
every man's education is that which he gives himself," [1] and in college he was following, without

---

[1] " Books and Libraries " in *Literary and Political Addresses,
Works,* vi. 83.

much reflection, the instincts of his nature, both
as regards his reading and his writing. His letters show him a schoolboy when attending to the
enforced tasks of the college, with occasional out-
breaks of enthusiasm for the more distinctly literary studies, but somewhat of an independent
voyager when launched on the waters of general
literature.

It was in the large leisure of his college days
that he formed an acquaintance which ripened into
intimacy with the great writers and with those secondary lights that often suit better the ordinary
mood. " I was first directed to Landor's works,"
he says, in 1888, when introducing some letters of
Landor to the readers of his own day, "by hearing
how much store Emerson set by them. I grew
acquainted with them fifty years ago in one of
those arched alcoves in the old college library in
Harvard Hall, which so pleasantly secluded without wholly isolating the student. That footsteps
should pass across the mouth of his Aladdin's
Cave, or even enter it in search of treasure, so
far from disturbing only deepened his sense of possession. These faint rumors of the world he had
left served but as a pleasant reminder that he
was the privileged denizen of another beyond 'the
flaming bounds of space and time.' There, with
my book lying at ease and in the expansion of intimacy on the broad window-shelf, shifting my cell
from north to south with the season, I made friend-
ships, that have lasted me for life, with Dodsley's
'Old Plays,' with Cotton's 'Montaigne,' with Hak-

luyt's 'Voyages,' among others that were not in
my father's library.   It was the merest browsing,
no doubt, as Johnson called it, but how delightful
it was!" [1]

The record of books withdrawn by Lowell from
the college library during his four years' residence
would of course furnish a very incomplete account
of his reading, since, as intimated above, he had his
father's well-stocked shelves, and access apparently
to the alcoves of Harvard Hall.   The record, nevertheless, is interesting as showing the range and the
drift of his reading.   Some of this reading is an-
cillary to his task work, but much is simply the
gratification of an expanding taste, and covers
such diverse works as Terence, Hume, the Antho-
logia Græca, Smollett, Hakluyt, Boileau, Scott,
and Southey.   It is noticeable that as his college
course proceeded the emphasis was laid on the
greater English literature.

Nor was he without the excellent ambition to
collect a library of his own.   " It is just fifty-one
years ago," he said 7 May, 1885, when unveiling
the bust of Coleridge in Westminster Abbey,
" that I became the possessor of an American reprint of Galignani's edition of Coleridge, Shelley,
and Keats in one volume.   It was a pirated book,
and I trust I may be pardoned for the delight
I had in it." [2]   His letters to his college friends
during these years contain frequent references to
the purchases of books he had made and the gifts

[1] *Latest Literary Essays and Addresses*, p. 43.
[2] *Literary and Political Addresses*, pp. 69, 70.

from his family which he prized. He has been
given a beautiful edition of Milton, which he had
looked forward to buying; he has been purchasing Samuel Butler and Beattie; a new edition of
Shakespeare has been announced, which he means
to buy if he can afford it; he has had a "detur"
of Akenside; he has laid his hands on a "very
pretty edition of Cowper;" and his frequent quotations from the poets show the easy familiarity he
had won in his reading.

Besides his continued friendship with Story and
other neighbors' sons, Lowell formed new alliances
among his college mates, and in his correspondence with two of them in this period he discloses
something of his character and tastes. One of
these friends, W. H. Shackford, was his senior by
two or three years, and Lowell's letters to him
show the boy's side turned toward one whom he
regarded with the friendly reverence which sixteen
pays to nineteen. On his part, Shackford seems
to have taken a violent fancy to Lowell, to have
made indeed the first overtures of friendship. To
this sager companion, who was a senior when
Lowell was a freshman, he reveals his more studi-
ous side. Shackford left college to teach at Phillips Exeter Academy, and Lowell wrote to him
from Cambridge and Boston, not much in the way
of college gossip, but of his own studies, the treasures he picked up at book-stores or auctions, his
plans for reading and travel, and brief comments
on his instructors. Through the correspondence
runs an affectionate current, an almost lover-like

tone of self-exculpation, the warm feeling of a boy
toward his mentor, and an impulse to make him
somewhat of a confessor.[1]

The earliest of these letters was written in the
middle of July, 1835, when Shackford had gone to
Portsmouth. It was a hasty shot fired after his
departing friend to assure him of his affection,
written under stress of headache from his brother's
office, and was followed the same day by a longer
letter. " When I wrote to you this morning," he
says, " I was laboring under three very bad com-
plaints enumerated in my other letter. I was then
at my brother's office. I am now at home, sitting
by an open window, with my coat off, my stock
do., with Coleridge's works before me wherewith
to consume the rest of the day, and also as cool as
a cucumber. Shack, if you are a victim to any
other disease, and are lying tossing with pain under
some physician's prescription (such, for instance,
as the pleasing draught concocted by Wm. Rufus,
or the Red King, composed of the following truly
delectable compounds, viz., ' rue, tansy, horehound,
coltsfoot, hyssop, and camomile flowers, farther
enriched by a handful of earthworms, half a dozen
wood lice and four centipedes '), if, I say, you
labor under all these misfortunes, devoutly thank
your more fav'ring stars, that you are not the
yawning victim of ennui, a disease which Æscu-
lapius himself could n't cure, and which I therefore humbly opine to have been the disease of

[1] Mr. Shackford did not live to continue his friendship with
Lowell. He died in 1842.

Achilles. . . . I hope you 'll be amused with this epistle (if perchance you are able to read it). But the fact is I can't write anything serious to save my life. Answer this the very day you get it. . . . "

At the end of the summer when more letters had passed between them, Lowell returned to his college work, and wrote from Cambridge a long letter dated 9 October, 1835, in reply to one long delayed. " My *dearest* friend," he writes, " I am rejoiced that you *have* broken the long silence that existed between us, not because I should not have written to you first, but because it shows that you were not grievously offended with me. I willingly confess myself to blame, but not in so great a degree as you may suppose. I *did* go to the White Mountains, and while travelling was not offended (do not use any stronger term) by not receiving any letters from you; on the contrary I expected none, for how could you have any knowledge of my ' whereabouts ' unless I wrote to you as I went along and told you where to direct? This I did not do, nor did I write any letters on my journey except one which I was obliged to write to Bob because I *promised* him I would. After I got home I was taken sick and kept my bed a week without being able to sleep most of the time on account of a raging sick headache which hardly allowed me to move. The day I saw you was the third time I had been out. I did go down, however, three times to see you, but could not find you, or saw you walking with somebody I did not know, and then I did not like to speak to you. Did you or could you think that I would forfeit your friendship, the most precious (because I believe it to be the truest) I ever enjoyed, because you did not find it convenient to write to me ? I hope you will not think that I say all this because I am *ashamed* to treat you coldly, or not to answer you. I am sure of one thing, that I have no such opinion of you. Your letter, Shack, was a *delight* to me (though I am not ashamed to confess that it [made] me cry). . . .

"I like Prof. Channing very much indeed, inasmuch as I sit where I can see his marks, and he has given me an 8 every recitation this term except once, and then he gave me 7. I went up to ask him something so as to see whether I was not mistaken (as he makes a 6 something like his 8's) and I found on the paper exactly what I expected. I have written one theme and got but two marks on the margin, one for a change required in the sentence, and another was a straight line drawn under the word ' to,' and also marked on the margin. Tell me whether you think this is good, as you have experienced. I study quite hard this term. I get on in German astonishingly ; it comes quite easy to me now. . . . I have written the longest letter I ever wrote in my life. I translated an ode of Horace into poetry the other day, and it was pretty good. Mathematics are my only enemies now. . . . I hope I may subscribe myself your *dear* friend."

A month later he writes his friend a lively account of a town and gown row, and notes his progress in reading Shakespeare. " I was surprised on looking over Shakespeare to find that I had read all his plays but two or three, among them 'Hamlet.' Only think, I have n't read 'Hamlet.' I will go at it instanter."

At the beginning of 1836, on returning to college after the holidays, he writes with a boyish bibliomaniac enthusiasm of the Milton and Coleridge which had been given him, and passes into comment on the books he is reading and those he means to buy. He grows more literary and political in the subjects of his letters, disclosing already not only a warm interest in public affairs, but a generous judgment. " I suppose you heard of the Seminoles massacring, as it is called, those companies of American troops. I think they are in the right of it; by ' they ' I mean the Seminoles. Not much danger of war with France now." Then follows an odd jumble of frank confessions of his likes and dislikes for his fellows, and his boyish passions, with a return to his hunt for books in special editions.

His letter of 22 April, 1836, is taken up with a long discussion in a semi-philological vein of love and friendship, but what would strike a reader of these letters most is the distinct change which now takes place in the handwriting, which has passed from a not always neat copy-book hand to one which suggests the delicacy of the hand he afterward wrote, though not its elegance; it is still constrained with the air of being the result of close attention. These gradual changes in style of handwriting rarely fail to mark a maturing of character, and it is interesting to observe, in Lowell's case, how they register a long period of vacillation and immaturity.

There is a gap of nearly a year in this correspondence as preserved, and the next letter, under date of 26 February, 1837, is filled with extracts from a long poem he is writing, in Spenserian stanza, and even occasionally with a word borrowed from Spenser; but the spirit that stirs the lines is Campbell. The theme is an imaginary journey up the Hudson, and West Point suggests the two stanzas :

> " Follow this narrow path to where the grass
>   Grows fresher on yon gently-rising mound,
>   To that lone brook, whose ripples as they pass
>   Spread to the air a sleep-compelling sound;
>   Here, Poland's hero erst a refuge found.
>   Go ask whose good right arm hurl'd back the slave,
>   When Russia's eagle o'er his country frown'd,
>   Who led her little band of patriots brave ;
> And weeping Freedom points to Kosciusko's grave.
>
> " Spirit of Freedom ! who didst erst inspire
>   Our nation ground beneath oppression's sway,
>   With trust in God, with thine own holy fire ;
>   Who nerv'dst the mother fond to send away
>   Her first-born boy to brave the bloody fray,
>   Bid him farewell, with full averted eyes,
>   Ne ask, though longing, for a moment's stay,
>   Still hover o'er us, if thou didst not rise
> With Washington's pure spirit to thy native skies ! "

The other correspondent whose letters from Lowell are preserved was George Bailey Loring, a boy of his own age, the son of a clergyman who was Dr. Lowell's friend, so that the friendship partook of an hereditary character; with him Lowell

had frank intimacy during their college days and
in the years immediately following. Their ways
in life separated, and they had less community of
interests and tastes when they came to manhood.
Dr. Loring went early into public life and held
various offices, being Commissioner of Agriculture
at one time and at another United States Minister
to Portugal.

In this fuller series of letters which is largely
contained in Mr. Norton's two volumes, Lowell is
the frank, unformed boy, giving vent to nonsense,
a lad's hasty impulse, and the foolery which goes on
in the name of sentiment. The equality of age created a different relation between them from that
which Lowell bore to Shackford, and the familiarity of their intercourse called out all manner of
intellectual pranks and youthful persiflage. The
jingle and lively verses which Lowell threw out for
the amusement of his comrade show him playing
carelessly with the instrument which he was already
beginning to discover as fitting his hand.

Lowell's unaffected interest in boyish things is
much more apparent in these random letters than
in the more careful epistles to his older friend,
though he is by no means silent on the side of his
intellectual life. In his first letter, dated 23 July,
1836, he talks about the things that two college
boys have on their minds at the beginning of vacation. " You must excuse me if this be not a very
long or entertaining epistle, as I am writing from
my brother's office (with a very bad pen) in a
great hurry. I shall not go to Canada and shall

not start for P[ortsmouth] probably for three
weeks.   My circular came on last night, 14 prayers,
56 recitations, whew!   The class supper was glorious, toasts went off very well.   Those about Parker
and the Temperance Society were most applauded.
I am going to join the ' Anti-Wine ' I think.   The
' Good Schooner Susan, R. T. S. L. owner and
master,' will make an excursion to Nahant this day.
Distinguished Passenger etc.   We shall go to
church at Nahant Sunday and return Monday
morning.   By the way I ' made up ' with —— and
—— at the supper.   I had a seat *reserved* (!) for
me (as an officer) on the right hand of the distinguished president (?)   A prettier table I never
saw."

The letters to his college friends were naturally
written mainly in vacation time, and in Christmas
week of the same year, 1836, he writes : " I am going to a ball to-night at the house of a young lady
whom I never heard of. . . . I 've begun and written about forty lines of my H. P. C. [1] prœmium.   I
shall immortalize I——k W——.   I extol him to
the skies and *pari passu* depreciate myself."   He
went to the ball, and a few days later wrote : " I
think I told you I was going to a party or ball
(call it what you will) : well, I went, made my
bow, danced, talked nonsense with young ladies
who could talk nothing but nonsense, grew heartily
tired and came away.   I saw a great many people

---

[1] The Hasty Pudding Club, a Harvard students' club, which
has always made much of literature of the lighter sort, its spe-
cialty now being amateur theatricals.

make fools of themselves, and charitably took it
for granted that I did the same. . . . I may add
something in the morning, so no more from your
aching headed and perhaps splenetic, but still affectionate friend, J. R. L."

In these letters Lowell twits his friend with his
attentions to girls, and intersperses his jibes with
poor verses; he has become a zealous autograph
hunter, and the letters he laid his hands on in his
father's house from home and foreign notabilities
illustrate the wide connections of the family, and
the part it had had in the great world.   In the
midst of it all he will burst forth into almost passionate expression of his love for nature and his
strong attachment to his birthplace and its neighborhood; and again quote freely from the books
he is reading, and tell of the progress he is making
in his more serious poetical ventures, and the books
he is adding to his library.   He made no boast of
immunity when he laughed at his friend for too
much susceptibility.   Here is a passage from a letter written in the summer of 1837, when he was
closing his junior year : —

. . . " Did n't I have a glorious time yesterday?
That I did if smiles from certain lips I

' prize
Above almost, I don't know what, on earth '

could make a day glorious.   Excuse me for quoting my own nonsense, but 't was more apt than
anything I could think of. . . . Imagine yourself
by the side of a young lady the perfection of
beauty, virtue, modesty, etc., etc., in whom you

entertain a pleasing interest, and you may form a
'faint imagining' of my situation. I am not calm
yet. In fact, every time I think of her eyes —
those eyes! Guido never could have conceived
her. Well, a truce with all recollections when
there is no hope."

A month later he gave a brief account of Commencement to his friend, and then speaks of a letter his brother Rob had received from their sister,
then in Glasgow. Lowell's father, mother, and
sister Rebecca went to Europe early in the summer of 1837. They were gone three years, and
during that time the young collegian found in his
brother Charles his nearest friend and adviser; his
house indeed was the student's home when he was
not in college, and his wife was the best of sisters
to him. Mrs. Anna Cabot Lowell was herself a
woman of fine culture and of unwonted intellectual
power. At a later period than this she opened a
school for girls, which is looked upon by many now
in mature life with warm gratitude. She edited a
choice collection of poems for the reading of school-
girls, and compiled also a little volume of suggestive thoughts called "Seed Grain." Dr. Lowell,
meanwhile, parted from his son with parental solicitude, and wrote him on the eve of sailing a
letter which is quaintly expressive of his own ingenuous nature and of the simplicity of the day,
and slightly indicative of his son's weaknesses as
they appeared to a father's eyes: —

NEW YORK, May 29th, 1837.

MY DEAR SON, — I wish you to write us once
a month, making an arrangement with Robert not
to write at the same time he does. You know the
necessity for economy, and you know that I shall
never deny you, but from necessity, what will
afford you pleasure. I shall direct Charles to pay
you half a dollar a week. If you are one of the
first eight admitted to the Φ Β Κ, $1.00 per week,
as soon as you are admitted. If you are not, to
pay you 75 cents per week as soon as you are admitted. If I find my finances will allow it, I shall
buy you something abroad. If you graduate one
of the first five in your class, I shall give you $100
on your graduation. If one of the first ten, $75.
If one of the first twelve, $50. If the first or
second scholar, $200. If you do not miss any
exercises unexcused, you shall have Bryant's ' My-
thology,' or any book of equal value, unless it is
one I may specially want.

My dear child, I wish you only to be faithful
to yourself. You can easily be a fine scholar, and
therefore in naming the smallest sum for your
weekly expenses, I feel no hesitation, as it depends
on yourself, with very little exertion, to secure the
second highest sum, and with not more exertion
than is perfectly compatible with health and sufficient recreation to secure the largest. *Use regular exercise. Associate with those who will exert
the best influence upon you.* Say your prayers
and read your Bible *every day*. I trust you have
made up all your exercises. *If not, make them up*

in one week, and let the president know it. Do
not get anything charged except with Charles's
knowledge and approbation. I have given him in-
structions respecting your expenses. . . .

Your affectionate father.

Dr. Lowell wrote many letters home and re-
counted the pleasant experiences of the little party
in Scotland and England, their foregathering with
the Traill family, and the visits they paid to
Wordsworth, Southey, Sir David Brewster, and
others. But he does not forget to continue his ad-
monitions and encouragements, as he receives his
son's reports of his doings. "Your office," he
writes from London, 13 December, 1837, "as one
of the editors of the ' Harvardiana ' may give you
a greater familiarity in composition. Be careful
that it does not abstract you from severer pursuits,
and that your style is not trifling, but the subject
and the manner useful and dignified. I do not
allow myself to doubt of your furnishing the crite-
rion of good standing which a membership of the
Φ B K will furnish, and I trust you will leave college with a high part and a high reputation.

"God bless you, my dear child. *Aim high, very
high*. I feel its importance for you more than
ever."

Harvardiana, to which Dr. Lowell refers, was
the college magazine of the day, started just as
Lowell entered college, and naturally inviting a
scribbler like Lowell to become one of the editors
when his senior year came round. His associates

were Rufus King, who later attained a leading position in the bar of Cincinnati, and wrote " Ohio " in the *American Commonwealths* series ; George Warren Lippitt, afterward for a long time secretary of legation at Vienna ; Charles Woodman Scates, a South Carolinian lawyer of great promise, who died young, and Nathan Hale, an older brother of Dr. Edward Everett Hale, and later a strong figure in Boston journalism. Lowell contributed twenty-four pieces in prose and verse, translations from the German, a bit of moralizing in the minor key which youth likes to pursue, some fierce sardonic verses, some sentiment, and then a mockery of sentiment. For the most part his contributions are the " larks " of students given to literature. With his associates he followed the example set by *Blackwood*, and imitated by the *Knickerbocker* and similar magazines, aiming at the sauciness and jocularity which were assumed to be the ordinary temper of editors gathered about their table, whereas in actual experience such editors are painfully at their wits' end. What most strikes one in these varied contributions is the apparent facility with which everything is thrown off, sense and nonsense coming with equal ease, but nonsense predominating.

Lowell's letters to his friends in his last year at college have frequent reference to his willing and unwilling labors on this " perryodical," as he was wont to call it in mimicry of Dr. Walker. In August, 1837, he sends Shackford a circular inviting subscriptions to *Harvardiana*, and on the blank

leaf writes one of the imitative letters in verse, for
which he had a penchant at this time : —

> " Dear Shack, a circular I send ye
>   The which I hope will not offend ye ;
>   If sae, 't wad tak' Auld Nick to mend ye
>   O' sic an ill
>   But, gin ye are as when I kenn'd ye
>   It never will !
>
> " Gin ye could get ae body's name
>   'T wad add forever to his fame
>   To help to kindle up the flame
>   O' sic a journal,
>   Whose reputation, though quite lame,
>   *Will* be eternal.
>
> " Now if ye do your vera best
>   In this maist glorious behest,
>   By gettin' names and a' the rest
>   I need na tell
>   Yese thus fulfil the airn'st request
>   O' J. R. L."

" King has been up here," he writes from Elmwood, 22 December, 1837, " for an article for the
' Perry,' but was unsuccessful in the attempt. The
fact is, it is impossible to read Lockhart's ' Life of
Scott' and attend to my illustrious nephew, ' the
corporal,' who is a very prototype of Jack Falstaff,
and write an article which requires such deep study
and abstraction."

The magazine was a part of that spontaneous
literary activity which is pretty sure to find vent in
college life outside of the class room, in independent reading, in societies sometimes secret, sometimes public, and in weekly, monthly, or quarterly
journals. Lowell, with his growing consciousness

of literary faculty and his naturally vagarious impulses, turned aside from the set tasks of college, as we have seen, and allowed himself to be indifferent to the routine imposed by college regulations. There are always men in college who undertake to be independent while living in it; sometimes the instinct is wise, sometimes it is merely the impulse of an indolent or conceited nature, but college authorities, like most constitutional governors, are bound to take more account of law than arbitrary and irresponsible rulers are, and their severity falls indiscriminately on the just and unjust. Lowell had made himself amenable to discipline on this score, but he might have escaped with reprimands only, had he not committed a breach of propriety in chapel which could not be overlooked. Such, at least, is the recollection of one of his college mates writing long afterward to Mr. T. W. Higginson, who prints his letter in " Old Cambridge."

The circumstantial account given in this letter has a plausible air, and may be wholly true, but if so, it was probably the final occasion rather than the cause of Lowell's suspension. The record of the Faculty is somewhat more general in its explanation. " 25 June, 1838. Voted that Lowell, senior, on account of continued neglect of his college duties be suspended till the Saturday before Commencement, to pursue his studies with Mr. Frost of Concord, to recite to him twice a day, reviewing the whole of Locke's ' Essay ' [On the Human Understanding], and studying also Mackintosh's ' Review of Ethical Philosophy,' to be examined in both on his return, and not to visit Cambridge during the period of his suspension."

Lowell seems to have taken his exile philosophically. The fact that he would not be able to read the class poem he had been chosen to give did not prevent him from writing it, and the isolation of his life gave him plenty of time for working at it. The mild discipline of " rustication " included, as the record shows, the requisite amount of study, and Concord, to which he was sent for a couple of months of study and reflection, was only fifteen miles from Cambridge. The Rev. Barzillai Frost, to whose oversight he was committed and with whom he lodged, was a young man, recently graduated from the Harvard Divinity School, and Mrs. Frost endeared herself to the young culprit by her affectionate care. In a speech which Lowell made at Concord, on the celebration of the 250th anniversary of the founding of the town, he introduced this slight reminiscence of his work with Mr. Frost : —

" In rising to-day I could not help being reminded of one of my adventures with my excellent tutor when I was in Concord. I was obliged to read with him ' Locke on the Human Understanding.' My tutor was a great admirer of Locke, and thought he was the greatest Englishman that ever lived, and nothing pleased him more, consequently, than now and then to cross swords with Locke in argument. I was not slow, you may imagine, to encourage him in this laudable enterprise. Whenever a question arose between my tutor and Locke, I always took Locke's side. I remember on one occasion, although I cannot now recall the exact passage in Locke, — it was something about continuity of ideas, — my excellent tutor told me that in that case Locke was quite mistaken in his views. My tutor said: 'For instance, Locke says that the mind is never without an idea; now I am conscious frequently that my mind is without any idea at all.' And I must confess that that anecdote came vividly to my mind when I got up on what Judge Hoar has justly characterized as the most important part of an orator's person."

Lowell knew something of Emerson when he went to Concord. His letters show him before that time going to hear him lecture in Boston, and years afterward he recalled with fervor the impression made upon him by Emerson's address before the Φ B K in Lowell's junior year. It "was an event," he says, "without any former parallel in our literary annals, a scene to be always treasured in the memory for its picturesqueness and its inspiration. What crowded and breathless aisles, what windows clustering with eager heads, what enthusiasm of approval, what grim silence of foregone dissent! It was our Yankee version of a lecture by Abelard, our Harvard parallel to the last public appearance of Schelling." [1] But in 1838 Emerson had published little, his fame resting mainly on his public lectures and addresses. In the address at Concord, quoted above, Lowell re-

[1] "Thoreau," in *Literary Essays*, i. 366.

cords a memory of the personal relations which he
then established with the elder poet: —

"I am not an adopted son of Concord. I cannot call myself that. But I can say, perhaps, that
under the old fashion which still existed when I
was young, I was 'bound out' to Concord for a
period of time; and I must say that she treated
me very kindly. I then for the first time made
the acquaintance of Mr. Emerson, and I still recall with a kind of pathos, as Dante did that of his
old teacher, Brunetto Latini, 'La cara e buona
imagine paterna,' 'The dear and good paternal
image,' which he showed me here; and I can also
finish the quotation and say, 'And shows me how
man makes himself eternal.' I remember he was
so kind to me — I, rather a flighty and exceedingly youthful boy, as to take me with him on
some of his walks, particularly a walk to the cliffs,
which I shall never forget."

Lowell formed at Concord the friendship which
lasted for life with E. R. Hoar, and the lady who
was to be Judge Hoar's wife. These two indeed
seemed to be excepted in his mind from the Concord people whom he met. He was plainly, as his
letters show, in a restless mood, dissatisfied with
himself, going through his appointed tasks with
the obedience which was habitual, and writing, as
the impulse took him, on his Class Poem, but
moody, irritable, and chafing at the bonds which
held him. There was the uncomfortable consciousness of serving out his time at Concord for a momentary jest, but there was also the profounder

unrest which came from the friction of discipline
with the awakening of powers not yet fully understood or determined. A few passages from his
letters to G. B. Loring will partially disclose the
way he tossed himself about.

July 1, 1838.

You must n't expect so long a letter from me
as the one you favored me with (and I hope sincerely you 'll favor me with many more such (for
nothing is more pleasant to me than a friend's letters) (except himself) (there, I have got into one
of my parentheses, which I can't help to save my
life — damnation! I 'm only making the matter
worse! so I 'll begin again. . . . This appears to
be a pretty decent sort of a place — but I 've no
patience talking about. I shall fly into a passion
on paper, and then — as Hamlet says — then what?
You can't guess, now you know you can't! Why,
I should be apt to "tear my passion to tatters."
Pretty good, eh! for an un-Sheridanic one? Well,
as I was saying, the poem has n't progressed (they
say that 's a Yankee word; it 's a damned good
word, as most Yankee things are) a line since I
left the shades of Alma Mater. I want the spirit
up here, I want

'Mine ancient chair, whose wide embracing arms," etc.

I shall take to smoking again for very spite. The
only time I have felt the flow of song was when I
heard the bull-frogs in the river last night. . . .

I shall do my best to please Mr. F. since I find
he does his best to please me and make me com-

fortable; "that's the ground I stand on." I feel
in a shocking humor, that is, not grouty (I'm not
such a damned fool; no offence I hope), but cursed
queer. I damn Concord, and as the man in a story
I read somewhere who was shot in a duel patheti-
cally exclaimed in his last struggle, I — " damn
everything." . . . I have written you more than I
intended, have two more to write to-night, and 50
pages in MacIntosh. . . . Don't for heaven's sake
think I write in such a hurry from affectation. I
wish with all my heart it were so.

                                                    July 8.

. . . I don't know that I shan't get gloomy up
here, and be obliged, like the gallant old Sir Hudi-
bras's sword,

> "To eat into myself, for lack
>   Of something else to cut and hack."

Everybody almost is calling me "indolent,"[1]
"blind, dependent on my own powers" and "on
fate." . . . I acknowledge that I have been some-

---

[1] There is a letter from Mrs. Anna Cabot Lowell, 3 July, 1838,
to her brother-in-law, which throws a little light on the way in
which his friends regarded Lowell at this time : " Aunt S. was
here last evening and depicted in a lively manner the grief of
Scates for your idle courses. She says he went to you with tears
in his eyes to implore you to persevere, and that he told his
friends in faltering accents that you had but this one fault in the
world. Being desirous to know the exact nature of that fault,
that you might apply the specific remedy, I asked her what the
fault was. She said 'indolence to be sure : indolence and the
Spence negligence.' I quote her very words. My opinion of the
case is that it proceeds more from negligence than indolence, and
more from a blind confidence in your powers and your destiny
than either."

thing of a dreamer and have sacrificed perchance too assiduously on that altar to the "unknown God," which the Divinity has builded not with hands in the bosom of every decent man, sometimes blazing out clear with flame (like Abel's sacrifice) heaven seeking, sometimes smothered with green wood and earthward like that of Cain. Lazy, quotha! I have n't dug, 't is true, but I have done as well, and "since my free soul was mistress of her choice and could of books distinguish her election," I have chosen what reading I pleased and what friends I pleased, sometimes scholars and sometimes not. . . .

July 12.

For the Campbell I trust I need n't let my thanks stare me in the face, so I shall leave you to put yourself in my place and imagine them. If you see Scates tell him to write, or I shall — excommunicate, or something dreadful. If you happen to go down by the bath house I wish you would take a look after the skiff and write me about it. Because perhaps I might come down to the Supper in a wagon and bring it up; at any rate, there will be nobody there to take care of it when you leave (or rather to lay claim to it), and it may be lost, for which I should be sorry, for I hope to have considerable navigation out of her yet.

August 9.

I shall be free as a bird in a fortnight, and 't will be the last Concord will ever see of me I fancy. . . . I am again in doubt whether to have my "Poem" printed or no. I have n't written a

line since I have been in this horrible place. I feel
as queer as a woman does probably (unmarried of
course) when she finds herself in what Dante calls
" mezzo cammin del nostro vita." . . . I 'm homesick and all that sort of thing. Miss —— being
the only being I have actually sympathized with
since I have been in Concord has made me feel like
a fool. I must go down and see Emerson, and if
he does n't make me feel *more* like a fool it won't
be for want of sympathy *in that respect*. He is a
good-natured man, in spite of his doctrines. He
travelled all the way up from his house to bring me
a book which had been sent to me *via* him.

August 17.

The first eight pages of the " Poem " are probably printed by this time, and the proof on its
winding way, as Charlie Foster would say to me.
I wrote to the President requesting him to let me
go home to-morrow, but have n't yet received any
answer, and doubt much whether I ever shall.

I don't know what to do with Miss ——. She
runs in my head and heart more than she has any
right to, but then

> A pair of black eyes
> Of a charming size
> And a lip so prettily curled, O!
> Are enough to capsize
> The intention wise
> Of any man in the world, O!
>
> For a pretty smile
> Is a mighty wile
> For a heart, for a heart that is light, O!

And a girl like a dove
Makes a man fall in love,
Though he knows that it is n't right, O!

For love is a thing
That will quit the lonely king
To make sunny the cot of the peasant, O!
And it folds its gauzy wing —
In short — it is a thing —
'T is a thing — that is deuced pleasant, O!

Oh a gentle heart
Is the better part
Of a lovely woman's looks, O!
And I totter on the brink
Of love when I think,
When I think, when I think of Miss B——, O!

For a thousand girls
Have hair that curls,
And a sort of expressive face, O!
But it is n't the hair
Nor the genteel air —
'T is the heart that looks bright and gives grace, O!

Ay, lasses are many
Without e'en a penny,
But with hearts worth their weight in gold, O!
Whom I 'd sooner wed —
Yea, and sooner bed
Than a princess rich, ugly, and old, O!

No bee e'er sucked honey
From gold or silver money,
But he does from the lovely flower, O!
Then give me a spouse
Without fortune, land, or house,
And her charming self for a dower, O!

By Jove, I like that better than anything I 've
written for two years! I wrote it *con amore* and

currente calamo. 'T is yours now, but by your
leave I 'll copy it off, alter it a little and send it
down as "a song" for *Harvardiana,* for which I
protested I would write nothing O! Why, it 's
good! It sings itself! I don't think I shall alter
anything but Miss B.'s name, for it ran off the end
of my pen so that it must be better than I can
make it. Why, I *like* it, I do. There is n't anything good in it either, except in the last passage.
It has really put me in good spirits. Between
Sunday and Wednesday I added about 250 lines
to the "Poem." It is not finished yet. I wish it
were.

The Class Poem, which he printed since he was
not permitted to be present at his class celebration,
when he would have read it, is a somewhat hap-
hazard performance, as Lowell intimates in his letters. He says naïvely in one of the notes to the
poem, of which there is a liberal supply in an appendix, that he suddenly discovered his subject
after he had begun writing, by happening to refer
in an off hand way to Kant.

> "Kant, happy name! change but the K to C,
> And I will wring my poem out of thee.
> Thanks, vast Immanuel! thy name has given
> The thing for which my brains so long have striven.
> ·　　·　　·　　·　　·　　·　　·
> Cant be my theme, and when she fails my song,
> Her sister Humbug shall the lay prolong."

The satire of a young collegian is apt to be
pretty severe, and Lowell runs amuck of Carlyle,
Emerson, the Abolitionists, the advocates of Wo-

man's Rights, and the Teetotallers. For the most part the poem runs along glibly in the decasyllabic verse so handy to familiar poetry, and though there are many lame lines, there are more instances of the clever distichs which Lowell knocked off so easily in later years than one would have guessed from the examples of his verse which appear in his early letters. Here, for example, are some of his lines on Carlyle : —

> " Hail too, great drummer in the mental march,
> Teufelsdröckh ! worthy a triumphal arch,
> Who send'st forth prose encumbered with jackboots,
> To hobble round and pick up raw recruits,
> And, able both to battle and to teach,
> Mountest thy silent kettledrum to preach.
> Great conqueror of the English language, hail !
> How Caledonia's goddess must turn pale
> To hear the German-Græco-Latin flung
> In *Revolutions* from a Scottish tongue ! "

In the more serious and practical part of the poem there is an impassioned burst imitative of Campbell, in which he imagines the farewell words of the Cherokee Indians, who at this time, to his indignation, were being pushed westward from Georgia.

To the debit of his youthful zeal may be set down the lines on Emerson which were his footnote to the famous address to the Divinity School delivered 15 July, 1838 : —

> " Woe for Religion, too, when men, who claim
> To place a ' Reverend ' before their name,
> Ascend the Lord's own holy place to preach
> In strains that Kneeland had been proud to reach,
> And which, if measured by Judge Thacher's scale,

Had doomed their author to the county jail!
When men just girding for the holy strife,
Their hands just cleansed to break the bread of life,
Whose souls, made whole, should never count it loss
With their own blood to witness for the cross,
Invite a man their Christian zeal to crown
By preaching earnestly the gospel-down,
Applaud him when he calls of earthly make
That ONE who spake as never yet man spake,
And tamely hear the anointed Son of God
Made like themselves an animated clod ! "

To the credit of his manliness may be set down, *per contra*, the following letter which he wrote after the publication of the poem : a letter, which, for all its boyish assumption of the *toga virilis*, has a ring of sincerity about it : —

CAMBRIDGE, Sept. 1st, 1838.

DEAR SIR, — In my class poem are a few lines about your " address." My friends have expressed surprise that after I had enjoyed your hospitality and spoken so highly of you in private, I should have been so 'ungrateful' as ever to have written anything of the kind. Could I have ever dreamed that a man's private character should interfere with his public relations, I had never blotted paper so illy. But I really thought that I was doing rightly, for I consider it as virtual a lie to hold one's tongue as to speak an untruth. I should have written the same of my own brother. Now, sir, I trouble you with this letter because I think you a man who would think nowise the worse of me for holding up my head and speaking the truth at any sacrifice. That I could wilfully malign a man whose salt I had eaten, and whose little child I had danced on my knee, — he must be a small man who would believe so small a thing of his fellow.

But this word " ingratitude " is a very harsh and grating word, and one which I hope would never be laid to my charge since I stood at my mother's knee and learnt the first very alphabet, as it were, of goodness. I hope that if you have leisure, sir, you will answer this letter and put me at rest. I hope you will *acquit* me (for I do not still think there is aught to *forgive* or *pardon*, and I trust *you* will not after reading this letter) of all uncharitableness.

Of course no one can feel it as strongly as I do, for since my friends have hinted at this " ingratitude " I have felt a great deal, and scarcely dare to look at the Tennyson you lent me without expecting some of the devils on the cover to make faces at me.

I hope you will find time to answer this and that I may still enjoy your friendship and be able to take you by the hand and look you in the face, as honest man should to honest man.

   I remain yours with respect,
     JAMES RUSSELL LOWELL.

P. S. I have sent with this a copy of my " poem " — if it be not too tiresome, you would perhaps think better of me, if you were to read it *through*. I am not silly enough to suppose that this can be of any importance to you (if, indeed, you ever heard of the passage I refer to), but it is of very great importance to me.

J. R. L.

Lowell's own comment on the poem years after was in the lines : —

> " Behold the baby arrows of that wit
>   Wherewith I dared assail the woundless Truth !
> Love hath refilled the quiver, and with it
>   The man shall win atonement for the youth." [1]

In this the earliest of his acknowledged publications, as so often in his later poems, satire and sentiment jostle each other.   The predominant note, indeed, is satire in the lofty tone of nineteen, but the invocation and the close are in a different strain.   Here, too, there is the exaltation of a very young man, and one may read phrases which perhaps said more than Lowell meant to say ; but it was a ruffled youth with which his college career closed, and this period of his life was not to know as yet any steadying force.   It is not strange that he grasped at somewhat illusory phantoms in his eagerness to stay himself.   Here are the invocation and epilogue : —

> " Oh thou ! to whom, where'er my footstep roam,
>   My restless soul would spread its pinions home, —
> Reality ! more fair than any seeming
> E'er blest the fancy of an angel's dreaming, —
> Be thou my muse, in whose blue eye I see
> The heaven of my heart's eternity !
> Oh, hover like a spirit at my side,
> In all my wanderings a heavenly guide,

[1] Letters, ii. 302.

Then, if in Cant's dim mists I lose my way,
Thy blessed smile shall lead me back to day,
And, when I turn me from the land of night,
Thou, morning star of love, shalt herald light!

" Lady! whom I have dared to call my muse,
        With thee my day began, with thee shall end —
Thou can'st not such a poor request refuse
        To let thine image with its closing blend!
As turn the flowers to the quiet dews,
        Fairest, so turns my yearning heart to thee,
For thee it pineth — as the homesick shell
        Mourns to be once again beneath the sea —
Oh let thine eyes upon this tribute dwell,
        And think — one moment kindly think of me!
Alone — my spirit seeks thy company,
        And in all beautiful communes with thine,
In crowds — it ever seeks alone to be
        To dream of gazing in thy gentle eyne! "

After all, the irregular impulses of the class
poem point to what is of more consequence, the
beginning of Lowell's manhood. Until the summer of 1837, he had been a happy-go-lucky boy,
sunning himself in literature, in nature, and in his
friends; then there set in a period when he was
at odds with fortune, and a stirring of half-under-
stood desires arose; the consciousness of power
was struggling with the wilfulness of youth.

CHAPTER III

As his college course drew near its close, Lowell began to forecast his immediate future. His growing devotion to letters, especially to poetry, and perhaps the wish to linger a little longer within the shelter of the academic life, led him to cherish the notion of studying a while in Germany, and he wrote to his father, who was still abroad, in pursuance of this plan; but he received no encouragement. Germany, it was properly said to him, was no place for the study of law by an American, and the law was regarded as his vocation.

Vaguely conscious of his real calling, Lowell passed in review the two professions of the ministry and the law, which at that time would be likely to attract one who had begun to use his pen with as much assiduity as an embryo artist plies his pencil in sketches. Unquestionably the ministry opened a fair way of life to him, somewhat as it had, less than a score of years earlier, to Emerson, though the conditions had already begun to change. Lowell shrank from adopting that calling with an instinct which sprang in part from his sense of its traditional sacredness, in part from

an increasing consciousness of his own separation
from the form of religious teaching which would
naturally be looked for in him. There was a
preacher in Lowell not merely by inheritance, but,
even at this time of nonsense and idle levity, in
the stirring of a soul that hated evil, and longed
to exercise an active influence in righting wrongs.
The full strength of this impulse was to be developed shortly, and thenceforward to find constant expression through his life, for a preacher at
bottom he was throughout his career. An undercurrent of feeling persuaded him that he might
even take to preaching, if he could be sure of being
a celibate, and independent of any harassing anxiety respecting his support. But as he wrote of
himself a few years later to his friend Briggs: "I
believe my religion (I am an infidel, you know, to
the Christianity of to-day, and so my religion is
something palpable to me in case of strait) arms
me against any sorrows to come." The youthful
protest in the parenthesis must be taken seriously,
but not subjected to microscopic analysis. Reverence was an abiding element in his nature, and it
was early displayed, but it was reverence for what
was intrinsically to be revered, and that very spirit
carried with it an impatient reaction against conventional religion. In the letter to Dr. Loring, in
which he discussed the question of going into the
Divinity School, he was led, from a slight reference
to the doctrines which Emerson was announcing, to
speak more directly of personal religion.

"I don't know," he says, "whether we poor little

worms (who though but little lower than the angels are [but] a little higher than those whom our
every step annihilates) ought not to *condescend* to
allow that there may be something *above* his reason. We must sometimes receive light like the
Aurora without knowing where it comes from.
And then, on the other hand, we may be allowed to
doubt whether our wise Creator would have given
us a dispensation by which to govern our everyday
life, any part of which was repugnant to our reason. It is a question which every man must settle
for himself : indeed he were mad to let any settle
it for him."

An independence of judgment did not lead him
to throw away a fundamental faith in spiritual
realities, but it made him ready to refuse conform-
ity with the nearest form of religion. At the
time he was writing, Lowell thought he saw the
churches, if not tolerant of a great evil, at least
mainly silent before it, and with the radicalism
which was as integral a part of him as his conservatism, he broke away from associations which
seemed thus inert and false to the very ideals they
professed to cherish. Had not the poetic impulse
and the artistic temper been so strong in him, it is
quite possible that as Emerson in his philosophic
idealism had let the minister's gown slip from his
shoulders, yet had remained on the platform, so
Lowell in his moral earnestness might, if he had
really gone into the ministry, have shortly become
a witty reformer, preaching with the prophet's
leathern girdle and not in the priest's cassock.

But heredity and an impulse to deliver his mind
were not strong enough to take him into the pulpit
against the clear dictates of a reasonable judgment, and with apparently no disposition toward
medicine, he turned almost from necessity to the
law. The law, at first, at any rate, did not so
much attract him, as it was reached by a process
of elimination. The substantial motive which
urged him was his need of a livelihood. Although
his father at this time was in what is quaintly
termed " comfortable circumstances," Lowell, like
his fellows everywhere in America, most certainly
in New England, never would have entertained the
notion of living indefinitely at his father's expense.
As a matter of course he must earn his living, and
he was so meagrely supplied even with pocket
money at this time that his letters contain frequent
illustration of his inability to indulge in petty pleasures — a short journey, for instance, the purchase
of a book or pamphlet, even postage on letters.

So, in the fall of 1838, when he was living at
Elmwood with his brother Charles, he began to
read Blackstone " with as good a grace and as few
wry faces " as he could. But suddenly, a fortnight only after making this assertion, he had
abandoned the notion of studying law, out of utter
distaste for it. It was after a great struggle, he
says, but the struggle was evidently one of those
occasional self-communings of the young man who
is not predestined to any profession, and yet is
unable to respond to the half articulate demands
of his nature. We can read Lowell's mind at this

time in the fragmentary confessions of his letters, and see that the controlling influence was to secure ultimately the right to devote himself to literature. The law is a jealous mistress, and Lowell was sagacious enough to perceive that to secure success in the profession he must needs devote himself to it with long and unremitting attention, and he was sure a real love for the study of law was a condition precedent to success. So again he weighed the chances. Once more he considered the ministry ; he even speculated over the possibilities of medicine — his friend Loring had taken up that for his profession ; but with a certain common-sense view of the matter, he argued that if his occupation were to be merely a means to an end, why, trade was the logical road to money-making, and he set about looking for a " place in a store."

" I must expect," he writes ruefully, " to give up almost entirely all literary pursuits, and instead of making rhymes, devote myself to making money." But with a whimsical attempt after all to join his ideals with this practical course, after saying that in abandoning the law he gives up the chance of going to Europe, since his father had promised him this plum if he would stick to the law for three years, he closes his letter : " I intend to go into a foreign store so that I may be able to go to Europe yet. I shall have to brush up my French so as to write foreign letters."

This was written on Tuesday the 30th of October. The next Monday, when he had gone to Boston to look for a place, he dropped in at the United

States court where a case was on in which Webster
was one of the counsel. His imagination took fire.
" I had not been there an hour," he writes, " before
I determined to continue in my profession and
study as well as I could." By an unexpected circumstance, however, he was within a month interrupted in his study. His brother Robert, who was
in the counting-room of a coal merchant, was laid
up with a lame hand, and so James took his place
at the desk. It is not impossible that he was se-
cretly glad of making thus, with a good conscience,
a little test of his aptitude for business.

His position as a substitute gave him a breathing spell, and he plunged again into rhyming.
His letters during the winter were full of experi-
ments in verse, and he was, moreover, giving serious attention to the technique of poetry, having
recourse to such manuals as Sidney's "Defense of
Poesie" and Puttenham's "Art of English Poesie,"
a characteristic act, for he had the same instinct
for the great genetic period of English poetry as
Lamb and his fellows in England had a generation
earlier. He even began to throw out lines in the
direction of self-support through literature. Besides his trials in the newspapers and magazines, he
took the chance given him to lecture in Concord,
and he wondered if his friend Loring could get
him an opportunity at Andover. He had " quitted
the law forever" on the 26th of February, 1839,
but the mood of exhilaration over a possible mainte-
nance through lecturing evaporated after a return
from Concord with four dollars, less his travelling

expenses, as the result of his first experiment. And yet business was as repellent to him as law. In a letter to G. B. Loring of March, 1839, he bursts forth into a cry of bitterness : —

"I don't know what to do with myself. I am afraid people will think me a fool if I change again, and yet I can hardly hope ever to be satisfied where I am. I should n't wonder if next Monday saw me with Kent's Commentaries under my arm. I think I might get to take an interest in it, and then I should not fear at all about the living. If I had not been thrice a fool, I should have been in Dane Law College reciting at this very moment. And what makes me feel still worse is that nobody knows or can know my motive for changing, and the struggle which kept me irresolute.

"I am certainly just at present in a miserable state, and I won't live so long. You must excuse the shortness of this letter, for my feelings are in such a distracted sort of a state that the more I write the less do I feel able to write.

> "Dear George, when I am set at table
> I am indeed quite miserable,
> And when as that I lie in bed,
> Strife and confusion whirl my head ;
> When I am getting up at morn
> I feel confoundedly forlorn,
> And when I go to bed at eve
> I can do nought but sigh and grieve.
> When I am walking into town
> I feel all utterly cast down,
> And when I 'm walking out from it
> I feel full many a sorrow fit."

The struggle in his mind went on through the

rest of the spring. He kept doggedly at his desk, apparently, but wrote more verse, especially of a serious sort. At last, on the 20th of May, he could write in a somewhat forced strain of exultation: " Rejoice with me! For to-morrow I shall be free. Without saying a word to any one, I shall quietly proceed to Dane Law College to recitation. Now shall I be happy again as far as *that* is concerned. Nature will smile for me yet again. I shall hear the merry tinkle of the brook and think not of the tinkle of dollars and cents. Upon the ocean I may look, nor dream of the rates of freight. Let us rejoice, George, in the days of our youth. We shall find it very different when we come to support ourselves. Good old Homer in the Odyssey makes Telemachus tell Minerva, ' Well may they laugh and sing and dance, for they are eating the bread of another man.' Now we who eat our father's bread at present may be as merry as we will. But very different will it be when every potato that we eat (lucky if we can get even those) shall seem watersoaked with the sweat of our brow. I am going to be as happy as the days are long."

A little later he wrote: "I am now a law student, and am really studying and intend to study. I shall now be able to come and spend some Saturday with you and come down Monday morning. . . . To-day I have been engaged an hour in recitation, 9 to 10, and then from 11 to $3\frac{1}{2}$ o'clock in studying law, which, as we only have one recitation a day, is pretty well. I have determined that I

will now *do* something.   I am lazy enough, heaven
knows, but not half so much so as some of my
friends suppose.   At all events, I was never made
for a merchant, and I even begin to doubt whether
I was made for anything in particular but to loiter
through life and then become manure."

From this time forward Lowell did not relin-
quish his study of law.   He confessed, indeed, to
a doubt if he should ever practice.   He had a
"blind presentiment of becoming independent in
some other way," and he allowed himself to dream
of cultivating literature in solitude on a little oat-
meal, but he pushed through to the nominal end,
and took his degree of bachelor of laws at commencement in August, 1840.[1]   Not long after, he
entered the law office in Boston of Mr. Charles
Greely Loring, and when the winter came he went
himself to Boston to live.

The vacillation and apparent irresolution outlined in his fickle pursuit of a profession in the
months after his graduation are unmistakable, but
there are expressions now and then in the letters
we have quoted that strike one as a little exaggerated even to one so open to attacks from conscience as was Lowell.   Why such a pother, one
might ask, over an embarrassment which is not
very uncommon, and after all touches chiefly the
prudential side of character ?   " Nobody knows or

[1] It was not uncommon in those days and long after for a student to take his degree at the Law School after a year or two only
of study and then to continue to hear lectures.   Lowell's name is
on the catalogue of the school for the year following his degree.

can know my motives for changing, and the struggle which kept me irresolute ; " but the boyish
companion to whom he wrote undoubtedly had an
inkling of his friend's perturbation, though frank
as that friend was in his correspondence and intercourse, he could surely have said, " the heart
knoweth its own bitterness."

The solution is simple enough in statement. Before his last year in college Lowell had met and
fallen fiercely in love with a beautiful girl, one of
the circle in which his family moved, and endowed
with intellectual grace and great charm of manner.
Then something came between them, and separation became inevitable, at least it became so in
Lowell's own view of the situation. The shock of
this rupture left not a shade of reproach for the
girl in Lowell's mind, but it broke up the fountains of the deep in his own life. He was scarcely
more than a boy in years, but he had in temperament and capacity for emotion a far greater maturity. He could write of himself a few years
later : " Brought up in a very reserved and conventional family, I cannot in society appear what
I really am. I go out sometimes with my heart so
full of yearning toward my fellows that the indifferent look with which even entire strangers pass
me brings tears to my eyes." There was indeed
an extraordinary frankness about him in these
early days, filling his letters with expressions which
might easily have made him wince in later years ;
but the spontaneity of his nature, which was always
seen in the unguardedness of his familiar writing

and his conversation, had in these days the added ingenuousness of youth.

The experience thus referred to in the summer of 1837 was no short, sharp passion burning itself out in quick rage; it smouldered and leaped up into flame at intervals for two years, fed moreover by the consciousness of his own impotence and the predicament into which he was helplessly drawn; and it was during these two years that this restlessness and vacillation of temper were almost ungovernable. Later in life even he looked back with horror upon this time, saying half in pity, half in contempt for himself, that he put a cocked pistol to his forehead in 1839, and had not finally the courage to pull the trigger.

It would be easy to fill many pages with illustrations drawn from unprinted poems written during this period, and they would have the added value of disclosing the fact that poetry was fast becoming the natural expression of his mind, even while he was fashioning it with constantly better art. In a letter written to Loring, 26 July, 1839, containing two bits of verse lyrically interpretative of his experience, he says : " You must not be surprised if I don't write again for some time, but the next time I do write I trust my letters will be better worth the postage. At any rate, it shall be filled more with my *real* than with my *poetical* me; although now they are synonymous terms, as they should be, for my poetry answers me very much as a sort of journal or rather nousometer."

It is hard for most of us to escape the lurking

judgment that the man, or boy either, who throws
his spiritual experience into verse is more or less
consciously dramatizing, and we are apt to credit
greater honesty to the one who does not than to
the one who does poetize his disappointments; but
in spite of the artfulness which betrays itself in
the effort of one who has not yet perfect command
of his instrument, there is a ring of sincerity about
Lowell's poetic journal which, without juggling, we
both infer from his nature as it is otherwise disclosed, and make illustrative of the real life of the
spirit. Here are some verses which occur in a letter to Dr. Loring in the summer of 1839. In
writing of them to his friend a few days later,
Lowell says: "The lines I wrote to you the other
day were improvised, and you must judge them
leniently accordingly. I do not think now, as I
did 'two years ago,' that poetry *must* be an inspiration, but am convinced that somewhat of care,
nay, even of thought, is requisite in a *poom*."

> "Turn back your eyes, my friend, with me
> Upon those two late parted years —
> Nay, look alone, for I can see
> But inward through these bitter tears:
> Deep grief sometimes our mind's eye clears.

> "How much lies in that one word 'Past'!
> More than in all that waits before;
> How many a saddened glance is cast
> To that stern wall of nevermore,
> Whose shadow glooms our heart's deep core.
> .   .   .   .

> "As hard it is for mortal glance
> To pierce the Has been's mystery
> And force of iron circumstance

Which said let these and these things be,
As to resolve futurity.

" A many streams that once ran full
Of joy or Marah waves of pain,
Wasting or making beautiful,
Have sunk no more to flow again,
And scarce the tracks they wore remain.

" And many shades of joy and woe
Pass cloudlike, silent, o'er my soul,
Which not one being else may know,
And into utter darkness roll,
Links lost from out my being's whole.
. . . .

" This Present is becoming Past ;
Live then each moment manfully
If you would wish your deeds to last,
Sowing good seed continually
Whose harvest time is yet to be.

" In our great pride we think that we
Build up our high or low estate,
Dimly half conscious that we see
The paths which lead to small and great
Through the fixed eye of settled Fate.

" The Past may guide the Future's ways :
Seeds cast far up the stream of time,
Returning after many days,
May grow to their ordained prime
Of fruitage in another clime. "

As if to reinforce our confidence in the genuine-
ness of the emotion which prompted these moral
verses, written apparently to the sound of Longfellow's " Psalm of Life," which had just appeared
in the *Knickerbocker*, we come in a few weeks to a
rhymed letter in which a reminiscence of the same

experience is recorded with simplicity and natural-
ness in a homely poetic strain : —

> "Two years ago, in days how like to these,
>   Yet how unlike ! beneath the changing trees
>   I walked with her full many a happy hour,
>   Pausing to gather some belated flower,
>   Or to pick up some nut half eaten, dropt
>   By a scared squirrel as away he hopt.
>   The jest, the laugh, and the more high debate
>   To which the forest aisles seem consecrate,
>   Nay, even the jest, and the dark plaided shawl
>   That loved her light form — I remember all :
>   For then I entered that fair gate of love
>   On whose bright arch should be inscribed above,
>   As o'er that other in the Tuscan's story —
>   ' Per me si va ne l' eterno dolore.'
>   The leaves were falling round us then, and we
>   Talked of their many meanings musingly.
>   Ah, woe is me ! we did not speak at all
>   Of how love's leaves will wither, change, and fall —
>   Full silently — and how the pent up breast
>   Will hide the tears that cannot be represt."

In this same letter Lowell enumerates at the
close the books he is reading and about to read . —

> " I 'm reading now the Grecian tragedies,
>   Stern, gloomy Æschylus, great Sophocles,
>   And him of Salamis whose works remain
>   More perfect to us than the other twain.
>   (Time 's a gourmand, at least he was so then,
>   And thinks his leavings good enough for men.)
>   When I have critically read all these,
>   I 'll dip in cloudy Aristophanes,
>   And then the Latin dramatists, and next
>   With mathematics shall my brain be vext.
>   So if I carry all my projects through
>   I shall do pretty well, I think, don't you ? "

What most impresses the attentive reader of
Lowell's verses and letters as the two years, to

which he so often refers, draw to a close, is the evidence that the young man was finally emerging from the mist and cloud through which he had been struggling, and was getting his feet upon solid ground, so that not only was his irresolution changed for a fairly diligent pursuit of his profession, but he had acquired a greater robustness of spirit and was squaring himself with life in earnest. The internal conflict had been fought out and the substantial victory gained was showing itself in greater self-reliance and a growth in manly ways.

It is therefore with especial satisfaction that the chronicler of his external history comes upon an event which was to mark emphatically the attainment of his intellectual and spiritual majority. Near the end of the year 1839 he made the acquaintance of Maria White. She was the daughter of Mr. Abijah White, a farmer in Watertown, whom Lowell characterized on first meeting him as "the most perfect specimen of a bluff, honest, hospitable country squire you can possibly imagine." Mr. White had a family of sons and daughters who thenceforward became Lowell's familiar acquaintance. One of the sons, William A. White, had been a classmate at Harvard, — he speaks of him once as his "quondam chum," — and it was by him that Lowell was introduced to his home. As Lowell had written with great freedom to his friend Loring of his troubled experience, so now one may trace in this very frank correspondence the manner in which this new affection displaced the mournfulness of that experience and substituted great peace and content for the soreness which still remained after a struggle that had resulted in substantial self-mastery.

In his earliest, hardly more than casual reference to Maria White he characterizes her as " a very pleasant and pleasing young lady " who " knows more poetry " than any one he is acquainted with. " I mean," he says, " she is able to repeat more. She is more familiar, however, with modern poets than with the pure well-springs of English poesy." His changing mood during the winter months that follow is visible in the poetry which he writes and copies in his letters, but in the early summer there is a bolder and franker tone, until the acquaintance which has ripened into intimacy culminates in an engagement not long after the completion of the lover's law studies.

June 13, 1840. I got back from Watertown, whither I went to a gathering at Miss Hale's (whose family are boarding at the Nonantum). I spent the night at W. A. W.'s. Lovely indeed it was with its fair moon and stars and floating cloud mist. I walked back with M. W. on my arm, and not only did my body go back, but my spirit also over the footsteps of other years. Were not the nights *then* as lovely . . . and the river that we gazed down into — think you those water-parties are so soon forgotten ? When we got to the house we sat upon the steps and talked, —

> And then like a Spring-swollen river
> Roll the full waves of her tumultuous thought,

Crested with glittering spray;
Her wild lips curve and quiver,
And my rapt soul on the deep stream upcaught,
Lulled by a dreamful music ever,
Unwittingly is borne away.

.   .   .   .

I float to a delicious land,
By a sunset Heaven spanned,
And musical with streams.
Around, the calm majestic forms
And Godlike eyes of early Greece I see,
Or listen till my spirit warms
To songs of courtly chivalry,
Or weep, unmindful if my tears be seen,
For the meek suffering love of poor Undine.

She is truly a glorious girl with her spirit eyes.
On the mantel is a moss rose she gave me and
which when it withers I shall enshrine in my
Homer. This morning I drove her up to Waltham. They tell me I shall be in love with her.
But there is but one *Love*. I love her because she
is a woman, and so was another being I loved.

August 18, 1840. Since you heard from me I
have been at Nantasket and had a fine time. I
found M. W., her brother, and Page,[1] down there,
and I carried Heath with me. I had one glorious
ride on the beach with M. W., I having hired a
horse and gig at Hingham. Hingham is a strange
place. I walked through the greater part of it
one day and did not even see a living soul. . . .

Nantasket is a beautiful place. The beach is
five miles long, smooth, hard sand without a pebble. When the wind blows on shore you may see

[1] William Page, the artist, whom Lowell first knew through
the Whites.

one line of unbroken white foam, five miles long,
roll up the beach at once. I spent one whole evening alone on the rocks with M. W. A glorious
evening it was. Page's portrait of M. W. is going
to be fine, at least I hope so. It *ought* to be. . . .

August 25, 1840. I have just finished reading Goethe's correspondence with a child, Bettina
Brentano. I had long tried (rather wished) to get
it, the more so from some beautiful extracts which
M. W. read to me, but had never seen it till now.
It is *beautiful*. It is wonderful when we think
that Bettina was a child. It is like sunshine on
grass newly rained upon — like the smell of a
flower — like the song of a bird. We are given
to look into the very core of the most loving heart
that ever came directly from God and *forgot not
whence it came*.

But it was mournful to think that all this love
should have been given to the cold, hard Goethe.[1]
I wanted such a soul for myself. M. W.'s is
nearer to it than any I have ever seen. But I
should have seen her three years ago. If that
other love could raise such a tempest in my soul
as to fling up the foul and slimy weeds from the
bottom, and make it for so long sluggish and
muddy, a disappointment from her would I think
have broken my heart.

George, twice lately I have had a very strange

[1] " Goethe's poetic sense was the Minotaur to which he sacrificed everything. To make a study he would soil the maiden
petals of a woman's soul." — " Lessing," in *Literary Essays*, ii.
195.

dream. Byron says that dreams "shake us with
the vision of the past." Do they not also shake us
with the vision of what is to come? I dreamed
that I went to see M. W., that I saw her walking
just before me, and that when I strove to overtake
her, she vanished. I asked a man whom I met if
he had seen her (describing her). He said "yes,
she has gone down the happy road." I followed,
but could get no glimpse of her. Does this mean
that I shall love M. W. and that she will die?
Homer says that there are two gates of quickly
fading dreams, one of sawn ivory, and the other
of polished horn. Those dreams that pass thro'
the ivory gate are liars, but those that forth issue
from the polished horn tell truth to any one of
mortals who sees them. Did my dream come thro'
the horn or the ivory? Are you oneirocritical
enough to say? At any rate, remember this.
M. W. lent me a "sweet" book (*she* did not call
it so and I don't know why *I* did), "Philothea," by
Mrs. Child. If you ever come across it, read it.
It is, as Mr. Emerson called it, "a divine book."
. . . To-day is (or was) Commencement. I was
standing in the pew listening to the music when I
looked round and saw a pair of eyes fixed on me
that made me feel glad; they were M. W.'s. I
thought she was in Beverly. I managed to squeeze
my way up to her at last and walked with her to
Judge Fay's, stayed there a little while and then
went to take my degree of LL. B. After dining
with the alumni, I walked round to the President's
in the faint hope of seeing her again. Just as I

got nearly there, I saw her go in.   I went in after.
The man she was with left her, and I enjoyed her
for more than two hours.   Scates made his appearance here to-day, so that my day has been a very
happy one.

P. S.   There are more lies contained in the
piece of parchment on which my degree is written
than I ever before saw in a like compass.   It
praises me for assiduous attention at recitations,
etc., etc.   (This letter seems to be all about M. W.)

Good by,   J. R. L.

Sunday, [31 August, 1840.]   I have received
your letter and had also written an answer to it,
which I just burnt.   It was written when I was
not in a fit state of mind to write.   I had been
feeling very strongly that

> " Custom lies about us with a weight
>   Heavy as frost, and deep almost as life."

If I had written this an hour ago, it would have
been black and melancholy enough, but I have
smoked three cigars and ruminated and am calm —
almost. . . .

If I had seen her three years ago things might
have been not thus.   But yet I would not give up
the bitter knowledge I gained last summer for
much — very much.

> " Who never ate his bread in sorrow,
>   Who never passed the lonesome hours,
>   Weeping and watching for the morrow,
>   He knows ye not, ye Heavenly powers."

I have been calmer and stronger ever since.   Oh
the glory of a calm, still soul !   If we could keep

our souls ever in a holy silence, we should be wise,
we should hear the music of the spheres. But they
will ever be talking to themselves. If we could
but become so, we should then ever have at our
beck those divine messengers which visit us also as
well as Abraham. . . .

Do "they say" that she is "transcendental"?
Yes, she does indeed go beyond them. They cannot understand a being like her. But if they mean
that she is unfit for the duties of life, they are
entirely wrong. She has more "common sense"
than any woman I have ever seen. Genius always
has. Hear what Maria herself says in one of her
glorious letters to me. "When I said that I loved
you, I almost felt as if I had said 'and I will
espouse sorrow for thy sake,' for I have lived long
enough and observed life keenly enough to know
that not the truest and most exalted love can bar
the approach of much care and sorrow." And all
these she is ready and able to bear. Yes, she will
love you, for she loves everything that I love.

The first volume of poetry which Lowell published, "A Year's Life," is, as its name intimates,
a poetic record of the time covered by these and
other passages from his correspondence. It appeared in January, 1841, and he was moved to
print it both because Miss White desired it, and
because it was so full of her. The love which
found expression, as we have seen, in letters to a
familiar friend, could not fail of an outlet in verse,
and was but thinly concealed from the public in a

volume which, from Dedication to Epilogue, was
glowing with it.   Many of the poems he had already printed in the magazines for which he had
been diligently writing, and these poems, as they
appeared, were announcements, to those who knew
both the lovers, of the pure passion which was
flaming.

Two of the poems in particular reflect Lowell's
idealization of the lady and his consciousness of
what this experience meant to him.   " 'Ianthe,' "
he writes to Loring, "is good as far as it goes.   I
did not know her then.   She *is* a glorious creature
indeed ! "

> " Dear, glorious creature ! "

he exclaims, near the close of the poem,

> " With eyes so dewy bright,
>   And tenderest feeling
>   Itself revealing
>   In every look and feature,
>   Welcome as a homestead light
> To one long wandering in a clouded night;
>   O, lovelier far her woman's weakness,
>   Which yet is strongly mailed
>   In armor of courageous meekness
>   And faith that never failed ! "

The lines on pages 77, 78 are from the same poem,
which was written thus when the acquaintance was
ripening into intimacy.   The whole poem is a tribute to the visionary beauty of her face and character as revealed to him.   "There is a light," thus
the poem opens : —

> " There is a light within her eyes
>   Like gleams of wandering fire-flies;
>   From light to shade it leaps and moves

> Whenever in her soul arise
> The holy shapes of things she loves."

Throughout the poem runs, moreover, an undercurrent of holy awe and a presage of her short life, which drew from him the reflections on death that occur in his letters : —

> " I may not tell the blessedness
> Her mild eyes send to mine,
> The sunset-tinted haziness
> Of their mysterious shine,
> The dim and holy mournfulness
> Of their mellow light divine ;
> The shadows of the lashes lie
> Over them so lovingly,
> That they seem to melt away
> In a doubtful twilight-gray,
> While I watch the stars arise
> In the evening of her eyes.
> I love it, yet I almost dread
> To think what it foreshadoweth ;
> And, when I muse how I have read
> That such strange light betokened death, —
> Instead of fire-fly gleams, I see
> Wild corpse-lights gliding waveringly."

The closing section of the poem holds a reflection of that image which is after all most enshrined in the poet's heart, as one may gather not only from his after words concerning her, but from the influence manifest in his own early career from this time forward.

> " Early and late, at her soul's gate
> Sits Chastity in warderwise,
> No thought unchallenged, small or great,
> Goes thence into her eyes ;
> Nor may a low, unworthy thought
> Beyond that virgin warder win,
> Nor one, whose passion is not ' ought,'

May go without, or enter in.
I call her, seeing those pure eyes,
The Eve of a new Paradise,
Which she by gentle word and deed,
And look no less, doth still create
About her, for her great thoughts breed
A calm that lifts us from our fallen state,
And makes us while with her both good and great, —
Nor is their memory wanting in our need :
With stronger loving, every hour,
Turneth my heart to this frail flower,
Which, thoughtless of the world, hath grown
To beauty and meek gentleness,
Here in a fair world of its own, —
By woman's instinct trained alone, —
A lily fair which God did bless,
And which from Nature's heart did draw
Love, wisdom, peace, and Heaven's perfect law."

Lowell did not retain " Ianthe " in his later collections, but he reprinted to the last the other poem
especially identified with Miss White which bears
the significant title " Irene." This, as the reader
perceives, is more distinctly a piece of characteriza
tion, and its closing lines, wherein Irene is likened
to the lone star seen by sailors tempest-tost, may
be read as carrying more than a pretty poetic
simile, for it cannot be doubted that the love which
now possessed the poet was in a profound sense a
word of peace to him. Something of the same
strain, though more remote and dramatic, may be
read in the poem " The Sirens," which is also retained by Lowell in his later collections, and is
dated in " A Year's Life " " Nantasket, July, 1840,"
a date which has an added interest when one refers
to the letter given above on page 78. One more

passage may be read from his letters as giving his own final word of retrospect and prospect. It occurs in a letter to G. B. Loring, 2 January, 1841.

" Yes, my friend, it is most true that I have changed. I thank *her* and one other, under God, for it. . . . Had the love I bore to a woman you know of three years ago, been as pure, true, and holy as that I bear to her who ' never from me shall be divided,' I had been a man sooner. My love for her was fierce and savage. It rose not like the fair evening star on the evening I first saw her (I remember it well), but (as *she* has said of such love) like a lurid meteor. And it fell as suddenly. For a time I was dazed by its glare and startled by the noise of its bursting. But I grew calm and soon morning dawned. . . .

" And I mean to live as one beloved by such a woman should live. She is every way noble. People have called ' Irene ' a beautiful piece of poetry. And so it is. It owes all its beauty to her, and were it a thousand times as beautiful would not be so much so as she is to me."

The strong emotional experience which thus possessed Lowell came to him when he was largely under the sway of sentiment, but though, as we have seen, it was translated into poetry very freely, it is not so much the immediate expression in literary form which concerns us as it is the infusion of an element in the formation of character. Lowell was overcharged in his youth with sensitiveness in affection. There was a fitfulness in his demonstration of it, an almost ungovernable outflow of feeling, which left him in danger of coming under the control of morbid impulse. What he required, and what most happily he found, was the serenity and steadfastness of a nature, exalted like his own, but glowing with an ardor which had other than purely personal aim.

Miss White was a highly sensitive girl of a type not unknown, especially at that time, in New England. Of delicate sensibility, she listened eagerly to the voices rising about her which found their choragus in Emerson. It was before the time of much organization among women, but not before the time when one and another woman, inheritors of a refined conscience, stirred by the movement in the air, sought to do justice to their convictions in espousing this or that moral cause, not at all necessarily in public championship, but in the eloquent zeal of domestic life. As her brother William was to become an active reformer, so she fed her spirit with aspirations for temperance, and for that abolition of slavery which was already beginning to dominate the moral earnestness of the community, holding all other reforms as subordinate to this. Lowell, seeing in her a Una, was quickened in the spirit which had already been awakened, and instantly donned his armor as her Red Cross Knight.[1]

At this period there was a much greater homogeneity in New England life than there has been at any time since. The democratizing of society

[1] It is very likely under the impetus given by Maria White that Lowell took a place as delegate to the Anti-Slavery Convention held in Boston, 17 November, 1840.

had been going on under favoring conditions, for industry was still at the basis of order, less was made of the distinction of wealth, more of the distinction of education, the aristocratic element was under the same general law of hard work, and a proletariat class had not been created by an inflow of the waste of Europe which inevitably accompanied the sturdy peasants. The city had not yet swept ardent youth into its rapids, and the simplicity of modes of life was hardly more marked in the country than in the town. Whoever recalls the now old-fashioned tales by Miss Catherine Sedgwick will have a truthful picture of a social order which seems Arcadian in the haze of sixty years since.

It was, in some aspects, the culmination of the ingrowing New England just before the Atlantic ocean became contracted to a broad stream, the West was clutched by iron hands, and all manner of forces conspired to render this secluded corner of the earth a cosmopolitan part of a larger community.

One of the most characteristic phases of this life was the attention paid by all classes to the awakening which was going on in education, reform, politics, and religion. Mr. Norton has printed a letter [1] of Lowell's in which he gives an animated picture of a temperance celebration in Watertown, at which Maria White appeared in a sort of New England translation of a Queen of the May, as the celebration itself was a festival in the moral vernacular.

[1] *Letters*, i. 67–69.

Lowell's own delight in her was unbounded, and the scene as he depicts it, was a New England idyl.

Maria White and her brother belonged to a group of young people on most friendly terms with one another, and known offhand by themselves as the Band. They lived in various places, Boston, Cambridge, Watertown, Salem, and were constantly seeking occasions for familiar intercourse. Dr. Hale has given a lively account of their fellowship and summons a witness who was herself a member of the company.[1] To this coterie Lowell was now introduced, and the relations between him and Miss White made the pair the centre of attraction. Miss White's spirituelle beauty and poetic temperament and Lowell's spontaneity of wit and sentiment were heightened in the eyes of these young people by the attachment between them, and they were known with affectionate jesting as the Queen and King of the Band. In the exalted air upon which the two trod, stimulating each other, their devotion came to have, by a paradox, an almost impersonal character, as if they were creatures of romance; their life was led thus in the open, so much so that, as has been said more than once, the letters exchanged by them were passed about also among the other young people of the circle.[2] Be this as it may, the assertion is rendered

[1] *James Russell Lowell and His Friends*, pp. 72–76.

[2] "I have enjoyed the society of my fair cousin Maria very much. She has shown me several of James's letters, and I think I never saw such perfect specimens of *love-letters*, — those in any novel you ever read are perfectly indifferent compared to them. Without being silly in the least, they are full of all the fervor and

credible by the highly charged atmosphere in which
they were living.   The two young poets — for
Maria White was not only of poetic temperament,
but wrote verses, some of which found place in
current magazines — were lifted upon a platform
by their associates, and were themselves so open
in their consciousness of poetic thinking and acting that they took little pains to abscond from this
friendly publicity.   It is a curious instance of freedom from shamefacedness in so native a New Englander as Lowell, but his letters, his poems, and
common report, all testify to an ingenuousness of
sentiment at this time, which was a radical trait,
and less conspicuous later in life only because like
other men he became subject to convention.

But though Lowell lived in this exhilarated
state, he was not likely to be led away into any
wholly impracticable scheme of living.   His own
good sense could be relied on, and his independence of spirit, as could his detestation of debt,
which kept him all his life a frugal liver.   He was,
besides, brought up sharply at this time by the
necessity suddenly laid on him to earn his living, if
he would be married, since his father, always generous to him, had now lost almost all his personal
property, and was land poor ; it was clearly understood, too, that the young people must rely on
themselves for support.   Fortunate was it for him
that he was to have a wife who shared to the full
his views on living.   " It is easy enough," wrote

extatification which you would expect from the most ardent lover."
— L. L. Thaxter to T. W. Higginson, 19 January, 1842.

Maria White to Levi Thaxter, " to be married —
the newspaper columns show us that every day;
but to live and be happy as simple King and
Queen without the gifts of fortune, this is, I confess, a triumph which suits my nature better."

Lowell, who had been lodging in Cambridge,
moved into Boston when he was established in
Mr. Loring's office, but in the spring of 1842 went
back to Elmwood to live. Dr. Lowell had returned
from Europe with his wife and daughter in the
early summer of 1840. It is probable that the return of Lowell to his father's house was due to the
declining health of his mother, who showed symp-
toms of that disorder of the brain which clouded
her last years, and is graphically depicted in her
son's poem, " The Darkened Mind." From this
time her husband and children watched her with
solicitude and tried various remedies. She was
taken on little journeys to Saratoga and elsewhere,
in search of restoration, but in vain. In this case,
as so often happens, the sufferer who draws largely
on one's sympathy is the faithful, despairing husband.[1]

Although Lowell had been admitted to the bar,
and was ready to practice, clients were slow in
coming, and with his resources in literature it was
natural enough that he should use his enforced
leisure in writing for publication. There were few

[1] " I am obliged to stay at home whenever Father goes to Boston, and as he usually goes thither on the four first days of the
week, I am rather closely prisoned." — J. R. L. to R. Carter, 31
December, 1843.

periodicals in America in 1840 that could afford
to pay their contributors, and the sums paid were
moderate. But the zeal of the editors was not
measured by their ability to reward contributors,
and both editors and writers fed a good deal at the
table of the Barmecides spread in the somewhat
ramshackle House of Fame. The *Southern Literary Messenger* was one of these impecunious but
ambitious journals, and the editor teased Lowell
constantly for contributions. Lowell gave them
freely, for writing was his delight, and he was not
unwilling to have a hospitable and reputable magazine in which to print what he wrote, both for the
slight incentive which publication gave, and because
he could thus with little effort "make believe" that
he was a popular author. He used frequently
the signature Hugh Perceval. He liked the name
Perceval, which had been borne by his earliest
American ancestor, and regretted that it had not
been given him at his birth, as had then been proposed. In the *Southern Literary Messenger* he
could publish half personal poems to be read between the lines by his intimate friends; but he
grew impatient of this unprofitable business.

"Have you got the August S. L. M. yet?" he
writes to Loring, 18 August, 1840. "I have not.
White [1] wrote to me a short time since that the
July and August numbers were coming out together, and at the same time asking me to translate a long poem of Victor Hugo's. I have not
answered him yet. But when I do I shall tell him

[1] Thomas W. White, the editor.

that ' reading and writing come by nature, but to
be a translator is the gift of Fortune,' so that if he
chooses to pay me he shall have translations. I
don't think I shall write any more for him. 'T is
a bad habit to get into for a poor man, this writing
for nothing. Perhaps if I hang off he may offer
me somewhat."

The publication of " A Year's Life " was a more
definite assertion of his place as a poet. He had
been encouraged to publish both by the confidence
of Miss White and by the practical aid of friends,
like his friend J. F. Heath, who engaged to secure
the sale of at least a hundred copies. Lowell
watched the fortunes of his first open venture
eagerly, from a conviction that it would have some
influence on his further efforts. " I have already,"
he writes to Loring, 18 February, 1841, " been
asked to write for an annual to be published in
Boston, and 'which is to be a fair specimen of
the arts in this country.' It is to be edited (sub
rosa) by Longfellow, Felton, Hillard, and that set.
Hawthorne and Emerson are writing for it, and
Bryant and Halleck have promised to write. The
pay for poetry is five dollars a page, at any rate,
and more if the work succeeds according to the
publishers' expectation. So you see my book has
done me some good, although it does not sell so
fast as it ought, considering how everybody praises
it. If you get a chance to persuade anybody to
buy it, do so. The praise I don't care so much
about, because I knew just how good and how bad
the book was before I printed it. But I wish, if

possible, to get out a second edition, which will do
me more good, as an author, than all the praise
and merit in the world. My father is so very
much pleased with the book that he wishes me to
publish a second edition at any rate, and he will pay
all expenses, and be responsible for its selling."

The little volume was the first fruits of Lowell's
poetic harvesting, and the promise it gave of poetical genius was by no means inconsiderable. In
his maturer judgment, to be sure, Lowell preserved
but seven of the thirty-three poems and two of the
thirty-five sonnets contained in it, — in all, thirty-
five of the one hundred and eighty-two pages of
the book, and had he been drawn off from poetry,
supposing this possible, the book would have been
reckoned as lightly in the general account of his
production as Motley's fiction was in his full measure. But he was not drawn off from poetry, and
the early note here struck was a dominant one
afterward. In most poets of any consequence the
disciple is pretty sure to be evident in early work,
and Lowell in " A Year's Life " unmistakably
owned himself an ardent lover of Keats and to a
less degree of Tennyson, who had been caught up
by the lively circle in which he moved with the
eagerness of an American discovering, as one so
often did, the old world of contemporary England.
In copying Keats, Lowell was indeed copying the
Keats who copied, and it is not at all unlikely that
when he was enamored of " Fancy," " Lines on
the Mermaid Tavern," " Robin Hood," and the
like, and echoed them faintly in " The Bobolink,"

"Ianthe," "Irene," and others, he was harking back also to Wither and other Elizabethans whom Keats loved, and whose light touch was caught so deftly by Milton in his "L'Allegro" and "Il Penseroso." Be this as it may, Lowell was most outspoken at this time in his admiration of Keats. He had become acquainted with him, as we have seen, in that volume which contained the triad, Coleridge, Keats, and Shelley, which was the fountain of modern English poetry to which so many thirsty Americans went. Lord Houghton's memoir of Keats had not appeared, and Lowell himself, in 1840, contemplated writing a life, going so far as to concoct a letter to Keats's brother George, which, however, he never sent. His admiration, besides taking the form of frank imitation, displayed itself in his early sonnet, "To the Spirit of Keats," which he contributed to the New York literary journal *Arcturus*, conducted by the brothers Duyckinck. His letter to Evert A. Duyckinck, accompanying the sonnet, is interesting for its tribute to the two modern English poets who, after Spenser, were his nearest friends.

BOSTON, Dec. 5, 1841.

MY DEAR SIR, — I address you rather than your brother editor, because I judge that the poetical department of *Arcturus* is more especially under your charge. I have to thank you for your sympathizing notice of my verses last spring. I thought then that you might like to have a contribution occasionally from me, but other engagements which

it were tedious to specify hindered me from doing
what my sympathy with the aim of your magazine
dictated.   I subscribed for your *Arcturus* before I
had seen a number of it (though I can ill afford
many such indulgences of taste) because I liked
the spirit of your prospectus.   For the same reason
I sent you my volume — of which I sent but a bare
half-dozen to " the press " — because I despise our
system of literary puffing.   Your notice of Keats,
in the number for this month, a poet whom I especially love and whom I consider to be one of the
true old Titan brood — made me wish to see two
of my own sonnets enshrined in the same volume.
One of them you will see is addressed to the same
" marvellous day."   I cannot help thinking that
you will like both of them.[1]

In your " News Gong " I see that you suggest a
reprint of Tennyson.   I wish you would say in
your next that he is about to reprint a new and
correct edition of his poems with many new ones
which will appear in a few months.   I think it
would be a pity to reprint his poems at all — for he
is poor and that would deprive him of what little
profit he might make by their sale in this country
—especially would it be wrong to reprint an incor-
rect edition.   (Moxon will be his publisher.)

I do not wish you to state your authority for this
— but you may depend on it, for my authority is
the poet himself.   I have the great satisfaction of
thinking that the publication is in some measure

[1] The sonnet, " To the Spirit of Keats," was the first of the
two ; the other was " Sunset and Moonshine," not retained by the
poet in his final collection.

owing to myself, for it was by my means that he was written to about it, and he says that " his American friends " are the chief cause of his reprinting.

Wishing you all success in the cause of true and good literature,

I remain your friend,

J. R. LOWELL.

The little book was received with an attention which seems to suggest the paucity of hopeful literature at the time and the Marchioness spirit of the critics. Lowell's eager friends came forward with their notices, but there were then fewer journals even than now that could be looked to for careful judgment. In *Graham's Magazine* there was a long account of the book headed " A New School of Poetry at hand," and the writer, who hides behind the letter C., after crediting Lowell with ideality, enthusiasm, love for his fellow-men, freshness, and delicacy, finds fault with him chiefly for affectation of language and carelessness ; but he welcomes him as the herald of a new school which is to be humanitarian and idealistic. It is amusing to find our familiar friend, the " great original American poem," looked for confidently from this new poet. Lowell warmed himself with this praise.[1]

[1] " [Mrs. Longfellow] was the first stranger that ever said a kind word to me about my poems. She spoke to me of my *Year's Life*, then just published. I had then just emerged from the darkest and unhappiest period of my life, and was peculiarly sensitive to sympathy. My volume, I knew, was crude and immature, and did not do me justice ; but I knew also that there was a *heart* in it, and I was grateful for her commendation." — J. R. L. to H. W. Longfellow, 13 August, 1845.

The most serviceable vehicle for Lowell's literary endeavors at this time was *The Boston Miscellany* projected by Nathan Hale, Lowell's associate in *Harvardiana*, and published by two young Boston men, Bradbury and Soden. The *Miscellany* had the short life characteristic of American literary magazines in the early half of the century, but it showed the sound literary judgment of its editor in the list of contributors he attracted. Lowell entered heartily into the plans for the new magazine. He wrote for it, among other things, a sketch, "My First Client," which is in its form as near an approach to fiction as he ever attempted, and is a slightly embellished narrative of his own clientless experience as a lawyer. He thought so ill of it that he refused to allow it to be reprinted, a few years later, in one of the annuals then popular.

The most significant contribution which he made to the *Miscellany* was a series of papers on the Old English Dramatists, begun anonymously, but continued with his name. These were readings in Massinger, Marlowe, and others, with running comments, and reflected the keen interest which he took then and all his life in that great quarry of noble thoughts and brave images. The series was the forerunner of his labors in the field of criticism of literature, and the pleasure which he took in the work, as well as the appreciation which the papers received, gave him a hopeful sense that he might trust to letters for support, and abandon the law, which he hated, and which naturally returned the compliment. In September, 1842, he had become so sanguine that, after mysteriously hinting at an even more substantial means of support, he wrote to his friend Loring : —

"I think I may safely reckon on earning four hundred dollars by my pen the next year, which will support me. Between this and June, 1843, I think I shall have freed myself of debt and become an independent man. I am to have fifteen dollars a poem from the *Miscellany*, ten dollars from *Graham*, and I have made an arrangement with the editor of the *Democratic Review*, by which I shall probably get ten or fifteen dollars more. Prospects are brightening, you see."

It was the prophecy of a sanguine young man, but unhappily the plan which seemed to him to promise most was instead to plunge him into debt. The *Miscellany* had closed its short career by merging itself in the *Arcturus* of New York, and taking courage from the brilliancy of the journal rather than caution from its brevity of life, Lowell, in company with Mr. Robert Carter, projected a new Boston literary and critical magazine to be issued monthly. The Prospectus has all the bravery and gallant dash of these forlorn hopes in literature.

The contents of each number will be entirely Original, and will consist of articles chiefly from American authors of the highest reputation.

The object of the Subscribers in establishing *The Pioneer*, is to furnish the intelligent and reflecting portion of the Reading Public with a

rational substitute for the enormous quantity of
thrice-diluted trash, in the shape of namby-pamby
love tales and sketches, which is monthly poured
out to them by many of our popular magazines, —
and to offer instead thereof, a healthy and manly
Periodical Literature, whose perusal will not necessarily involve a loss of time and a deterioration of
every moral and intellectual faculty.

The Critical Department of *The Pioneer* will
be conducted with great care and impartiality, and
while satire and personality will be sedulously
avoided, opinions of merit or demerit will be can-
didly and fearlessly expressed.

The Pioneer will be issued punctually on the
day of publication, in the principal cities of the
Union.   Each number will contain 48 pages, royal
octavo, double columns, handsomely printed on fine
paper, and will be illustrated with Engravings of
the highest character, both on wood and steel.

Terms : Three Dollars a year, payable, in all
cases, in advance.   The usual discount made to
Agents.   Communications for the Editors, letters,
orders, &c., must be addressed, *postpaid*, to the
Publishers, 67 Washington St. (opposite the Post
Office,) Boston.

LELAND & WHITING.

October 15th, 1842.

The publishers appear to have had no pecuniary
interest in the venture, the editors being the proprietors as well.   Mr. Carter was a young man of
Lowell's age, living at the time in Cambridge,
where he afterward married a daughter of Mr.

George Nichols, long known for his scholarly attainments as printer and corrector of the press, and for a short time also as a publisher. Mr. Carter was a man of wide reading and tenacious memory and a good writer, as his breezy book, "A Summer Cruise on the Coast of New England," testifies. His encyclopædic mind stood him in good stead when, later, he held a position in the publishing house of D. Appleton & Co., and superintended the "New American Encyclopædia."

The *Pioneer*, though it might be called a continuation of *The Boston Miscellany*, had characteristics of its own which show that its conductors had a clearly defined ideal in their minds and did not lack the courage and energy to pursue it. The *Miscellany* had made concessions to the supposed taste of the day, and had tried to catch subscribers with fashion plates and articles, while really caring only for good literature. The *Pioneer* discarded all adventitious aid, and, with fidelity to its name, determined to break its way through the woods of ignorance and prejudice to some fair land beyond. Upon its cover page it bore a sentence from Bacon: " Reform, therefore, without bravery or scandal of former times and persons ; but yet set it down to thyself as well to create good precedents as to follow them." It is easy to see that Lowell, with his love of good letters, and with a zeal for reform just now quickened by the fine fervor of Maria White, meant with his individual means to do very much what the proprietors and conductors of the *Atlantic Monthly* attempted on a larger scale fifteen

years later. But those fifteen years made a good
deal of difference in the attitude of men toward the
greatest of national evils, and in 1843 Lowell was
not likely to be a trenchant political writer, or to
think of literature and anti-slavery sentiment in the
same breath. The vague spirit of reform which
stirred him was rather a recurrence to fundamental
ideas of freedom which made him impatient of for-
mality and provincialism in literature, and led him
to associate American political ideas with large
independence of intellectual life. He had been
breathing the atmosphere of the spacious England
of the dramatists, and it was the nature of this literature which attracted him, as it was its art which
drew Lamb, Hazlitt, and Keats.[1] Hence, when he
planned the *Pioneer*, he was not projecting a journal of national reform under the mask of literature; he was ambitious to bear his testimony to
the ideal of a national literature springing from
a soil of political independence, and akin to great
literature the world over. In a word, he knew
the exhilaration of a native spirit, not in spite but
because of his feeding upon great and not superficial, modish letters; and he was eager to demon-
strate both creatively and critically the possibility
of a genuine and unaffected American literature.
In the Introduction to the *Pioneer*, for every new
journal then had its salutatory, — and the valedic-

[1] " Especially grateful is the praise of one in whose conversation I have marked a hearty appreciation of those greatest reformers, our glorious old English Poets." — J. R. L. to Robert Carter,
2 September, 1842.

tory was likely to follow shortly, — he sets forth
this principle of a native literature. After com-
plaining of the derivative character of current criticism and opinions, — derived, that is, from the
latest English quarterlies and monthlies, — he continues : —

" We are the farthest from wishing to see what
many so ardently pray for, namely, a *National* literature : for the same mighty lyre of the human
heart answers the touch of the master in all ages
and in every clime, and any literature, as far as it
is national, is diseased, inasmuch as it appeals to
some climatic peculiarity, rather than to the universal nature. [Moreover, everything that tends
to encourage the sentiment of caste, to widen the
boundary between races, and so to put farther off
the hope of one great brotherhood, should be steadily resisted by all good men.] But we do long for
a *natural* literature. One green leaf, though of
the veriest weed, is worth all the crape and wire
flowers of the daintiest Paris milliners. For it is
the glory of nature that in her least part she gives
us all, and in that simple love-token of hers we
may behold the type of all her sublime mysteries ;
as in the least fragment of the true artist we discern the working of the same forces which culmi-
nate gloriously in a Hamlet or a Faust. We would
no longer see the spirit of our people held up as a
mirror to the Old World ; but rather lying like
one of our own inland oceans, reflecting not only
the mountain and the rock, the forest and the red
man, but also the steamboat and the rail car, the

cornfield and the factory. Let us learn that romance is not married to the past, that it is not the
birthright of ferocious ignorance and chivalric bar-
barity, but that it ever was and is an inward quality, the darling child of the sweetest refinements
and most gracious amenities of peaceful gentleness,
and that it can never die till only water runs in
these red rivers of the heart, that cunning adept
which can make vague cathedrals with blazing
oriels and streaming spires out of our square meet-
ing-boxes,—

" ' Whose rafters sprout upon the shady side.'

" In this country where freedom of thought does
not shiver at the cold shadow of Spielberg (unless
we name this prison of ' public opinion ' so), there
is no danger to be apprehended from an excess of
it. It is only where there is no freedom that an-
archy is to be dreaded. The mere sense of freedom
is of too fine and holy a nature to consist with in-
justice and wrong. We would fain have our journal, in some sort at least, a journal of progress,
one that shall keep pace with the spirit of the age,
and sometimes go near its deeper heart. Yet,
while we shall aim at that gravity which is becoming of a manly literature, we shall hope also to
satisfy that lighter and sprightlier element of the
soul, without whose due culture the character is
liable to degenerate into a morose bigotry and selfish precisianism. To be one exponent of a young
spirit which shall aim at power through gentleness,
the only means for its secure attainment, and in

which freedom shall be attempered to love by a
reverence for all beauty wherever it may exist, is
our humble hope. . . ."

Here was a literary creed, expressed in no very
exact formulas, and really declarative of little more
than an individual purpose that the *Pioneer* should
contain good and not dull or imitative literature.
A good beginning was made, for the three numbers
which were published contained poems and papers
by Dr. Parsons, Story, Poe, Hawthorne, Jones
Very, John Neal, John S. Dwight, and the two
editors. Lowell continued his studies in the Old
English Dramatists, printed several poems, and
wrote apparently much of the criticism, but there
were no papers of a directly didactic character; it
was clear that the editor relied on criticism for a
medium of aggressive preaching of sound literary
doctrine. Here also Lowell had his opportunity
to fly the flag of anti-slavery, and he did it with a
fine chivalry in a notice of Longfellow's "Poems on
Slavery," when he used the occasion to pay glowing
tribute to the earlier fighters. Garrison, " the half-
inspired Luther of this reform, a man too remarkable to be appreciated in his generation, but whom
the future will recognize as a great and wonderful
spirit ; " Whittier, " the fiery Koerner of this spiritual warfare, who, Scævola-like, has sacrificed on
the altar of duty that right hand which might have
made him acknowledged as the most passionate
lyrist of his time ; " the " tenderly-loving Maria
Child, the author of that dear book, ' Philothea,'
a woman of genius, who lives with humble content

in the intellectual Coventry to which her conscientiousness has banished her — a fate the hardest for genius to bear. Nor ought the gentle spirit of Follen, a lion with a lamb's heart, to be forgotten, whose fiery fate, from which the mind turns horror-stricken, was perhaps to his mild nature less dreadful than that stake and fagot of public opinion, in dragging him to which many whom he loved were not inactive, for silence at such times is action."

Lowell threw himself into this literary venture with resolution and hope. He had the double motive of making a vehicle for sound and generous literature, and of securing for himself a rational means of support. Those nearest to him watched the experiment with solicitude, for magazine making on a small scale was as perilous then as it is now on a scale of magnitude. His sister, Mrs. Putnam, wrote him a most anxious letter called out by the fact that her brother was in New York and Carter in charge, a man too easy and good-natured she thought for such a position. She begged him to consider that his first number was better than his second, and that in turn seemed likely to be better than the third, and she dreaded a decline in the magazine. As for Miss White, she looked upon the scheme, when it was taking shape, with mingled pride and anxiety. She shared Lowell's lively trust in the pioneer character of the journal, but she had a prudent mind, and saw with a woman's instinct the possibility of failure, where Lowell would listen to nothing but the note of success.

The *Pioneer* lived but three months. The os-

tensible cause of its failure was the sudden and
lamentable breakdown of its chief supporter, as
shown in the following card printed at the close of
the third number.

" The absence of any prose in the present number of *The Pioneer* from the pen of Mr. Lowell,
and the apparent neglect of many letters and
contributions addressed to him personally, will be
sufficiently explained by stating that, since the
tenth of January, he has been in the city of New
York in attendance upon Dr. Elliot, the distinguished oculist, who is endeavoring to cure him of
a severe disease of the eyes, and that the medical
treatment to which he is necessarily subjected pre-
cludes the use of his sight except to a very limited
extent.   He will, however, probably be enabled, in
time for the fourth number, to resume his essays on
the Poets and Dramatists, and his general supervision of the magazine.   R. C."

It is plain that when the third number appeared
the conductors expected to bring out a fourth, but
the enforced abstention from work of the principal
editor and writer and the lack of resources in
money made the discontinuance of the magazine
inevitable.[1]   In spite, however, of the disastrous

---

[1] Mr. Woodberry, in editing "Lowell's Letters to Poe," in
Scribner's Monthly for August, 1894, explains the situation thus :
" The contract bound Lowell and Carter to furnish the publishers
five thousand copies on the twentieth of each month under a pen-
alty of five hundred dollars in case of failure and the publishers
to take that number at a certain price.   The March number was
eight days late, and the publishers, in the face of what was probably seen to be an unfortunate speculation, claimed the forfeit
but offered to waive it if the contract should be altered so as to

experience and the debt which it entailed, the activity of mind which the venture called forth was worth much to Lowell. He had not a specially orderly or methodical habit, and he lacked thus the equipment which an editor requires, but he had great fertility, and was under an impulse which at this time he turned to account in literature. Could he have been associated with some well organized nature, it is not impossible that the *Pioneer* would have become established on a sound basis and have been the vehicle for Lowell's creative and critical work in literature. Such work would have attracted the best that was to be had in America, and the periodical might have been an important factor in the intellectual life of the day.

The persistence with which the magazine idea was exploited hints at the possibilities which lay for a rising literature in this particular form. The vigorous John Neal wrote to Lowell when he was projecting the *Pioneer :* " Persevere ; be bold and fear not. A great change is foretelling itself in the literature of the day. Magazines are to supersede newspapers, and newspapers novels among light readers." The criticism which Lowell wrote or commanded for the *Pioneer* was frank, fearless, and sure to arrest attention. It pointed the way, and might easily have done much to shape the course of letters and art. In the absence of such

require them to take only so many copies as they could sell. The result was that the editors were obliged to stop printing from a lack of credit, and were left with a large indebtedness for manufacture as well as to contributors. It appears from Poe's letters that he was paid his small claim a year later."

a serviceable vehicle, Lowell was left to his own resources, and having no organ at hand he dropped criticism for the time and concentrated his mind on his poetry.

As Mr. Carter's apologetic note intimates, Lowell was obliged to go to New York early in January, 1843, for treatment at the hands of the oculist, Dr. Elliot. A few extracts from his letters to Mr. Carter during his absence show something of his life and interests in this enforced absence.

January 15, 1843. . . . My course of life is this. Every morning I go to Dr. Elliot's (who, by the way, is *very* kind) and wait for my turn to be operated upon. This sometimes consumes a great deal of time, the Dr. being overrun with patients. After being made stone blind for the space of fifteen minutes, I have the rest of the day to myself.

Handbills of the *Pioneer* in red and black with a spread eagle at the head of them face me everywhere. I could not but laugh to see a drayman standing with his hands in his pockets diligently spelling it out, being attracted thereto doubtless by the bird of America, which probably led him to think it a proclamation of the President — a delusion from which he probably did not awake after perusing the document. . . . I shall endeavor while I am here to write an article on Pope. *Something* I will send you for the next number, besides what I may possibly glean from others. A new magazine has just been started here, but it is illiberal and will probably fail.

January 17, 1843. I shall only write a word
or two, as I have already been writing, and my
eyes, having been operated on yesterday *with the
knife*, must be used charily. . . . I hope to hear
better accounts of money matters in your next.
Explain as to the 500 copies you speak of as sold
the day before. Remember how interesting the
least particle of news is to me, and I may be at
home under three weeks from this, though I hope
to be in a fortnight. . . .

January 19. So you are fairly bewitched![1]
Well, I might have expected it, but still it was no
reason that you should have told me so little about
the magazine. *I* should not have talked wholly
about one individual — of course not. *I* should
not have been bewitched. . . .

Have you got any copy for the third number?
Do not ask any conservatives to write, for it will
mar the unity of the magazine. We shall be surer
of success if we maintain a uniform course, and
have a decided tendency either one way or the
other. We shall, at least, gain more influence in
that way.

I have picked up a poem by Harry Franco
against capital punishment. It has a good deal of
humor in it and is striking. A woodcut of a poor
devil hanging with the crows discussing his fate
will perhaps accompany it. Prose I have got no
scent of as yet. . . .

January [20]. I have received *all* your letters, and like to have you send by express. I

---

[1] Carter had just been to see Maria White.

should like to see Miss Gray's and Miss Peabody's articles before they go to press. I am a better judge of that kind of merchandise than you. The second number is a good one, but *full* of misprints. The notices in the cover, if printed at all, should have been expurgated. See to it next time, and do not let your kind heart seduce you into printing any more puffs of *me* personally. What do you mean by that notice of Emerson? I shall have to write to him. Your notice of De Quincey was excellent.

I send herewith a poem of Miss Barrett[1] which came with the letters you sent me. She sent *three* others, and promises more in a very pleasant letter. I shall send on quite a budget of prose, I hope, soon, but cannot use my eyes much. I am going to answer an article on the copyright question by O'Sullivan in the forthcoming *Democratic Review*. I must see proofs of Miss Barrett and all my own pieces. . . . I must not write any more or I shall not get home these six months.

January 22. . . . My dear, good, kindest, best friend, you know that I would not write a word that should knowingly pain your loving heart. So forgive whatever there has been in my other letters to trouble, and only reflect how anxious I must naturally feel, away from home as I am, and left a great part of the time to the solitude of my own thoughts by the total deprivation of the use of my eyes.

Willis is under Dr. E.'s care also, and yester-

[1] "The Maiden's Death."

day introduced himself to me, and said all manner
of kind things.   He had meant to write to me,
giving me his experience in editing, and had long
been anxious to know me, &c., &c.   This morning
he came and took me to church with him, and altogether overwhelms me with attention.   His wife is
a very *nice* pretty little Englishwoman, with a very
sweet voice.   W. said he wrote the notice in the
Jonathan as the most judicious way of helping the
magazine, giving your own philosophic theory as
to its possible results. . . .

January 24. . . . I *must* write an article for
the next number, and yet I do not see very well
how I am to do it.   For I can scarcely get through
one letter without pain, and everything that I write
retards my case and so keeps me the longer here.
But I love Keats so much that I think I can write
something good about him.

Willis continues very kind, and I begin to
think that he really likes me.   At least he said
the same to Dr. E. about me that he told me to
my face.   He told the Dr. (I copy it the more
readily that I know it will delight *you*) that I had
written the most remarkable poem that had been
written in this country, and that I was destined to
be the brightest star that had yet risen in American literature.   He told me, also, that I was more
popular and more talked about and read at this
time than any other poet in the land, and he is
going (or was) to write an article in the *Jonathan*
to that effect.   These things *you must keep in
your own heart*.   He promises to help the *Pioneer*

in every way he can, and he will be able to do us a great deal of good, as he has last week taken half the ownership of the *Jonathan* on condition of solely editing it. He talks of paying me to write letters for him from Boston. . . .

John Neal lectures here to-night. I have not seen him, and I do not know whether I shall hear him, for if I get a package from you to-day, as I hope I shall, I shall hardly have 25 cents left to buy a ticket with. So you think we have succeeded. They are the pleasantest words I have heard since I have been here. But we must not feel too sure yet. I think we *shall* succeed. Folks here (some of them) say that we shall beyond our utmost expectation. . . .

Saturday. . . . You shall have some copy from me on *Wednesday* morning if I get blind by it. Where is Brownson? Don't print nonsense. Better not be out till the middle of March. But you are only trying to frighten me. Do not print nonsense, for God's sake. Print the history of Mesmerism. Write an article on Japan. If I were to read over your letters again in order to answer them categorically, I should not be able to use my eyes for a week. You do not recollect that I undergo an application or an operation *every day*. If I could *see* you for ten minutes I could arrange all. I perhaps may come on and return hither again. *Do not hint* this to any one, for if Maria heard of it, she would be expecting anxiously every day. I am sick to death of this place, yet it does me good spiritually to stay here. I

must not write any more. In your next letter ask
all questions and I will answer. . . .

Lowell stayed on in New York on account of his
eyes till the end of February. At a period when
Mrs. Child could gravely write and publish in a
book "Letters from New York," to go to New
York from Cambridge was nearly equivalent to
a winter abroad. As his letters to Carter show,
with the disabilities under which he labored Lowell
could do little at reading or writing, and he used
the opportunity for social occupation. Page he
had already come to know, and he had made the
acquaintance through the *Miscellany* of Charles F.
Briggs, whom now he took into warm friendship.
Mr. Briggs was a diligent man of letters, best known
to the public of that day as " Harry Franco," and
through him Lowell fell in with many writers
and book people. But he was most impatient to
return, and now that his magazine had ceased he
found himself with no routine labors, but with a
mind full to overflowing.

The real pursuit of Lowell during 1843 was
poetry, and poetry of a lofty character. In the
Ode which he wrote in 1841 beginning, — *page 11*

" In the old days of awe and keen-eyed wonder " —

he had outlined the function of the poet ; and the
whole set of his nature in the months between his
engagement and his marriage was in the direction
of poetic earnestness. His conception was dominated by moral enthusiasm : the preacher in him

was always thrusting himself to the front, and the reformer of the day sometimes masqueraded in his verse in very antique forms.   But his genuine love of art above all his unfailing apprehension of poetry as an end in itself saved him from a merely utilitarian notion of his high calling.   And it is safe to say that he never was so happy as when he was abandoning himself to the full enjoyment of poetic composition.   He diverted the streams of love and of anti-slavery fervor into this full current, and could say of his " Prometheus " that it was " overrunning with true radicalism and anti-slavery ; " but the exhilaration which fanned his wings was the consciousness of youth and love finding an outlet in the natural voice of poetry.   " I was never so happy as now," he writes to Loring, 15 June, after telling of his " Prometheus " and " A Legend of Brittany," on which he was at work.   " I see Maria every other day.   I am embowered in leaves, have a voluntary orchestra of birds and bees and frogs, and a little family of chickens to whom I have a sort of feeling of paternity, and begin to believe I had some share in begetting them."

Page painted Lowell's portrait when he was in New York and exhibited it in the spring.   This picture is at once a likeness of the poet and an expression of the painter.   Page was an idealist who found a most congenial subject in Lowell. Out of the dark canvass — for the painter, pursuing the elusive phantom of a recovery of the art of the Venetians, succeeded at any rate in giving to his work an ancient air — there looks forth a face which is the very apparition of poetry. Far removed from the sentimental aspect, it has depth of feeling, a serene assurance, and a Shakespearean ideality. It is not difficult to see that Page was not painting in Lowell a young Cambridge author, but the student of the English dramatists and the inheritor of all the ages of poetry. To his own neighbors and friends Lowell had much of this air in his presence. His flowing chestnut hair falling in rich masses from an equally dividing line, his unshorn face, his eyes with their kindly wistful look, his tremulous mouth, — all served to separate him in appearance from common men and to mark him as an unusual person.

How affectionately Lowell regarded Page and what admiration he had for his genius may be read in the dedication to him which was prefixed to his "Poems" issued in 1843 and retained in later collections. The frankness with which he avows his love for his friend is a witness to that openness of Lowell's nature which we have already noticed, and the terms in which he speaks of Page's art and of the artistic faith which they held in common give a hint of the basis of their comradery. Lowell disclaimed any special knowledge of painting, and always brought to bear, in his discussions on art, the principles which he had learned through his devotion to the art of poetry. In the relation of the two men to each other one is half tempted to recall the friendship of Keats and Haydon. In each case the poet believed in the painter less by reason of the work done than because of the ideals

Mr. Lowell in 1843

W. PAGE. PINX. 1843.

W.H.W.BICKNELL. SC

held and aimed at.   Page was an enthusiast, and a
man of mingled imaginative and speculative powers.   As Haydon preached the Elgin marbles to
Keats, so Page discoursed on the old masters to
Lowell.   But the reciprocal admiration of Lowell
and Page was really for the man behind the art.
" I am glad you like my poems," Lowell wrote to
Mrs. Shaw ; " Page is wiser than you and likes
them because he knows I am better than they ; "
and to Mr. Briggs he had written shortly before :
" You are a great deal better than anything you
write, and Page than anything he paints, and I
always think of you without your pen, and of him
.without his brushes."

The admiration and affection with which Page and
Briggs regarded Lowell were only more intimate
than the feelings which were generally aroused.
He had come to be looked on as a new poet.   So
Hawthorne, in his " Hall of Fantasy," as first published, characterized him as " the poet of the generation that now enters upon the stage."   When
the *Pioneer* was started Lowell's was a name to
conjure with.   " The principal editor," says the
Tribune, " is well and widely known as one of the
most gifted and promising poets in America ; " and
a Philadelphia paper speaks of the journal as
" edited by a man whose genius and originality is
at once the praise and wonder of his countrymen."
To be sure, newspaper praise is apt to be pitched in
a high key, and the army of independent admirers
on closer examination turns out to be a company
of the author's enthusiastic friends marching and

countermarching across the stage, disappearing in one wing only to come out from another. But after all allowance has been made, it is clear that in a community which was eagerly expecting great things in literature, Lowell, though he had published little and much of that anonymously, was already one of the candidates for fame. He himself did not need this incentive. He had the consciousness of power and that audience of one which stimulated him to the exercise of his power.

"A Year's Life" had been frankly autobiographic. The poems written afterward and now collected in the 1843 volume were the distinct outgrowth of a nature stimulated by this new experience of love and at last both fully alive to the consciousness of poetic feeling and eager with a desire to act out the aspirations which had been blown into flame by the breath of love. Hence the volume, in its contents, is of varied character, as the poet himself held within his restless life the somewhat contradictory elements which go to make up a poet and a reformer. "A Legend of Brittany," which is the substantial piece, and stands at the front, is a piece of pure romance, pretty evidently sprung from the soil in which grew Keats's "Isabella ; or the Pot of Basil." The underlying theme is not dissimilar, the measure is the same, and there is something of the same richness of color and delight in the beauty of single, even unfamiliar words. Yet the reader feels that Keats not only had the more vivid imagination, but a clearer sense of the beauty that lies in intensity of expres-

sion — an intensity so great that one almost holds
one's breath as he reads. Lowell, as we know, rarely
essayed anything in the nature of story-telling ; the
dramatic faculty was not his, and keen as was his
appreciation of the power of the elder dramatists,
his criticism shows that he dwelt most emphatically
on those passages and lines which disclose poetic
beauty, rather than the features of construction.
But Keats's warmth and richness of decorative
painting appealed to him with peculiar force at a
time when he himself had come out into the sunshine and was intoxicated with his own happiness.
It is clear that when he was writing " A Legend
of Brittany " he was revelling in the possession of
poetic fancy, and drawing himself to the height of
his enjoyment of pure poetry unmixed with elements of didacticism. He wrote to G. B. Loring,
15 June, 1843, " I am now at work on a still
longer poem [than " Prometheus "] in the *ottava
rima* to be the first in my forthcoming volume. I
feel more and more assured every day that I shall
yet do something that will keep my name (and
perhaps my body) alive. My wings were never so
light and strong as now. So hurrah for a niche
and a laurel." The poem did not apparently call
out any strong response, nor has it, I suspect, ever
been read with very great admiration — certainly it
cannot for a moment be compared in popularity
with " The Vision of Sir Launfal," which followed
five years later, and the explanation is perhaps to
be found mainly in its derivative character, even
though readers might not be acutely aware how far
it owed its origin to Keats.

Mr. Briggs, who was the stanchest of Lowell's literary friends at this time, wrote with enthusiasm of the volume, using terms of admiration which must have been grateful indeed, since they were charged with discrimination and just appreciation; but he was frank and honest in his friendly judgment, and he wrote to Lowell of "A Legend of Brittany:" "It is too warm, rich, and full of sweet sounds and sights; the incense overpowers me, and the love and crime, and prayers and monks and glimpses of spirits oppress me. I am too much a clod of earth to mingle well in such elements. I feel while reading it as though I were lying upon a bed of down with a canopy of rose-colored silk above me, with gleams of sunshine darting in the room and half revealing and at times more than revealing strange figures painted upon the walls of my chamber. But I do not wonder that M. W. should like it. It is the proper reading for pure-minded loving creatures, from whose eyes knowledge with its hard besom has not yet swept away the golden cobwebs of fancy. I like her the better myself for liking it." [1]

This long poem is not the only one in the book which springs from pure delight in poetic imagination; but it is by far the most full and unalloyed expression of this pleasure. When one reads, however, such a poem as "Rhœcus," with its preface

46

---

[1] In a letter written after he had at last seen Miss White, Mr. Briggs writes: "I hardly know what I could say to M. W. unless what I felt inclined to when I saw her, 'Sancta Maria, ora pro nobis.'"

apologizing for so much paganism, and its application, and especially when one reads " Prometheus," one is aware how largely Lowell was dominated, even in this time when his soul was flushed with the sense of beauty and awake to the tendrils it was putting forth, by a strong purpose to read the lesson of beauty and love to his fellows. The seriousness of life was indeed charged with an exalted meaning by the revelation which came to him when he was admitted into the intimate companionship of a woman who had in her something of the spirit of a prophetess, but it would be untrue to say that Maria White handed him the torch ; she kindled to a greater brilliancy that which he already held, and his love transmuted the vague stirrings of his own nature into more definite purpose. Keats, to refer again to one with whom Lowell certainly had spiritual kinship, was mildly affected somewhat in the same way by the friendship which he formed in his impressionable years with Hunt and his circle, and if we could imagine Fanny Brawne a Mary Wollstonecraft, we might speculate on the effect she would have had on his poetry. Even Keats, with his passionate devotion to beauty, could dig a subterranean passage under the opening of the third book of " Endymion " for the purpose of blowing up the " present ministers ; " and Lowell, taking the world-worn myth of Prometheus, could write into it reflections apposite to what he regarded as a tremendous upheaving force just ready to manifest itself in society. The poem of " Prometheus," however, justly stands high in the estimation of Lowell's

readers, for the thought involved in it rises above
the level of a didactic utterance, and carries with it
an impersonation of human dignity which saves it
from the reproach of making the myth a mere text
for a modern discourse. The poem is the most comprehensive and largest expression of the mind of
the poet at this period of emancipation, and the
fine images with which it abounds spring from the
subject itself and are not mere decorations.

Here, again, a comparison of "Prometheus" with
Keats's "Hyperion" illustrates the infusion of
moral ardor which separates the disciple from the
master.   Keats summed up his poetic philosophy
in the lines —

> "For 't is the eternal law
> That first in beauty should be first in might," —

and he was fain to see the operation of Nature's
law by which one race of conquerors would dispos-
sess another.

> "So on our heels a fresh perfection treads."

Lowell, speculating on the eternal struggle, figured
in "Prometheus," of right and wrong, of darkness
and light, bids Jove heed that he —

> "And all strength shall crumble except love" —

and sees in a vision —

> "Peaceful commonwealths where sunburnt Toil
> Reaps for itself the rich earth made its own."

Mr. Briggs, writing to him on the appearance of
the poem in the *Democratic Review*, reminds him
that he had read a bit of it when visiting him in
his house at Staten Island, and adds: "But I did

not anticipate that you could or would lengthen
out those few lines into a poem so full of majesty
and sweetness. So far as my observation will allow
me to judge, it is the best sustained effort of the
American Muse. The structure of the verse is exceedingly fine to my ear, although it may not be as
acceptable to the public ear as the almost emascu-
late smoothness of Bryant, to which it has been
accustomed. The bold bright images with which
'Prometheus' abounds would be sufficient of themselves to give you a name among the wielders of
the pen, but the noble and true spirit of Philosophy
which they help to develop makes them appear of
secondary importance, and gives you a claim to a
higher renown than the mere word-mongers of
Parnassus can ever aspire to." Lowell, in replying
to this letter, wrote : " My ' Prometheus ' has not
received a single public notice yet, though I have
been puffed to repletion for poems without a tithe
of its merit. Your letter was the first sympathy I
received. Although such great names as Goethe,
Byron, and Shelley have all handled the subject in
modern times, you will find that I have looked at
it from a somewhat new point of view. I have
made it *radical*, and I believe that no poet in this
age can write much that is good unless he give himself up to this tendency. For radicalism has now
for the first time taken a distinctive and acknowledged shape of its own. So much of its spirit as
poets in former ages have attained (and from their
purer organization they could not fail of some) was
by instinct rather than by reason. It has never till

now been seen to be one of the two great wings that upbear the universe." In the same letter he says: " The proof of poetry is, in my mind, whether it reduces to the essence of a single line the vague philosophy which is floating in all men's minds, and so renders it portable and useful and ready to the hand. Is it not so? At least no poem ever makes me respect its author which does not in some way convey a truth of philosophy."

In the same temper which produced " Prometheus," he wrote what he regarded as in some way a companion piece, " A Glance behind the Curtain," in which he imagines a conversation between Cromwell and Hampden. There is no seeming endeavor at characterization of either figure, dramatically, but the poem, which is an attempt to read Cromwell's mind, is a stirring and indignant demand that Freedom shall do her perfect work.

" Freedom hath yet a work for me to do," he makes Cromwell exclaim : —

> " So speaks that inward voice which never yet
> Spake falsely, when it urged the spirit on
> To noble deeds for country and mankind.
> And for success, I ask no more than this, —
> To bear unflinching witness to the truth.
> All true whole men succeed ; for what is worth
> Success's name, unless it be the thought,
> The inward surety, to have carried out
> A noble purpose to a noble end,
> Although it be the gallows or the block ?
> 'T is only Falsehood that doth ever need
> These outward shows of gain to bolster her."

Thus, in the guise of Cromwell, speaks the young man dimly conscious, in a travailing age, of work

needing to be done, and stirred too by the high
emotions of the woman he loved, yet not quite able
to translate his vague desire to be a champion of
Truth into deeds. To be sure, at the close of this
poem he remembers that Cromwell was the friend
of Milton,

> " A man not second among those who lived
> To show us that the poet's lyre demands
> An arm of tougher sinew than the sword."

In the dreams of his youth I think he saw himself
playing a part in the drama that was opening, and
wondering how he could wield the pen so as to
make it a weapon for slaying wrong or defending
right. Yet direct as he might wish his attack to
be, he was held back by an equally potent impulse
to fulfil the demands of art. "A Chippewa Legend," in this same volume, though used as a parable for an impassioned denunciation of slavery,
has touches of nature in the unfolding of the story
which show clearly how much delight he took in
the story itself, and how easily he might have
stopped short as a singer, if the preacher in him
had not made the song turn out a sermon.

The autobiographic element in this volume of
"Poems" is most distinctly summed up in a sonnet
which dropped out of later collections containing
most of the other poems. It bears the title "On
my twenty-fourth Birthday, February 22, 1843,"
and marks well his own sense of a certain transition which had taken place in his growth.

> " Now have I quite passed by that cloudy If
> That darkened the wild hope of boyish days,

> When first I launched my slender-sided skiff
> Upon the wide sea's dim, unsounded ways;
> Now doth Love's sun my soul with splendor fill,
> And Hope hath struggled upward into Power,
> Soft Wish is hardened into sinewy Will,
> And Longing into Certainty doth tower:
> The love of beauty knoweth no despair;
> My heart would break, if I should dare to doubt,
> That from the Wrong, which makes its dragon's lair
> Here on the Earth, fair Truth shall wander out,
> Teaching mankind, that Freedom's held in fee
> Only by those who labor to set free."

In "A Year's Life" the l'envoi of the volume is a timid poem, "Goe, little booke!" in which the poet, sending his venture out among strangers and most likely among apathetic readers, comforts himself with the reflection : —

> " But, if all others are unkind,
>   There's *one* heart whither thou canst fly
>   For shelter from the biting wind;
>   And, in that home of purity,
>   It were no bitter thing to die."

The " L'Envoi " of " Poems " is addressed to M. W. and is an open confession of the indebtedness of his love, three years after the veiled disclosure in " Ianthe," " Irene," " Isabel," and other figurings of his affection, and runs like a golden thread through all the warp and woof of his imagination and fancy. In this serious poem, which he retained in his later collections, though without the declarative initials,[1] Lowell intimates very clearly that his maturer outlook on life, and his attitude toward poetry are due largely to the inspiration

---

[1] " L'Envoi," beginning
" Whether my heart hath wiser grown or not."

which he has derived from the aspirations of his
betrothed. Not only has his love for her quickened his eye of faith, but he has caught a wider
view and a firmer hold on the great realities of the
spirit through the contagion of her lofty idealism
and its fervent expression in a moral ardor. This
is especially manifest in a long passage which has
been omitted from the poem in later collections.
There are portions of this omitted passage which
are little better than a dissertation on the poet's
mission, and they were wisely dropped, but they
drew after them by necessity a few verses which
have an interest as recording in a candid fashion
the change which had come over the poet's mind in
these three years just past. After the introductory
lines, in which he speaks rather disdainfully of
" A Year's Life," and intimates that he has grown
a sadder and a wiser man, yet with no lessening of
that trust in God which was so marked a characteristic of his betrothed, he goes on · —

> " Less of that feeling which the world calls love,
>   Thou findest in my verse, but haply more
>   Of a more precious virtue, born of that,
>   The love of God, of Freedom, and of Man.
>   Thou knowest well what these three years have been,
>   How we have filled and graced each other's hearts,
>   And every day grown fuller of that bliss,
>   Which, even at first, seemed more than we could bear,
>   And thou, meantime, unchanged, except it be
>   That thy large heart is larger, and thine eyes
>   Of palest blue, more tender with the love
>   Which taught me first how good it was to love;
>   And, if thy blessed name occur less oft,
>   Yet thou canst see the shadow of thy soul
>   In all my song, and art well-pleased to feel

> That I could ne'er be rightly true to thee,
> If I were recreant to higher aims.
> Thou didst not grant to me so rich a fief
> As thy full love, on any harder tenure
> Than that of rendering thee a single heart;
> And I do service for thy queenly gift
> Then best, when I obey my soul, and tread
> In reverence the path she beckons me."

It would be joy enough, he proceeds, if he could so measure joy, to rest in this contentment of loving and being loved, but life had nobler destinies, and he rejoiced that she who gave him her love had a larger conception of poetry, and so he passes to an analysis of the true aims of poesy, which finally takes the turn of considering the possibility of satisfying these aims by rendering the landscape of America into verse, —

> "They tell us that our land was made for song," —

and so continues as preserved in the present form of the poem.

It will be seen thus that this volume of "Poems," taken as a register of Lowell's development, marks a greater sureness of himself, a more definite determination of aim, a confidence in powers whose precise range he cannot yet measure, and with all this a swaying now toward the expression of pure delight in art, now toward the use of his art for the accomplishment of some great purpose. It is noticeable, also, that in "A Year's Life" there is no trace of humor and scarcely any singular felicity of phrase; in "Poems," wit and humor begin to play a little on the surface. There can be little doubt that the direct influence of Maria White was toward what may without offence be called the practical issue, and this not because she was utilitarian — on the contrary, Lowell felt called on to defend her against the charge of being a transcendentalist, the charge implying a reproach as of a mere visionary; no, it was a certain high, even exalted and enthusiastic allegiance to Truth which dominated her nature, made her in a degree to accept this allegiance as sign of a mission which she was to fulfil, rendered her eager to have the close coöperation of her lover, and made him almost feverishly desirous of justifying her faith by his works. A letter which she wrote to Mr. Briggs, though it anticipates a little the course of this narrative, may be cited here as throwing some further light on her nature.

WATERTOWN, Dec. 12th, 1844.

MY DEAR FRIEND, — James is so hurried with his book that he has not an instant to spare, and has therefore commissioned me to answer your letter, and account to you for his long silence. The truth is, he delayed writing his articles on Poets and Old Dramatists, or rather delayed arranging them in the form of conversations, until he had only two months left for what really required four. The book must be out before we are married; he has three printers hard upon for copy, for which he has to rise early and sit up late, so that he can only spare time to see me twice a week, and then I have but transient glimpses of his dear face.

The pears were thought delicious, and James would have told you that we all thought so, had

not these troubles about his book just been dawning
upon him. The basket still remains upon a shelf
in my closet, and when I look at it a pleasant train
of thoughts comes up in regard to my housekeep-
ing, in which I see it filled, with eggs white as snow,
or apples from our little plot, though never again
with pears like those which first consecrated it.

Both James and myself feel greatly interested
in your journal,[1] in spite of its proposed name.
James told me to express his horror to you at the
cockneyism of such a title. *The Broadway Chronicle* chronicles the thoughts and feelings of Broadway, not those of the New England people whom
you seem willing to receive somewhat from. Should
not a title have truth for its first recommendation ?
Do you write from the meridian of Broadway ? I
think you write from a sturdy New England heart,
that has a good strong well-spring of old Puritan
blood beating therein, with all its hatred to forms
and cant, to fashion and show. If ' Pistol speaks
naught but truth,' should his name be a lie ? Pistol's is not; it expresses the man truly. I wish
yours did as much to us here, though if it *really*
gratifies your taste and judgment, if it is not a
whim, but a *thought*, we shall all like it in time, I
suppose, if we do not now. If it is good we shall
of course come round to it. I always say just what
I think, as you see, and I trust it will not seem
harsh and unlovely to you in me as a woman. I
do not wish to appear so ever, but I had rather

[1] *The Broadway Journal*, which Mr. Briggs was just projecting.

than give up what I think is truly and undeniably one of *woman's* rights in common with man.

James says he cannot say anything now with certainty in regard to his contributions to your paper, except that he will give you, of course, the best he has. Mrs. Putnam, I believe, has nothing translated at present, but James will ask her, also William Story and Nathan Hale. I have some translations I made from the German, songs, ballads, etc., which are at your service if you care to have them. I hope to write somewhat when I can have James always by my side to encourage me, and in time it may be something more than a source of pleasure to us. Carter has seen your letter, and I do not doubt will be ready to do all he can, ready and glad.

I intended to have written to you and Mrs. Briggs expressly to invite you to our wedding, but I cannot do it now with much force or grace after your paragraph on the subject.[1] To us who have been married for nearly five years, it is of course no spiritual change; but if it were merely for the fact that from that day we can always be together, it would be well worth celebrating by some rite

[1] Mr. Briggs had written to Lowell: "I suppose that you are going to impose upon yourselves the heathenish ceremonies of a wedding, and in the most solemn period of your lives, give yourselves up to the most foolish of all the world's follies. Tut! you will be sick of white satins and raisins for the next century. Is't the first of the month that you are to be married? I would like to know the day that I may keep you in remembrance. Page will be here and I will have him down to Bishop's Terrace, and we will keep it up with becoming solemnity. One of my darling fowls shall be sacrificed."

and calling our friends about us to participate in
it.   What that rite is does not greatly matter, but
I prefer that which time has consecrated.

> " I can scorn nothing which a nation's heart
>   Hath held for ages holy."

That is, nothing in the form of rite or observance
for things in themselves sacred, for you will tell
me the Ages held the gibbet, the scourge and rack
holy, if I let it pass without qualification.   Still,
I bid you to our marriage, though I trust even if
you do not come you can see it whenever you see
us.   Some have great need to ask their friends at
such a time, that they may afterwards certify such
a thing has taken place because no trace of it remains.   It can never be so with us, it could never
be so with any who hold love sacred. . . .

We shall be married the night after Christmas,
and go on to New York after one day and night
spent at home.   We should love to stop there to
see you as long as you would like to have us, but
our present engagements in Philadelphia will take
us directly on there.   We shall be in New York
on Sunday, *where* is not decided yet.   With love
to your wife, yours with friendly heart,

MARIA WHITE.

The book which this letter speaks of as absorbing Lowell's time and thought was his " Conversations on Some of the Old Poets," for which Miss
White made a cover design and which was published by John Owen early in January, 1845.   It
will be remembered that Lowell began in the

Boston Miscellany and continued in the *Pioneer*
some studies on the Old Dramatists. The series
might have gone on at greater length, for he was
working a vein which yielded him great delight,
and never indeed ceased to engage his attention.
He resumed the theme in the last considerable
venture of his life, and gave a course of lectures
at the Lowell Institute in the spring of 1887, which
was in effect a series of readings from the dramatists with running comments. "When I selected
my topic for this new venture," he said to his audience at the opening of the course, "I was returning to a first love. The second volume I ever
printed, in 1843 I think it was,[1] — it is now a rare
book, I am not sorry to know; I have not seen it
for many years, — was mainly about the Old English Dramatists, if I am not mistaken. I dare say
it was crude enough, but it was spontaneous and
honest."

The suspension of the *Pioneer* left Lowell without any convenient vehicle for carrying further
these appreciative papers, and he projected a book
partly because the subject was in his mind, partly
because he was anxious to turn his printed matter
to fresh account, but chiefly, it must be inferred
from the contents of the book, because he was
eager to have freedom of speech on several matters which lay close to his mind. He resolved,
therefore, to remodel his papers, so far as he used

[1] The exact succession of his books was *A Year's Life*, 1841 ;
Poems, 1843 (dated 1844) ; *Conversations on Some of the Old Poets*, 1845.

them at all, into a series of conversations. His
work upon the book was hurried, as the letter last
quoted from Miss White intimates. In September, 1844, he was planning a course of four or five
lectures on English poetry, beginning with Chaucer, which he proposed delivering in Philadelphia
in the winter immediately after his marriage; but
he seems suddenly to have changed his mind, and
to have tossed what he might have prepared into
this new book, which opens with a long conversation on Chaucer, — a conversation split in the next
edition into two. The passages from Chaucer
which he quotes are drawn sometimes from the
modernization by Wordsworth, but are also, in
some cases, his own much closer simplification of
the original. To the ear they depart very little
from the original, the widest departure being in
getting rid of the final *e*. The talk on Chaucer is
followed by comments on Chapman and Ford, with
reference by easy suggestion to Shakespeare, Marlowe, Fletcher, Pope, and Wordsworth.

But though the staple of the "Conversations" is
poetry, and there are generous examples and much
keen appreciation of the poets discussed, the book
would interest a reader to-day less by its treatment
of the subjects which gave it excuse for being than
by its free and careless exhibition of Lowell's mind
on topics of current concern. There is very little
of dramatic assumption in the interlocutors. Philip
and John are simply convenient personages playing at a battledore and shuttlecock game of words.
Philip is the major character, who does all of the

reading and advances most of the propositions, but
John, whose chief part is to start Philip by questions, and to interpose occasional jibes or independent observations, is not differentiated in manner;
he is another of Lowell's many selves, and may be
taken as the critical, interrupting side of his mind.[1]
But both speakers are after the same game.

One of the agreeable touches in the volume is in
the asides with which Lowell refers to contemporary authors like Hawthorne and Longfellow, to
Page, to Dwight, and to such beginners as W. W.
Story and R. C., and when he takes up for discussion a recent address by the Rev. Mr. Putnam.
These references and allusions help one to understand the attitude which Lowell took toward his
book. He did not deceive himself as to its importance. It was a prolongation of his magazine work
and gave him an opportunity to free his mind.
The form, as I have intimated, was not that of a
true conversation; it is far removed from such
excellent exemplars as the " Imaginary Conversations " of Landor, the first of which had appeared
a score of years before; it had but little of the
graceful fencing which brings the talkers closer and
closer to the heart of a subject, till one makes the
final thrust that disarms his antagonist. No; it
was simply a device to secure flexibility and dis-

[1] Mr. Evert A. Duyckinck, in March, 1846, replying to a suggestion by Lowell of " specimens of old translators " for Wiley &
Putnam's Library, doubts the practicability, but adds, " You will,
I hope, not lose sight of so good a topic which might provoke a
new conversation between yourself and your Mrs. Harris (Philip
and John) very profitably."

cursiveness, and is talk run mad, sometimes an
harangue, sometimes an epigram, most often a
rapid flow of views on literature and life. "If
some of the topics introduced seem foreign to the
subject," says Lowell, in his prefatory address To
the Reader, "I can only say that they are not so to
my mind, and that an author's object in writing
criticisms is not only to bring to light the beauties
of the works he is considering, but also to express
his own opinions upon those and other matters."

The reading which lies behind the talk is varied,
and the talker speaks from a full mind, but there is
none of that restraint of art which gives weight to
the words and makes one wish to read again and
again the reflections. The cleverness is of the
showy sort, and an interesting comparison could be
drawn between the portions of the book which relate directly to the dramatists and the more mellow
discussion of the same subject in the latest of Lowell's published prose. But despite the crudeness
which marks the earlier book, it shares with the
later that delightful spontaneity and first hand
intelligence which make Lowell always worth attention when he speaks on literary art. It was
characteristic of him that when at sixty-eight he
discoursed on the dramatists whom he had been
reading all his life, he had not the need and apparently not the curiosity to turn back and see what
he said about them at twenty-five. There was little,
if any, of the careful husbandry of his ideas which
marks some men of letters ; out of the abundance
of the heart his mouth spoke.

In no one of his books can the reader discern
better the spontaneous element in Lowell's mind,
and the length to which he could go under the impulse of the immediate thought. So fluent was he,
so unaware of any effort, and so swept away for
the time being by the stream of his ideas, that he
seemed to himself as one possessed, and more than
once he hinted darkly that he was not writing the
book, but was the spokesman for sages and poets
who used him as their means of communication.
The visionary faculty which he possessed could
easily be confused at this time with the half-rapt
condition of the mind fed with emotional ardor.
The book, as we have seen, was written at full
speed, and it reflects the generous nature of the
writer; but it reflects also the untempered thought,
and registers judgments in the process of making.

Running through the entire book, and making
the real excuse for it, is Lowell's study of the essence of poetry. This is what gives to the volume
its chief interest; it is really a half-conscious expli-
cation of the concern which was most agitating his
mind at this time. What was poetry? Could
it be the substance of a man's life? There is a
prosecution of some of the same problems which
recently he had been trying to solve in his own volume of poems. He had to ask himself if he was a
poet. The witness for that was to be found not so
much in his taste and his preferences in literature,
nor solely in the delight which he took in versification; he felt the stirring in his nature of that
high vocation of the poet which makes him a seer

and an interpreter. His impulse was to yield to it, but the question arose, What was he to interpret? What was there in life about him which was crying out for articulation? And here, if I mistake not, he fell into some confusion of mind through the insistence of one particular incarnation of divine thought. He was conscious and aware of a momentous idea, that of freedom expressed in terms of human brotherhood, words which even then had the dull ring of cant when they were used by counterfeit-minded men, yet had in the minds of genuine men and women a vibrant and exultant sound as if they were to pay all the debts of poor human nature. Remembering that this was on the eve of '48, when the visionaries of Europe and America were very sure that they saw a great light, one sees how forcible this idea could be as a motive in the throbbing and ingenuous heart of a young American who was quite sure he was called to high endeavor.

But with the shrewdness which belonged to his mother wit, Lowell could not satisfy himself with merely windy utterances. He needed emphatically to kindle something with his divine flame. As he says of Lessing: "His genius was not a St. Elmo's fire, as it so often is with mere poets, — as it was in Shelley, for example, playing in ineffectual flame about the points of his thoughts, — but was interfused with his whole nature and made a part of his very being." Now he found himself confronting a monstrous denial of this truth of freedom issuing in human brotherhood when he

contemplated slavery in America, and his natural
indignation was heightened by the ardor of the
woman he loved. Was he not, after all, to be a
reformer beyond everything else? and where was
the point of contact between the poet and the reformer? His mind circled about this problem; his
convictions called upon him with a loud voice to
make good his professions; his instinctive sense of
congruity, which is hardly more than an alternate
form of the sense of humor, forbade him to make
poetry the maid of all work for the anti-slavery
cause, and he sought diligently to resolve this particular form of spiritual activity into the elemental
properties of freedom, and so to find therein a true
medium for the sustenance of poetry. Moreover,
though he described himself not long after, in "A
Fable for Critics," as —

> " striving Parnassus to climb
> With a whole bale of *isms* tied together with rhyme," —

it must be said with emphasis that he held these
isms too lightly for them to become the determin-
ing factor in his intellectual and spiritual growth.
They did hamper him, as he says a little ruefully
in the next line, and while it is idle business to
speculate on what a man might have become in the
absence of the very conditions that made him what
he was, one is tempted to wonder if with his en-
dowments Lowell might not, under less strenuous
conditions, have been exclusively a poet. What is
one man's meat is another man's poison, says the
homely adage, and it is a curious fact that but for
the same flame of anti-slavery passion Whittier

might never have been more than a verbose Quiet-
ist versifier.

In his dedication of the volume to his father,
Lowell speaks of it as "containing many opinions
from which he will wholly, yet with the large charity of a Christian heart, dissent," and the most fla-
grant of these is probably in a passage in which he
speaks with vehemence of the church and religion.
As falls to the hearer of many impulsive utterances of young men, one is apt to see in them
rather the impatience of a generous heart ("why
so hot, my little man?") than the deliberate convictions into which one has been forced reluctantly,
but the passage is so characteristic of Lowell at
this period and so expressive of the turbulence of
his mind that it may well be read here. John has
been commenting on the innate piety of Chaucer
as illustrated by his glowing words on the daisy,
and Philip takes up the parable.

"PHILIP.

"Piety is indifferent whether she enters at the
eye or the ear. There is none of the senses at
which she does not knock one day or other. The
Puritans forgot this and thrust beauty out of the
meeting-house, and slammed the door in her face.
I love such sensuality as that which Chaucer shows
in his love of nature. Surely, God did not give us
these fine senses as so many posterns to the heart
for the Devil to enter at. I believe that he has
endowed us with no faculty but for his own glory.
If the Devil has got false keys to them, we must

first have given him a model of the wards to make
a mould by. The senses can do nothing unless the
soul be an accomplice, and, in whatever the soul
does, the body will have a voice. . . .

"JOHN.

"All things that make us happy incline us also
to be grateful, and I would rather enlarge than
lessen the number of these. Morose and callous
recluses have persuaded men that religion is a
prude, and have forced her to lengthen her face,
and contract her brows to suit the character. They
have laid out a gloomy turnpike to heaven, upon
which they and their heirs and assigns are privileged to levy tolls, and have set up guide-boards to
make us believe that all other roads lead in quite
an opposite direction. The pleasanter they are,
the more dangerous. For my part, I am satisfied
that I am upon the right path so long as I can see
anything to make me happier, anything to make me
love man, and therefore God, the more. I would
stamp God's name, and not Satan's, upon every
innocent pleasure, upon every legitimate gratification of sense, and God would be the better served
for it. In what has Satan deserved so well of us,
that we should set aside such first-fruits for him?
Christianity differs not more widely from Plato
than from the Puritans.

"PHILIP.

"The church needs reforming now as much as in
Luther's time, and sells her indulgences as readily.

There are altars to which the slaveholder is admitted, while the Unitarian would be put forth as unclean. If it be God's altar, both have a right there, — the sinner most of all, — but let him not go unrebuked. We hire our religion by the quarter, and if it tells any disagreeable truths, we dismiss it, for we did not pay it for such service as this. Christ scourged the sellers of doves out of the temple; we invite the sellers of men and women in. We have few such preachers now as Nathan was. They preach against sin in the abstract, shooting their arrows into the woundless air. Let sin wrap itself in superfine broadcloth, and put its name on charitable subscription papers, and it is safe. We bandy compliments with it, instead of saying sternly ' Get thee behind me ! ' The Devil might listen to some preaching I have heard without getting his appetite spoiled. There is a great deal of time and money expended to make men believe that this one or that one will be damned, and to scare or wheedle them into good Calvinists or Episcopalians; but very little pains is taken to make them good Christians. . . .

" JOHN.

" It has never been a safe thing to breathe a whisper against the church, least of all in this country, where it has no prop from the state, but is founded only on the love, or, if you will have it so, the prejudices of the people. Religion has come to be esteemed synonymous with the church; there are few minds clear enough to separate it

from the building erected for its convenience and
shelter.   It is this which has made our Christianity
external, a task-ceremony to be gone through with,
and not a principle of life itself.   The church has
been looked on too much in the light of a machine,
which only needs a little oil, now and then, on its
joints and axles, to make it run glibly and perform
all its functions without grating or creaking.   Nothing that we can say will be of much service.   The
reformers must come from her own bosom ; and
there are many devout souls among her own priests
now, who would lay down their lives to purify her.
The names of infidel and heretic are the *San beni-*
tos in which we dress offenders in the nineteenth
century, and a bigoted public opinion furnishes the
fagots and applies the match !   The very cross itself, to which the sacred right of private judgment
fled for sanctuary, has been turned into a whip-
ping-post.   Doubtless, there are no nations on the
earth so wicked as those which profess Christianity ; and the blame may be laid in great measure
at the door of the church, which has always sought
temporal power, and has chosen rather to lean upon
the arm of flesh than upon that of God.   The
church has corrupted Christianity.   She has decked
her person and embroidered her garments with the
spoils of pagan altars, and has built her temples of
blocks which paganism has squared ready to her
hand.   We are still Huns and Vandals, and Saxons and Celts, at heart.   We have carved a cross
upon our altars, but the smoke of our sacrifice goes
up to Thor and Odin still.   Lately I read in the

newspapers a toast given at a military festival, by one of those who claim to be the earthly representatives of the Prince of Peace. England and France send out the cannon and the bayonet, upon missionary enterprises, to India and Africa, and our modern Eliots and Brainerds among the red men are of the same persuasive metal.

"PHILIP.

" Well, well, let us hope for change. There are signs of it; there has been a growling of thunder round the horizon for many days. We are like the people in countries subject to earthquakes, who crowd into the churches for safety, but find that their sacred walls are as fragile as other works of human hands. Nay, the very massiveness of their architecture makes their destruction more sudden and their fall more dangerous. You and I have become convinced of this. Both of us, having certain reforms at heart, and believing them to be of vital interest to mankind, turned first to the church as the nearest helper under God. We have been disappointed. Let us not waste our time in throwing stones at its insensible doors. As you have said, the reformers must come from within. The prejudice of position is so strong that all her servants will unite against an exoteric assailant, melting up, if need be, the holy vessels for bullets, and using the leaves of the holy book itself for wadding. But I will never enter a church from which a prayer goes up for the prosperous only, or for the unfortunate among the oppressors, and not for the oppressed and fallen; as if God had ordained our pride of caste and our distinctions of color, and as if Christ had forgotten those that are in bonds. We are bid to imitate God; let us in this also follow his example, whose only revenge upon error is the giving success to truth, and but strive more cheerfully for the triumph of what we believe to be right. Let us, above all things, imitate him in ascribing what we see of wrong-doing to blindness and error, rather than to wilful sin. The Devil loves nothing better than the intolerance of reformers, and dreads nothing so much as their charity and patience. The scourge is better upon our backs than in our hands.

"JOHN.

" When the air grows thick and heavy, and the clouds gather in the moral atmosphere, the tall steeples of the church are apt to attract the lightning first. Its pride and love of high places are the most fatal of conductors. That small upper room, in which the disciples were first gathered, would always be safe enough."

These kindling words are those of a reformer dealing with existing conditions. It would be much more to the point if we could have in definite terms that revelation of the inner verity of religion which visited Lowell a little earlier than this, as may be seen by a passage from a letter to Dr. Loring, 20 September, 1842. " I had a revelation last Friday evening. I was at Mary's, and happening to say something of the presence of spirits (of whom, I said, I was often dimly aware), Mr. Putnam entered into an argument with me on spiritual matters. As I was speaking the whole system rose up before me like a vague Destiny looming from the abyss. I never before so clearly felt the spirit of God in me and around me. The whole room seemed to me full of God. The air seemed to wave to and fro with the presence of Something, I knew not what. I spoke with the calmness and clearness of a prophet." [1]

No doubt this ecstasy may be regarded as one manifestation of that psychical temper which caused him to see visions in his childhood, but it allied itself with intellectual processes, for he goes on to say: "I cannot tell you what this revelation was. I have not yet studied it enough. But I shall perfect it one day, and then you shall hear it and acknowledge its grandeur. It embraces all other systems."

We may not find a clear statement of this mystic revelation in the discursive "Conversations;" rather we should look for it in his poems of this period, and here, though we find nothing whatever to correspond to a system of divine order, we do find, recurring in various forms, a recognition of an all-embracing, all-penetrating power which through the poet transmutes nature into something finer and more eternal, and gives him a vantage ground from which to perceive more truly the realities of life. "The Token," "An Incident in a Railroad

[1] *Letters*, i. 69.

Car," " The Shepherd of King Admetus," all in a
manner witness to this, and show how persistently
in Lowell's mind was present this aspect of the
poet which makes him a seer. Perhaps there is a
more direct attempt at expressing this truth in one
of the poems not retained in later collections. It
is entitled " A Dirge," and is the imagined plaint
over a poet who has died. In this tumultuous period of Lowell's youth, when the tranquillity which
a returned love brought was after all a very self-
conscious tranquillity, there was always room for
morbid fancies, and the frequency with which in
his poetry he recurs to the images of death leads
one to suspect that he experimented a little with the
idea of his own death. And it may be that in this
poem, which a healthier judgment later led him to
suppress, he was dramatizing himself.

> " Poet ! lonely is thy bed,
> And the turf is overhead, —
>   Cold earth is thy cover ;
> But thy heart hath found release,
> And it slumbers full of peace
> 'Neath the rustle of green trees,
> And the warm hum of the bees
>   Mid the drowsy clover ;
> Through thy chamber still as death
> A smooth gurgle wandereth,
> As the blue stream murmureth
>   To the blue sky over.
>
> .   .   .   .   .
>
> Thou wast full of love and truth,
> Of forgivingness and ruth, —
> Thy great heart with hope and youth
>   Tided to o'erflowing ;
> Thou didst dwell in mysteries,
> And there lingered on thine eyes

Shadows of serener skies,
Awfully wild memories
        That were like foreknowing ;
Thou didst remember well and long
Some fragments of thine angel-song,
And strive, through want, and woe, and wrong,
        To win the world unto it ;
Thy curse it was to see and hear
Beyond to-day's scant hemisphere,
Beyond all mists of doubt and fear,
Into a life more true and clear, —
        And dearly thou didst rue it.

. . . .

"Poet ! underneath the turf,
        Soft thou sleepest, free from morrow ;
Thou hast struggled through the surf
        Of wild thoughts, and want, and sorrow ;
Now, beneath the moaning pine
        Full of rest thy body lieth,
While, far up in pure sunshine,
Underneath a sky divine,
        Her loosed wings thy spirit trieth ;
Oft she strove to spread them here,
But they were too white and clear
For our dingy atmosphere."

The limitations of his theme and measure forbid
more than a hint at this vocation of the poet, but
it happens that we have a somewhat more explicit
statement of the same general idea in a prose
form. A very few weeks after the revelation referred to in the letter to Dr. Loring, too soon certainly for it to have faded from his mind, he sat
down to write a paper on " The Plays of Thomas
Middleton," and the introductory passages contain
what may fairly be taken as snatches from that
music of the spheres which he seems suddenly to
have overheard.

" Poets are the forerunners and prophets of changes in the moral world. Driven, by their finer nature, to search into and reverently contemplate the universal laws of soul, they find some fragments of the broken tables of God's law, and interpret it, half conscious of its mighty import. While philosophers are wrangling, and politicians playing at snapdragon with the destinies of millions, the poet, in the silent deeps of his soul, listens to those mysterious pulses which, from one central heart, send life and beauty through the finest veins of the universe, and utters truths to be sneered at, perchance, by contemporaries, but which become religion to posterity. . . .

" The dreams of poets are morning-dreams, coming to them in the early dawn and day-breaking of great truths, and are surely fulfilled at last. They repeat them, as children do, and all Christendom, if it be not too busy with quarrelling about the meaning of creeds which have no meaning at all, listens with a shrug of the shoulders and a smile of pitying incredulity : for reformers are always madmen in their own age, and infallible saints in the next."

In such rhetorical terms did Lowell, all aflame himself with poetic zeal, try to outline the divine call of the poet, and the " Conversations " reënforce a doctrine which was held more firmly since the preacher was eager to display it in his own practice. At this time, certainly, Lowell's conception of the function of the poet was blended with his apprehension of the divine order, and he entered upon the discharge of poetic duties with the seriousness which a young priest might have carried to the sacred office. The very suppression of his native humor, so that it makes only a few furtive leaps in his poetry up to this time, — for we are setting aside his boyish pranks in verse, — illustrates the exalted mood in which he was living.

The "Conversations on Some of the Old Poets" was published, as we have seen, in January, 1845,[1] but as soon as his own part of the book was done, he was free for a more vital venture: on the 26th of December, 1844, after a five years' betrothal, he was married in her father's house at Watertown to Maria White.

[1] See Appendix B.

CHAPTER IV

IN THE ANTI-SLAVERY RANKS

1845–1849

In the spring of 1844 Mrs. White had taken her daughter Maria to Philadelphia to spare her the rigors of the North, and they had found lodgings at 127 Arch Street, with Friend Parker, a kindly Quakeress, who had made them acquainted with Mr. and Mrs. E. M. Davis, influential members of the Society of Friends. An intimacy grew up between them, for they had a strong bond of sympathy in their common zeal for the cause of anti-slavery and other reforms, and a few weeks after the return of the Whites to Watertown, Maria wrote to her new friends : " I have talked so much to James of Philadelphia, that I have inspired him with a desire to try its virtues if he has an opportunity. We shall probably be married in the spring and I wish very much to spend it there, instead of in our bleak New England, and we should do so if we heard of any opening or employment for him during so short a period as three months. I suppose the season for lectures would be over then, and I fear that Destiny has not been so kind as to arrange any exact labors for him then, simply because he wishes to go. But should you hear of any situation for a literary man at that time, however small the recompense, might I not depend on your kindness to let us know of it?"

For some reason the marriage took place as we have seen at the close of 1844, and not in the spring of 1845. Mr. and Mrs. Lowell stayed a day or two in New York at the New York Hotel, whose splendor amazed them, and reached Philadelphia on the first day of the new year. By a happy augury, the weather had been delightful on their journey, and they had almost a breath of summer in midwinter. They went at once to Friend Parker's, and settled down to happy work. The scheme of lecturing had come to nothing, but Mr. Davis had arranged that Lowell should do some editorial work on the *Pennsylvania Freeman*. That paper had taken the place of the *National Enquirer*, when Benjamin Lundy relinquished its management. Whittier went to Philadelphia in the spring of 1838 to edit the *Freeman*, and remained there two years, when his frail health compelled him to retire. The paper had been temporarily suspended in the interest of the *National Anti-Slavery Standard*, but had been revived and was now under the editorial control of C. C. Burleigh and J. Miller McKim.

The situation of the young pair is sketched in the following letter to Robert Carter : —

127 ARCH STREET, PHILADELPHIA,
Jan'y 14, 1845.

MY DEAR BOY, — Here we are situated as pleasantly as can be, and I write to inform you of the

fact a great deal sooner than you expected, having
been in Philadelphia just a fortnight to-morrow. I
shall not attempt to give you any statistical information with regard to anything here, for I know
that if I should try to describe the Hall of Independence, or anything else, you would contradict
me stoutly till I convicted you out of some Geography or other, and then you would manage to
change sides and appear to be confuting me. You
see that your obstinacy about Boston Common has
cheated you out of a minute detail of all the curi-
osities of this city, together with an account of the
riots, taken from the mouth of one of the leaders
of the mob who was shot dead at the first fire of
the military. But this is a melancholy subject.

Why did you not (you rascal!) slip even so
much as a little note into the package you sent
through the Anti-Slavery office ? Speaking of letters, I mailed one at Worcester from Maria to
Sarah Page, directed to your care, and the Post
Office being closed, I ventured to mail it without
paying the postage, trusting that the kind providence which has hitherto taken care of you above
your deserts may have enabled you to redeem it
from the claws of the Brookline postmaster.

Owen writes me that the " Conversations " is
selling well, and Peterson [1] says that the notices are
all of the most favorable kind. I have seen Graham
and shall probably be able to make a good arrangement for him after my new book has been puffed a
little more. He has grown fat, an evidence of suc-

[1] Editor of *Graham's Magazine.*

cess.   He lives in one of the finest houses in Arch
Street, and keeps his carriage.   He says he would
have given me $150.00 for the " Legend of Brit-
tany " for his Magazine without the copyright.   I
am sorry I did not think of this at the time.

I shall get along very easily while I am here.   I
am engaged to write leaders for the *Pennsylvania Freeman* (which comes out once a fortnight)
and am to be paid $5.00 for each.   I was unwill-
ing to take anything, but they say I must and I
suppose I ought.   I wrote one for the next Thursday's paper entitled " Our Position ; " it is not
very good, but I shall do better as I get used to it.

I have not seen the first number of the *Broadway Journal* yet, but the second is quite entertaining and well done.   The type is a little too large.
Are you going to write a notice of my book for the
paper?   Briggs has written to me since I got here,
but says nothing about it.   I unfortunately missed
seeing him in New York.

We have a little room in the third story (back)
with white muslin curtains trimmed with evergreen,
and are as happy as two mortals can be.   I think
Maria is better, and I *know* I am — in health I
mean, in spirit we both are.   She is gaining flesh
and so am I, and my cheeks are grown so prepos-
terously red that I look as if I had rubbed them
against all the red brick walls in the city.

I have seen your friend —— since I came here.
Somebody called on us the very evening after we
arrived, and on going downstairs who should it be
but our interesting friend.   He attacked me upon

the subject of a vegetable diet, and I replied by fun, which rather disconcerted him. He has not been here since.

I have felt a little of the swell of fashionable society since I have been here. Dr. Elwyn, a kinsman of mine, hearing that I was in town, called upon me and has been very attentive ever since. He is an agreeable man and somewhat literary for Philadelphia. His mother, who has lately quitted Episcopacy for Presbyterianism, called on us to-day, and told me that her " pastor," the Rev. Dr. Bethune, was coming to see me. Authorship might have taken the place of misery in Shakespeare's aphorism.

The abolitionists here are very pleasant and kind. . . . Maria sends her best love. I mean Mrs. Lowell sends it. Give my kind remembrances to Austin and to Owen. The package of the latter came safe.

God bless you ! Most lovingly yours,

J. R. L.

Mrs. Lowell sings her second in this duet in a letter to Mrs. Hawthorne, written two days later, in which she says: " We are most delightfully situated here in every respect, surrounded with kind and sympathizing friends, yet allowed by them to be as quiet and retired as we choose ; but it is always a pleasure to know you can have society if you wish for it, by walking a few steps beyond your own door. We live in a little chamber on the third story, quite low enough to be an attic, so that we feel classical in our environment: and we have one of the sweetest and most motherly of Quaker women to anticipate all our wants, and make us comfortable outwardly as we are blest inwardly. James's prospects are as good as an author's *ought* to be, and I begin to fear we shall not have the satisfaction of being so *very* poor after all. But we are, in spite of this disappointment of our expectations, the happiest of mortals or spirits, and cling to the skirts of every passing hour, though we know the next will bring us still more joy." [1]

The young couple had no resources save their faculty for writing. Mrs. Lowell brought no dowry, but she had poetic sensibility, and fell to translating into verse from German poetry, especially from Uhland. Lowell, with increased confidence bred of the facility with which he had dashed off the "Conversations," and with an unfailing spring of poetry, was ready for any sort of venture. His faithful friend, Mr. Briggs, who had just launched the first number of his new literary weekly, *The Broadway Journal*, was eager for contributions from both. "I am very proud," he wrote on receiving Mrs. Lowell's translation, "The Wreath," from the German of Uhland, "to be the first to introduce her new name to the public," and he proposed all manner of topics for Lowell to write on, such as a paper on Hawthorne and one on Emerson, for a series of articles on "Our American Prose Writers," which had been initiated with one on the now forgotten W. A. Jones.

[1] *Nathaniel Hawthorne and his Wife*, i. 283.

Lowell himself complained of a native indolence, and Briggs, who was skeptical of the force of this objection, proposed a very natural corrective : —

"There is no such stimulus to execution," he writes, "as a sure reward. Now I would like to make a contract with you to furnish me with a column or two, or more, of prose matter, to suit yourself, in the shape of criticism, gossip, or anything else, once a week for six months or a year. You have no idea how easy a thing of this kind becomes when you know that you must do it. If you get nothing else by such an undertaking than the business habit, it would be worth your while. What will you do it for? If our means were sufficient, or success were secure, I would make you an offer that would be sufficiently tempting, but I am loath to make you one that may seem too small. Consider now, and let me know."

Lowell's affection for Briggs and his sympathy with him in his risky venture of a weekly literary journal made him at first well-disposed to contribute freely in response to the editor's urgent invitation, and he was most generous in his attitude respecting payment. "You have been in business, my dear friend," he writes to Briggs, "and know exactly how much you ought to give me with a proper regard to your own balance sheet at the end of the year. I know that your inclination will be to give me more than that. But more you ought not to give nor I to take. I leave it for you to decide. I should not like to bind myself to write every week, though I have no doubt that I shall be able to, and I have some fears that a contingent want of money may hereafter prove as sharp a spur to me as a contract."

Mr. Briggs in reply was more explicit as to terms : " In regard to the compensation, it would be well to read Emerson's essay on that subject. According to him, compensation is inevitable, therefore one need never give himself any trouble on the subject. Nature settles the whole business. You will be sure to receive due compensation for whatever you may do for the *B. J.* Poe writes for me at the rate of one dollar a column. If you will do so, I shall esteem it a capital bargain. The poetry I will pay for separately on a different principle." Accordingly, a day or two after, Lowell wrote : " I send you the first of a series of four or five letters which you may print if you like it. If you do not like it, reject it without scruple. It may be a little too abolition for you as yet. I do not think it good at all, but Maria thinks better of it than I do (bating one or two coarse expressions in it). I do not consider it mine. I wrote it only in the hope of doing some good. So you may alter it as much as you please, if it will serve your turn. If, on the other hand, you like it, I think I may promise that the next will be better. I am in a great hurry, I have only time to say that I like your terms and am perfectly content to help you as much as I can. . . . I always expect to be taken at my word, so reject this without scruple."

The letter thus sent purported to be by one

Matthew Trueman, a country cousin to a supposed
Member of Congress, scalping him for his vote on
the question of the annexation of Texas. It was
intended to be the first of a series in which the
whole question of annexation was to be argued. It
was addressed to no one in particular, but only to
some hypothetical scoundrel. It will be remembered that annexation was the all-absorbing topic
of political discussion during the winter of 1844–
1845. Lowell could not do otherwise from his
anti-slavery principles than bitterly condemn the
action of Congress, and this letter was an out-
burst of satire and invective; but it did not see
the light, and it was not followed by others in the
same vein.

The editor of *The Broadway Journal* began
fencing with the author. He wondered to whom
it was addressed. He thought perhaps it would
be best not to print the whole. " Your satire," he
wrote, " bruises instead of cutting the flesh, and
makes a confounded sore place without letting out
any of the patient's bad blood. I will make as
full a selection as I can; but there are certain
expressions that could not be safely used in public."
He regrets that his friend should have lost so much
time over the letter, but thinks it must have done
him good by drawing off his superfluous zeal. " I
shall think better of you myself for knowing that
you can feel so strongly and write so harshly," he
adds: " it justifies the opinion that I expressed
of you in my notice of your ' Conversations ; ' " and
after a further discussion of abolitionism in prin-

ciple and practice, he begs him to write something
about Philadelphia, or art, the academy, the abominable white doors, the poor watery oysters, everything and anything. "Put all your abolitionism
into rhyme," he concludes: "everybody will read
it in that shape, and it will do good. Don't forget
that you are a poet and go to writing newspaper
articles."

The letter was shrewd, kind, reasonable to an
uninterested reader, but must have been exacer-
bating to Lowell. Mr. Briggs could not conceal
the final ground of his refusal, that to publish this
and similar letters would be to jeopard the fortunes
of *The Broadway Journal*, and in the sensitive
condition of the mind of the out and out abolitionist, this was arrant cowardice. A good deal of
correspondence followed, and Lowell lost his interest in the *Journal*, though he retained his strong
affection for his friend and sent him, as well as a
few poems, a slashing criticism of the exhibition in
the Pennsylvania Academy of Fine Arts, and a
review of Halleck's "Alnwick Castle, with other
Poems," but *The Broadway Journal* itself died out
of existence shortly, Mr. Briggs parting company
with it at the end of a half year.[1] In sending the
former of the two prose articles mentioned above,
Lowell wrote : —

[1] The circumstances pertaining to the close of Mr. Briggs's
connection with *The Broadway Journal* are detailed with some
particularity in letters from Mr. Briggs to Lowell, printed in
Mr. G. E. Woodberry's *Edgar Allan Poe* in the *American Men of
Letters* series. See pp. 234–239.

PHILADELPHIA, Feb'y 15.

MY DEAR FRIEND, — I send you something which will help you fill up, and will show my *willingness* to help till I can send something better. I am so continually interrupted here, and have been so long used to having all my time to myself, that I have not been able yet to acquire the habit of using anything but the very titbits of my time. I have begun several articles for you, but failed in satisfying myself, but before long hope to send you something to your taste. I will send a poem at any rate. Halleck, I see, is about to publish a new edition, which I should like to write a notice of if you have made no other arrangement.

This notice of the " Academy " I have written, you see, as editorial, and you can modify it as you please.

It is hard to write when one is first married. The Jews gave a man a year's vacation. I hope to serve you sooner, and meanwhile remain

Your loving friend,

J. R. L.

P. S.   Maria and I both like the *Journal* exceedingly.

The other vehicle for Lowell's more exclusively literary work during the winter of 1845 was *Graham's Magazine*, published in Philadelphia. He had been a contributor since the spring of 1841, when he used the signature " H. Perceval," which he had been employing in initial form in the *South-*

ern Literary Messenger. His contributions were
all poems, some of which he had preserved in the
two volumes already published, but in the number
for February, 1845, there appeared his biographical and critical sketch of Poe in the series "Our
Contributors," which ran for a score of numbers
and was accompanied by steel portraits. Graham
was desirous of including Lowell in the series with
a portrait by Page, but for some reason the plan
fell through. In this sketch of Poe, Lowell used
a discursive manner, giving expression in a lively
fashion to his judgments of other poets in the past,
but not hesitating to speak emphatically of the
genius of Poe, whom he did not know personally.

"Mr. Poe," he wrote, " is at once the most discriminating, philosophical, and fearless critic upon
imaginative works who has written in America.
It may be that we should qualify our remarks a
little, and say that he *might be*, rather than that
he always *is*, for he seems sometimes to mistake
his phial of prussic acid for his inkstand. . . . Mr.
Poe has that indescribable something which men
have agreed to call genius."

Lowell had offered to write this sketch in May,
1844, and had been supplied with biographical
material by Poe himself, who moreover read the
article in manuscript which Lowell sent at the end
of September through their common friend, Mr.
Briggs. During this winter of 1845 Poe was a
lively subject of discussion by Lowell and his
friends, for he was the most conspicuous figure in
American literature at that time. His " Raven "

appeared in *The American Review* for February,
and his series of papers on plagiarism, with their
acuteness, their ostentation of learning, and their
malice, was trailing through the *Mirror* and *The
Broadway Journal.* His name was linked with
that of Briggs in the editorship of the *Journal,*
and Briggs sometimes found it difficult to make
clear to his friends just how responsibility was ap-
portioned between them. It was impossible to
regard this very insistent figure as an intellectual
or æsthetic abstraction, and his personality was
always getting in the way of a fair judgment. In
a letter to Briggs, 16 January, 1845, Lowell remarks : " From a paragraph I saw yesterday in
the *Tribune* I find that Poe has been at me in the
Mirror. He has at least that chief element of a
critic—a disregard of persons. · He will be a very
valuable coadjutor to you." Briggs, who was at
this time a warm defender of Poe, had read the
article in the *Mirror,* which was a review of the
"Conversations," and assured Lowell that it was
extremely laudatory and discriminating, and a few
days later, after strongly praising " The Gold
Bug " which he had just read, he says : " Do not
trouble yourself about anybody's gloriometer. . . .
I have always misunderstood Poe from thinking
him one of the Graham and Godey species, but I
find him as different as possible. I think that you
will like him well when you come to know him
personally." Briggs copied " The Raven " into
his magazine and wrote enthusiastically to Lowell
about it. But Lowell was deeply offended by what

he termed "the grossness and vulgarity" of Poe's treatment of Longfellow, especially in his offhand allusion to Mrs. Longfellow and her children. Briggs again came to Poe's defence. "The allusion to Mrs. Longfellow," he wrote, "was only a playful allusion to an abstract Mrs. Longfellow, for Poe did not know even that Longfellow was married; look at the thing again and you will see that it contains nothing offensive. Poe has, indeed, a very high admiration for Longfellow, and so he will say before he is done. For my own part I did not use to think well of Poe, but my love for you and implicit confidence in your judgment led me to abandon all my prejudices against him, when I read your account of him. The Rev. Mr. Griswold, of Philadelphia, told me some abominable lies about him, but a personal acquaintance with him has induced me to think highly of him. Perhaps some Philadelphian has been whispering foul things in your ear about him. Doubtless his sharp manner has made him many enemies. But you will think better of him when you meet him."

Lowell, however, refused to be convinced. "The Rev. Mr. Griswold," he said petulantly, "is an ass, and, what's more, a knave, and even if he had said anything against Poe, I should not have believed it. But neither he nor any one else ever did. I remain of my old opinion about the allusion to Mrs. Longfellow. I remain of my old opinion about Poe, and I have no doubt that Poe estimates Longfellow's poetical abilities more highly than I do perhaps, but I nevertheless do not like his two last

articles. I still think Poe an invaluable contributor, but I like such articles as his review of Miss
Barrett better than these last."

Up to this time Lowell appears to have known
Poe only through correspondence.[1] A few weeks
later, when he was returning from Philadelphia to
Cambridge, he called upon him, but the interview
gave little satisfaction, due to the fact, mentioned
by Mr. Briggs, that Poe was tipsy at the time. A
few weeks later Lowell defended himself, in a
letter to Briggs, against a charge of plagiarism
made by Poe, and summed up his impressions as
follows : "Poe, I am afraid, is wholly lacking in
that element of manhood which, for want of a better
name, we call character. It is something quite distinct from genius, — though all great geniuses are
endowed with it. Hence we always think of Dante
Alighieri, of Michelangelo, of Will Shakespeare,
of John Milton, — while of such men as Gibbon
and Hume we merely recall the works, and think
of them as the author of this and that. As I prog-
nosticated, I have made Poe my enemy by doing
him a service. . . . Poe wishes to kick down the

[1] Lowell's letters to Poe may be found in an article with that
title, edited by Mr. Woodberry, and printed in *Scribner's Magazine*, August, 1894. Those of Poe to Lowell appear in Mr. Woodberry's volume on Poe in the *American Men of Letters* series.
Lowell's letters, which run from 19 November, 1842, when he
was beginning his *Pioneer* venture, to 12 December, 1844, just
before his marriage, are occupied mainly with solicitation of contributions, interest in Poe's work, and efforts at obtaining oppor-
tunities for Poe to lecture in Boston. They have slight value as
illustrations of Lowell's life, save as they show his eagerness to
help a brother author, and his keen interest in letters.

ladder by which he rose. He is welcome. But he does not attack me at a weak point. He probably cannot conceive of anybody's writing for anything but a newspaper reputation or for posthumous fame, which is much the same thing magnified by distance. I have quite other aims."

Finally, Briggs himself lost all patience with Poe, and replied to this letter: "You have formed a correct estimate of Poe's characterless character. I have never met a person so utterly deficient of high motive. He cannot conceive of anybody's doing anything except for his own personal advantage; and he says, with perfect sincerity and entire unconsciousness of the exposition which it makes of his own mind and heart, that he looks upon all reformers as madmen; and it is for this reason that he is so great an egoist; he cannot conceive why the world should not feel an interest in whatever interests him, because he feels no interest himself in what does not personally concern him."

In all his critical writing after this time, Lowell never discussed Poe. His offhand characterization in "A Fable for Critics,"

" Three fifths of him genius and two fifths sheer fudge,
.   .   .   .   .   .
Who has written some things quite the best of their kind,
But the heart somehow seems all squeezed out by the mind,"

passes at once into a lecture on his treatment of Longfellow. Poe was not a blackboard on which Lowell wrote his own virtues, but it is an illustration of the dominant ethical note in Lowell's nature, especially at this time, that open as he was

to the influence of poetry, and keenly sensitive to
the melody and color to be found in exquisite language, he could not detach poetry from character.
In his leaning toward reform, he tried to take
poetry with him as a fellow-worker, but I do not
think this really affected his judgment of Poe, and
Briggs's amusing report of Poe's consignment of
reformers to the mad-house was not likely to gall
him; his sense of humor would correct any irrita-
tion.   But Lowell did hold his head high and was
intoxicated with the spirit of idealism; he and his
wife stimulated each other, and breathing this air,
he was not in a mood to be indulgent toward what
he conceived to be lower ideals.   The biographical
essay which a few years later he wrote on Keats
shows clearly how desirous he was of bringing the
few known facts of that poet's life into accord with
a lofty conception of the poetic spirit; standing
uncomfortably near Poe, he was in danger of inter-
preting his poetry by the comment which his life
afforded.

Although literature then as always was the constant factor in Lowell's resolve, the circumstances
in which he was placed, and his own uneasy sense
that he ought to bear his part in the moral upris-
ing, led him to expend a good deal of energy this
winter in political and ethical writing.   He was
living in the midst of the Society of Friends and
breathing an atmosphere of anti-slavery reform;
the great debate on Texas was raging, and, more
than all, his wife by his side kept a steady flame
of zeal burning.   He let himself out once in verse

when he sent to the *Boston Courier* some stanzas
headed "Another Rallying Cry by a Yankee," in
which, with a vehemence that allowed little breathing space for wit or humor, he declaimed against
the iniquity of the Texas resolutions, then on the
eve of passage, and made a passionate appeal to his
native state to hold herself aloof from any compromise with slavery.

"O Spirit of the noble Past, when the old Bay State was free,"

he began, and employed all the resources of type
to make his protest heard : —

"And though all other deeds of thine, dear Fatherland, should be
Washed out, like writing upon sand, by Time's encroaching sea,
   That single word shall stand sublime, nor perish with the rest,
   'THOUGH THE WHOLE WORLD SANCTION SLAVERY, IN GOD'S
      NAME WE PROTEST!'"

The final stanza was a burst of state independence:

"No, if the old Bay State were sunk, and, as in days of yore,
One single ship within her sides the hope of Freedom bore,
Run up again the pine tree flag, and on the chainless sea
That flag should mark, where'er it waved, the island of the free!"

In these verses, as in others of a similar nature,
Lowell seems almost to have followed the lead of
Whittier, who employed the same stanza in several
of his anti-slavery poems written before this time.

In his eager, impulsive desire to right wrongs,
and his impatience at compromise, he chafed under
the restraints laid upon him. The rebuff he received when he undertook to scarify the conscience
of Congress in the pages of *The Broadway Journal*
irritated him. He had hoped that the *Journal*
would be a " powerful weapon in the hands of re-

form," and was disheartened. "The reason I have
written no prose for him (Briggs)," he wrote his
friend Carter, "has been because I knew not what
to write about.   The *Journal* shut its doors in the
face of every subject in which I was mainly interested, and I could not bring myself (in writing for
a friend especially) to undertake subjects in which,
feeling no interest, I could not possibly write
well."   He had engaged to write regularly for the
Pennsylvania Freeman, but even here he did not,
in his own mind, have a clear field. "I do not
feel entirely free," he says in a letter to Carter,
"in what I write for the paper, as its conductors
are rather timid."   That is the complaint of most
young reformers, and yet the constraint which appears in his articles is due rather to the caution
with which he feels his way along a path where he
is likely to be misjudged than to any outside re-
pressive influence.   At least this may be inferred
from a reading of two articles which he contributed
to the *Freeman* and which were no doubt looked
upon as very radical utterances. They had for
their heading "The Church and Clergy," and were
deliberate inquiries into the nature of the religious
bodies in America as tested by the attitude which
they took, organically, toward the great question
of political reform, especially as regarded the subject of slavery.   In a letter to Longfellow written
a few weeks after this date, Lowell puts his belief
into two or three pregnant sentences. "Christ,"
he says, "has declared war against the Christianity of the world, and it must down. There is no

help for it. The Church, that great bulwark of
our practical Paganism, must be reformed from
foundation to weathercock. Shall we not wield a
trowel, nay, even carry the heavy bricks and mor-
tar for such an enterprise? But I will not ride
over you with my hard-mouthed hobby."

In the two editorial articles referred to, Lowell
takes the ground that when there is dereliction to
pure ideals on the part of the more refined and
intellectual members of the church, especially of
those in the priestly order, there will be the
greater zeal of the more brutal and unintelligent
in defence of the church, and instances the cries of
the Jewish populace for the crucifixion of the Saviour, the mob at Athens that condemned Socrates
to drink the hemlock, and, taking a very recent
example : " It was the most brutal and degraded
of the English population which assaulted the
pure-minded Wesley, and cock-fighting, horse-
racing, drunken priests and justices established
their orthodoxy to the satisfaction of so competent
a constituency by reviling or indicting him. Now
that it has become necessary to protest against
Protestantism, it is the ignorant and unthinking
who are so eager to defend the right of private
judgment by tarring and feathering all who differ
with them." The mass of men, Lowell goes on to
say, love an easy religion, which affords a cheap
and marketable kind of respectability. " Puritan-
ism has always been unpopular among them as a
system which demands too much and pays too
little." The clergy, too, in the United States, being

dependent upon their hearers for support, unconsciously slip into the habit of adapting themselves to the prejudices and weaknesses of their supporters. Thus by degrees the church and religion are held to be synonymous terms, and the church becomes a kind of private estate, silent in the face of a great evil which the great body of Christian people has learned to tolerate. In point of fact true religious sentiment is the most powerful weapon in the world against slavery and all other social vices, but the religious system of the country as corrupted by connivance with evil is the greatest obstacle in the way. The only sure way of accomplishing its great object is for the church to keep in advance of popular morality, and " the surest and safest test for deciding when the time has arrived for the church to take another step forward is by observing whether it is reverenced by the wisest of its members as merely an external symbol of some former manifestation of Divinity, or is reverenced as containing in itself a present and living Divineness."

But why, it might be asked, should the clergy be picked out for blame in the matter of upholding slavery, rather than any other class, as that of the merchants for example ? The answer is plain. If the church professed to be no more than a society of private citizens meeting once a week, the clergyman would be simply the chairman of the gathering, and a mouthpiece of the majority. But the church sets up the claim to be of divine origin and the depository of truth. If this be so, it should always be in advance of public opinion. " It should not wait till the Washingtonians, by acting the part which, in virtue of the station it arrogates to itself, should have been its own, had driven it to sign the pledge and hold fellowship with the degraded and fallen. It should not wait until the Abolitionists, by working a change in the sentiment of the people, have convinced it that it is more politic to sympathize with the slave than with the slave-owner, before it ventures to lisp the alphabet of anti-slavery. The glorious privilege of leading the forlorn hope of truth, of facing the desperate waves of prejudice, of making itself vile in the eyes of men by choosing the humblest means of serving the despised cause of the master it professes to worship, all these belong to it in right of the position it assumes." And he calls upon the clergy to produce certificates of martyrdom before he will accept the claims they set up for themselves.

The whole discussion is characterized by sincerity and a scarcely veiled sarcasm, and is interesting not only as showing Lowell's thought at the time on a burning subject, but also as disclosing a certain academic air as if he had written carefully and with restraint, perhaps thinking how it would sound to his father's ear. There is hardly more than a faint suggestion of the wit and humor which marked his later political writing, and there is one passage which may be noted as distinctly literary in tone. " In many parts of Germany," he writes, " there are legends of buried churches and convents, whose bells are often heard, and in which, now and then, some person by a lucky chance can hear the monks chanting the ritual of many centuries ago. It seems to us that the religion of our churches is of very much the same subterranean and traditionary kind. To one walking in the pure light of upper day, the sound of their service seems dim and far off, and, if he catches a word here and there, it is an obsolete language which does not appeal to the present heart and soul, but only to a vague reverence for what is ancient, a mysterious awe for what is past."

The winter had been passed in this experimental fashion, Mrs. Lowell translating poems from the German by her husband's side, as he wrote now verse, now prose, intent on the questions of the day, yet never really giving himself out except now and then in some spontaneous bit of poetry. They made hosts of friends in Philadelphia and spent the last few weeks of their stay on a visit to the Davis family, with whom they had become close companions. Mrs. Hallowell, who was a child at the time, recalled the delight that attended their stay, especially the pleasure given the children by Mrs. Lowell, who told them fairy tales and recited ballads, giving the Caldon Low in a soft crooning voice sweeter than singing. They took a short driving tour with their hosts through Chester County, but near the end of May set out on their return to Cambridge, stopping by the way for a week's visit with Mr. and Mrs. Briggs in Staten Island. They went home by way of Albany in order

to see Page, and by the middle of June were established at Elmwood, where they formed one household with Lowell's father, mother, and sister.

Lowell had not found himself out yet.   He had,
indeed, a premonitory consciousness of his strength.
" I shall do something as an author yet," he wrote
to Briggs, 21 August, 1845.   " It is my laziness
and my dissatisfaction at everything I write that
prevents me from doing more."   But he adds,
" there is something, too, in feeling that the best
part of your nature and your performance lies un-
mined and unappreciated."   For the present he
seems to have written chiefly under the impulse
created by some sudden affair, as in the verses " On
the Capture of Fugitive Slaves near Washington,"
which appeared in the *Boston Courier*, 19 July,
1845.   The lines were prefaced by this note to the
editor, Mr. Buckingham : —

" Reading lately in the newspapers an account of
the capture of some fugitive slaves, within a few
miles of the Capital of our Republic, I confess my
astonishment at finding no comments made upon
what seemed to me an act of unparalleled inhuman-
ity.   Thirty unfortunate disciples of the Declaration of Independence pursued and captured by some
two hundred armed minions of tyranny !   It seems
strange that a burst of indignation from one end
of our free country to the other did not follow so
atrocious a deed.   At least it seemed a proper occasion for sympathy on the part of one of our daily
papers which a year or two ago indorsed Lord
Morpeth's sentiment that

'Who would be free themselves must strike the blow.'

Though such a mode of emancipation is totally abhor-
rent to my feelings, and though I would earnestly
deprecate any attempt at insurrection on the part
of our slave population, yet I confess to the weakness of being so far human in my feelings as to
sympathize deeply with these unhappy beings who
have been thwarted in their endeavor to convert
themselves from chattels into men by the peaceful
method of simply changing their geographical position.   Under these feelings, and believing you to
be a man with sufficient confidence in the justness
of your own opinions not to fear to publish sentiments which may chance to go beyond or even directly contravene your own, I wrote the following
lines."

There is a prophetic ring to the verses which
indicates how surely Lowell's poetic spirit had absorbed the underlying truth of abolitionism.   The
poem is far less declamatory, more profoundly
indignant than the Texas verses which he had
printed in the same paper.   The intimation which
he gave in his prefatory note, that his sentiment
might be unacceptable even to so hearty and honest
a hater of slavery as Mr. Buckingham, plainly
points to the doubt expressed whether a higher
allegiance might not demand a revolt from the constitution and union if they were found to be the
impregnable defence of slavery, — a doubt which
was already certainty in the minds of the most radical of the abolitionists ; but the stage of doubt was
as far as Lowell ever went, and this may be taken

as the utmost expression which he ever reached.[1]
The poem was vigorous enough to make an impression, and successive numbers of the *Courier* show
two long-winded writers knocking away at the
spectre of Dissolution which the poem had raised.[2]

Although the summer of 1845 does not seem to
have yielded much in the way of verse or prose,
Lowell had quite definitely taken ground as a man
of letters.   There was no more talk of the law, and
he even dropped lines of correspondence which had
marked his old carelessness of occupation.   " You
hint in your last letter," he wrote to E. M. Davis
in October, " that it must be very easy for me to
write, because writing is my profession, while in
truth this is precisely what makes it hard.   You
must recollect that it is vacation time with me when
the pen is out of my hand.   Before I became an
author I used to write multitudes of letters to my
friends.   Then, wherever I set my foot, thoughts
rose up before me short-winged and chirping as the
flights of grasshoppers which spring from the path
of one who walks in September stubble-fields.   The
post-office was my safety-valve, which eased me in
a trice of all my too explosive thoughts, humors,
and moods.   Now my thoughts take a higher and
wider flight, and are not so easily followed and

[1] It may be noted that at the New England Anti-Slavery Convention held in Boston, 28 May, 1844, the issue of disunion was
plainly presented in a set of resolutions.   The vote stood 250 in
favor to 24 in dissent.   Among the number who voted " nay "
were James Russell Lowell and Maria White.   See *William Lloyd
Garrison*, iii. 111, 112.

[2] For a striking use of the poem, see *infra*, vol. ii. p. 137.

defined by the eye.   I confess that my opinions seem to me of less importance." [1]

By his regular and his random writing Lowell had met the expense of his winter in Philadelphia, and with his simple mode of life and his horror of debt it was not a very serious problem which his livelihood presented.   Elmwood gave shelter, and the young couple shared the family economy.   A little more ease, however, was to come through the accession of Mrs. Lowell to a share in the estate of her father, who died suddenly in September of this year.   "I suppose," Lowell writes in the letter just quoted, "that when the estate is settled (Mr. White died intestate) we shall be the possessors of $20,000 or more.   I confess I hardly feel so independent as before.   I believe that in this age poverty needs to have apostles, and I had resolved to be one, but I suppose God knows what is best for me, or the event would not have happened.   That I should ever have lived to be such a nabob!" [2]

[1] But his talk went on as unrestrictedly as ever.   Longfellow records in his diary under date of 23 October, 1845: "Lowell passed the morning with me.   Amiable enthusiast!   He proposes to write a book in favor of fanaticism."

[2] It is a comment on Lowell's indifference to wealth that his imagination did not take fire at the announcement of the discovery of gold in California.   It may be said that his mind was directed toward the immediate political consequences, but he had occasion to write upon the subject of the discovery, when this alone engaged his attention.   He was struck with some of the picturesque situations, but his reflections were mainly summed up in these words: "We have never seen anything like the accounts from California since we read that chapter of *Candide*, in which Voltaire carries his hero to El Dorado.   Supposing all we hear to be true, it is hardly probable that gold will continue to be found

One of the effects of this modest fortune was to give the Lowells a further sense of independence and to lead them to form plans of travel and life abroad, for from the first the frailty of Mrs. Lowell's health had been a factor in all their problems. They meant to go again to Philadelphia the next spring, and they looked forward to going to Italy in the coming fall for a two or three years' residence. " Now that we know the amount of our property," Mrs. Lowell wrote shortly after to Mrs. Davis, " it seems quite doubtful whether we shall be able to travel much ; but we can live in Italy as cheaply as at home, and have all the advantages of climate and beautiful works of art besides."

On the last day of the year their first child was born, and they gave her the name of Blanche in gentle allusion to Mrs. Lowell's maiden name. Lowell wrote the news in a brief note on New Year's Day, 1846, to Mr. Davis: " Our little daughter Blanche was born yesterday afternoon at $3\frac{1}{2}$ o'clock. She is a very fine hearty child, very

there in such large quantities for any great length of time. It will doubtless become more and more scarce, and the difficulty of obtaining it greater. After all, the gold mines which give the surest and richest yield are the brain and the common earth. The discovery of a new fertilizer is of more practical benefit than that of the philosopher's stone would be ; the invention of the steam-engine has created more wealth than the richest gold mines ; and wise men are not wanting who believe that Fourier has given us something better than a California. And why travel fifteen thousand miles around Cape Horn for a place to dig in ? Heaven knows the earth wants more washing here than at Sacramento River. Moreover, every one of us has a vein more or less profitable, if it were only diligently worked." — " Eldorado," in *National Anti-Slavery Standard*, 21 December, 1848.

fair and white, with red cheeks, and looks already
a month old.   Maria, thank God, is quite well. . . .
Our fair has been eminently successful, more so
than any hitherto.   I received your tract only a
day or two since, having only been to Boston once
or twice for the last two months.   I am much
obliged to you for it, though my thankfulness is
almost used up by the baby."

How happy the parents were in their anticipation may be read in the affectionate terms in which
Lowell had confided their hopes late in August to
his friend Briggs.   " Never mind what our child
will be (if it should be born safely), we can at least
enjoy our parentship now and fancy what glories
we please of our little darling.   We have christened it long ago.   If she is a girl she is to be
named Blanche (White), a sweet name, thus unit-
ing Maria's family name with mine.   If a boy we
shall call him Perceval, that being the given name
of the first Lowle who set foot in America, and
having, moreover, a pretty diminutive (Percie), an
important thing for a boy.   Now, do not set your
wits at work to discover prophetically the unhear-
worthy nickname which the perverse ingenuity of
boys will twist out of it at school.   He shall never
go to school.   The only reason I have for a prefer-
ence of sex is that girls ordinarily resemble the
father most, and boys the mother.   Therefore I
hope for a boy, and if you knew Maria (I call her
mother already) as well as I do, you would hope
so too.   It is true I can never persuade her of
the force of this argument — because she does not

know how good she is. When people arrive at
that pitch of consciousness they are generally good
for nothing." And then follows the half-prophetic
passage : " I have never forgotten the sympathy I
felt with your hopes and your disappointment in a
similar case. . . . I look upon death so constantly
and surely as but a continuation of life (after the
glad removal or subsidence of the plethora of flesh
which now chokes half the spirit out of us) that I
shall be quite willing to send before us such an
ambassador as our little angel would be if he goes
sooner than we do. At all events, nothing can ever
take away from me the joy I have already had in
it." The haunting fear which every young father
has at such a time, and which Lowell intimates in
these lines, was not made real at once, but the child
lived with them only a brief fourteen months. It
is touching to find Mrs. Lowell a month before the
birth of her child writing verses of profound sympathy entitled " The Slave Mother," in which she
reflects the anguish such a mother feels on the
birth of her child ; and on the same day Lowell
was writing his poem " The Falcon," though in its
original form, entitled " The Falconer," it was
longer and filled with a certain savage indignation
over the quarry upon which the falcon, Truth, de-
scends. Both poems were contributed to " The
Liberty Bell," published for the anti-slavery bazaar which was held each December in Boston.
This was the social rally of the abolitionists and a
resource with which to meet the modest demands of
a crusade into which men and women threw them-

selves without counting the cost. Before and after
her marriage Mrs. Lowell took an active part in
the bazaar under the generalship of Mrs. Chapman.
Lowell hits off the characteristics of those who
were conspicuous in the local movement most wittily in his " Letter from Boston," which he sent to
the *Pennsylvania Freeman*, at the close of 1846.

The little child filled a large place in Lowell's
letters to his intimate friends. Briggs had sent
a message to the newcomer, and Lowell replied :
" Blanche was asleep when I read your kind wishes
about her, and I did not dare to disturb her in an
occupation in which she is sedulously perfecting
herself by the most diligent practice. She has not
yet learned our method of speech, and I to my sorrow have almost forgotten hers, so that I cannot
honestly send any authentic messages from her to
you. If you have been more happy than I in retaining a knowledge of the dialect of your infancy,
you will perhaps be able to make something out of
her remarks on hearing that she had loving friends
so far away. ' A *goo* (pianissimo) *ah* goo, errrrrr,
ahg — (cut off by a kind of melodious jug-jug in
her throat, as if she liked the phrase so well she
must needs try to swallow it) ah! (fortissimo) a
goo,' followed by a smile which began in the dim-
ple on her chin, and thence spread, like the circles
round a pebble thrown into sunshiny water, with
a golden ripple over the whole of her person, being
most distinctly ecstatic in her fingers and toes.
The speech was followed by a searching glance at
her father, in whose arms she had her throne, to

assure herself of his identity, and of her consequent security."

A more exact knowledge of the amount of the legacy received from Mr. White's estate and the income to be derived from it led the Lowells to abandon their first intention of going abroad soon, but, apparently in anticipation of such an emergency, Lowell had resolved to acquire a better colloquial knowledge of French. " As an evidence of my proficiency," he writes to Briggs, "let me set down here an impromptu translation of that Chevy Chace of the nursery, ' Three children sliding on the ice.' As it is my first attempt at the ' higher walks' of French poetry, you must read it with due allowance.

> " Trois enfants glissants sur la glace,
>   Tous en un jour d'été,
>   Tous tomberent, as it came to pass,
>   Les autres s'enfuyaient." [1]

There was an incident at this time which illustrates the sensitiveness of the anti-slavery mind. The weight of literature was thrown against slav-

[1] Mr. Briggs was highly entertained by the French exercise, and asked : " Who is your master ? But never mind. Let me recommend you to an incomparable one who had the honor of teaching Talleyrand a new language (English) to help him conceal his thoughts. I mean Cobbett. If you have never seen his French grammar, get it by all means and read it, if you do not study it ; and then read his English grammar, which you will find more amusing than the Comic Latin Grammar." Lowell does not seem to have followed his advice immediately. At least he wrote to me three or four years before his death : " I never read any English grammar in my life, thank God, except Cobbett's a few years ago, and in that I found errors of ignorance, — as was to be expected."

ery, and it was a matter of pride and rejoicing
that the most popular American poet, Longfellow,
should bear his testimony in a thin volume of
" Poems on Slavery." But a Philadelphia publishing house, Cary & Hart, brought out a handsomely illustrated volume of his poetical works,
from which this group of poems was omitted, and
the leaders of the anti-slavery movement were
indignant at what they regarded as the poet's
pusillanimity. Their journals attacked him bitterly, especially the *National Anti-Slavery Standard*, edited by Mrs. Chapman, Edmund Quincy,
and Sydney Howard Gay. Lowell's comments on
the matter are interesting as throwing light on the
attitude of his mind upon the question of the poet
and his mission, which we have seen was so vital
a one in his early history. He wrote to Briggs 18
February, 1846 : . . . " I never wrote a letter
which was not a sincere portrait of my mind at
the time, and therefore never one whose contents
can hold a rod over me. My pen has not yet
traced a line of which I am either proud or
ashamed, nor do I believe that many authors have
written less from *without* than I, and therefore
more piously. And this puts me in mind of Longfellow's suppression of his anti-slavery pieces.
Sydney Gay wishes to know whether I think he
spoke too harshly of the affair. I think he *did*,
even supposing the case to be as he put it, and this
not because I agree with what he tells me is your
notion of the matter — that it is interfering with
the freedom of an author's will (though I think

you were *ironing* with that grave face of yours) — for I do not think that an author has a right to suppress anything that *God* has given him — but because I believe that Longfellow esteemed them of inferior quality to his other poems. For myself, when I was printing my second volume of poems, Owen wished to suppress a certain 'Song sung at an Anti-Slavery Picnic.' I never saw him, but he urged me with I know not what worldly arguments. My only answer was — 'Let all the others be suppressed if you will — *that* I will never suppress.' I believe this was the first audible knock my character made at the door of Owen's heart — he loves me now and I him. My calling is clear to me. I am never lifted up to any peak of vision — and moments of almost fearful inward illumination I have sometimes — but that, when I look down, in hope to see some valley of the Beautiful Mountains, I behold nothing but blackened ruins, and the moans of the downtrodden the world over, but chiefly here in our own land, come up to my ear instead of the happy songs of the husbandmen reaping and binding the sheaves of light — yet these, too, I hear not seldom. Then I feel how great is the office of Poet, could I but even dare to hope to fill it. Then it seems as if my heart would break in pouring out one glorious song that should be the gospel of Reform, full of consolation and strength to the oppressed, yet falling gently and restoringly as dew on the withered youth-flowers of the oppressor. That way my madness lies."

In the same letter, with the long-reaching speculation of a father over his first child, the subject
of Blanche's training is touched upon with a half
serious, half playful exaggeration. Lowell had
been writing humorously of his chivalric feelings
toward dependents like the maid of all work in the
house, and he breaks out: " I mean to bring up
Blanche to be as independent as possible of all
man kind. I was saying the other day to her
mother (who has grown lovelier than ever) that
I hoped she would be a great, strong, vulgar, mud-
pudding-baking, tree-climbing little wench. I shall
teach her to swim, to skate, and to walk twenty
miles a day as her father can — and by the time
she is old enough, I do not despair of seeing the
world so good that she can walk about at night
alone without any danger. You ask the color of
her eyes.   They are said to be like her father's, —
but, in my opinion, they are of quite too heavenly
a blue for that. But I do not think the color of
the eyes of much import. I never notice it in
those I love, or in any eyes where I can see deeper
than the cornea and iris. I do not know the color
of my father's eyes, or of any of my sisters' (except from hearsay), nor should I know that of
Maria's except from observations for that special
end. But where your glance is arrested at the surface, where these windows are, as it were, daubed
over with paint (like those of rooms where menial
or unsightly offices are performed which we do not
wish the world to see, or where something is exhibited for pay) to balk insight — then the color is

the chief sight noticeable. I do not believe that the finest eyes have any special hue — and this is probably the ground for the fallacy that poets' eyes are gray — a kind of neutral color."

In January, 1846, the publication was begun of the *London Daily News*, a paper which represented the most advanced liberal thought in politics and was for a short time conducted by Dickens. For this paper Lowell agreed to write a series of articles on "Anti-slavery in the United States." His name was not to appear. Indeed, the scheme intended an historical sketch of the reform by one in sympathy with it, but not confessedly by an abolitionist. In pursuance of the plan four articles appeared in the months of February, March, April, and May, 1846, and the manner of treatment plainly supposed a much longer continuance, but it is probable that certain changes in the management of the paper rendered a continuance inexpedient ; for in June the paper was lessened from a double sheet of eight pages to a single one of four, and the price reduced, leaving small opportunity for the leisurely essays which had formerly found place. The four papers did little more than clear the way, and really brought the historical sketch only down to the establishment of *The Liberator* by Mr. Garrison. For the most part the treatment is little more than an orderly and somewhat perfunctory recital of well-known facts, but once or twice the writer breaks forth into his more personal speech. Thus in the first article occurs this passage : —

"Unless we draw an erring augury from the past, that devoted little band who have so long maintained the bleak Thermopylæ of Freedom, remembering those in bonds as bound with them, as now they are the scoff and by-word of prospering iniquity, so will they be reckoned the Saints, Confessors, and Martyrs in the calendar of coming time, and the statues of Garrison, Maria Chapman, Phillips, Quincy, and Abby Kelley will fill those niches in the National Valhalla which a degraded public sentiment has left empty for such earthen demi-gods as Jackson, Webster and Clay." Again the final article, after dealing with the Missouri Compromise, introduces Mr. Garrison upon the scene by quoting the preface to the first number of *The Liberator*, and goes on to say : —

"Now for the first time indeed Slavery felt itself assailed genuinely and in thorough earnest. But editors and other proprietors of public opinion manufactories in the Free States were slower of perception. They had not the warning of that instinctive terror which informed the slaveholder of the approach of danger. But they were soon satisfied of the dreadful truth that there existed in their very midst one truly sincere and fearless man, and instantly a prolonged shriek of execration and horror quavered from the Aroostook to the Red River. They saw, with a thrill of apprehension for the security of their offices or of their hold upon public consideration what treasonable conclusions might be legitimately drawn from their own harmless premises, harmless only so long as there was no man honest enough to make an application of them, and so cast suspicion on the motives of all. If the pitch and tow fulminations of Salmoneus had been suddenly converted into genuine bolts of Jupiter, he could not have dropped them from his hands with a more confounded alacrity. Here was a man gifted with a most excruciating sincerity and frankness, a hungry conscience that could not be sated with the cheap workhouse gruel of smooth words, and inconveniently addicted to thinking aloud."

The article closes with this striking diagnosis: —

"The advent of Garrison was indeed an event of historical moment. The ban of outlawry was set on Slavery, and its doom was sealed. It matters not that since that time Slavery has won some of its most alarming victories. The nucleus of a sincere uncompromising hostility to it was formed. A clear issue between right and wrong, disentangled from the mists of extraneous interests, was presented to men's minds. The question was removed from the dust and bewilderment of political strife to the clear and calm retirements of God's justice and individual conscience. Henceforth the struggle must be not between the Northern and Southern States, but between barbarism and civilization, between cruelty and mercy, between evil and good. This was already in itself a victory, a triumph which would have been enough to round the long life struggle of a reformer with peace. Exaltation was achieved by the mere look, as it were, of an unknown, solitary, and friendless youth,

so full was it of the potent conjuration of honesty
and veracity.   Whatever may be the contents of
government mails and official bulletins, the shining
feet of the messengers of Nature are constant and
swift to bring to the ears of the lowly servant of
Truth at least the sustaining news — that God still
exists, and that He may select even the bruised
reed for his instrument."

It is not materially anticipating to record here
what Lowell wrote of Garrison a couple of years
later, when he was defining his own position on
abolitionism, to his friend Briggs : " Garrison is so
used to standing alone that, like Daniel Boone, he
moves away as the world creeps up to him, and
goes farther into the wilderness.   He considers
every step a step forward, though it be over the
edge of a precipice.   But, with all his faults (and
they are the faults of his position), he is a great
and extraordinary man.   His work may be over,
but it has been a great work.   Posterity will forget his hard words, and remember his hard work.
I look upon him already as an historical personage, as one who is in his niche. . . . I love you
(and love includes respect) ; I respect Garrison
(respect does not include love).   There never has
been a leader of Reform who was not also a black-
guard.   Remember that Garrison was so long in
a position where he alone was right and all the
world wrong, that such a position has created in
him a habit of mind which may remain, though circumstances have wholly changed.   Indeed, a mind
of that cast is essential to a Reformer.   Luther

was as infallible as any man that ever held St. Peter's keys." But the most condensed expression of his feeling toward this remarkable man, who so dominated the anti-slavery movement, is to be found in the verses addressed to him beginning—

"In a small chamber, friendless and unseen."[1]

In May, 1846, occurred one of those personal incidents which stirred deeply the heart of the anti-slavery crusader and was made the occasion of public testimony. The Rev. Charles Turner Torrey, who had been an active writer and worker in the cause, and in 1834 was shut up in the penitentiary in Baltimore for having aided slaves to escape, died in May, 1846, of disease brought on by ill usage. He was of New England birth and his body was brought to Boston for burial. Besides the burial service there was a public meeting in Faneuil Hall on the evening of 18 May. Dr. Henry I. Bowditch, an ardent supporter of the anti-slavery cause and one of the committee in charge, wrote to Lowell on the 3d of the month, telling him that private advices led them to expect hourly the news of Torrey's death, and that the plan was on foot for a public funeral service. "If this is done," he says, "we shall hope to hear from the poets of our land, the true ministers of God and of Christ, at the present

[1] At the close of 1866 a testimonial was presented to Mr. Garrison when he retired from active service, and Lowell was the medium of certain English subscriptions, among them that of John Bright. In sending this Lowell writes to Mr. Garrison: "Nothing could have been more in keeping with the uniform wisdom of your anti-slavery leadership than the time you chose for resigning it."

era. . . . May I receive from your heart of love
and high-souled honor sentiments such as I have
not a few times obtained from your free-hearted
poetry?" No appeal could have used so cogent an
argument as that which thus characterized the poet,
and Lowell responded with the lines, "On the
Death of Charles Turner Torrey," which were read
at the meeting in Faneuil Hall by Dr. Channing.
Dr. Bowditch thanked the poet for the response to
his request, but doubted if the poem was not of too
charitable a tenor. "Your poetry," he says, "is a
harbinger of better hours, but not for this century,
as I fear we have missed the great idea of our existence and a new cycle of time must pass its round,
and a new, a lovelier race of beings must settle on
this earth ere man shall truly appreciate the divine
doctrine you enunciate in the last line of your
verses."

Lowell had now become clearly identified with
the anti-slavery cause and did not shrink from using
the phrase "we abolitionists." His reputation as
a poet had steadily risen. He was contemplating
a second series of his "Conversations," and though
he rarely used the instrument of poetry in direct
attack, much of his verse sounded those notes of
freedom and truth which were, even when ab-
stractly used, rightly regarded as dominant notes
in the songs of the times. The leaders of the anti-
slavery cause welcomed him as an important coadjutor. At this time the *National Anti-Slavery
Standard* was passing through one of the several
changes sure to overtake the management of a

journal which was the organ of such a bundle of
individualities as would make up a reform party.
The *Standard* was the official paper of the American Anti-Slavery Society, as the *Liberator* was
the individual mouthpiece of Mr. Garrison. The
Standard had been conducted successively by Mrs.
Lydia Maria Child and her husband, David Lee
Child. The former, who had marked literary ability and a fondness for the art of literature, had
directed the paper in such a way as to win the
attention of other than pronounced abolitionists;
the latter had a stronger interest in legal and constitutional questions, and his disquisitions, which
were inordinately long, must have wearied the
readers whom it was desirable to gain over. Those
who merely wished to hear their beliefs sounded
may have had no fault to find, but these did not
need conversion. The paper, therefore, passed in
1844 into the hands of Mrs. Chapman, Edmund
Quincy,[1] and Sydney Howard Gay, who augmented
the energy and diversity of the journal, but did
not succeed in arresting the decline of its subscription list. In the spring of 1846 the paper had
only about 1400 paying subscribers.

A further change seemed desirable, and the sensible one was made of concentrating the responsibility in the hands of one person, Mr. Gay, and
endeavoring to reënforce him with an imposing list
of regular contributors. This list was published

[1] It is greatly to be regretted that the important correspondence of Quincy and Lowell does not exist. By agreement each
destroyed the letters of the other.

11 June, 1846, and comprised these names: Eliza
Lee Follen, Rev. John Weiss, Charles F. Briggs,
Wendell Phillips, James Russell Lowell, Maria
Weston Chapman, Rev. William F. Channing,
Rev. Thomas T. Stone, Edmund Quincy, and, a
little later, Rev. Samuel May. It will be seen thus
that there was a tolerable admixture of literature
with polemics. Lowell had been urged to take a
prominent place, and consented out of readiness to
cast in his lot with the men and women who were
heading the forlorn hope. He was perfectly aware,
however, of a certain incompatibility of temper and
aims which disqualified him from an unreserved
submersion of his powers in this cause. The letter
in which he gives in his adherence to the plan
defines with much clearness his own consciousness
of his vocation, and the very humorousness of the
introduction intimates that he held off from the
task of stating his position, as well as exhibits a mer-
curial temperament that would inevitably refuse
to be kept within very exact limits. The letter is
so important a disclosure of Lowell's mind at this
time that it must be given entire, though the most
significant part has already been printed by Mr.
Norton. Mr. Gay had written him under date of
May, 1846: "It is with no little satisfaction that I
welcome you into our company of standard-bearers
to the anti-slavery host. I have long wished to see
you actively engaged among us, and even had I no
personal interest in the matter, the position you
have chosen is precisely the one I should best like
to see you in. You could nowhere do more good,

and in no other way could you become so thoroughly
identified with the cause.   It is the historical
cause of our day, and as the Future will know you
as a Poet, she should find in our records additional
evidence that you understood and fulfilled your
mission."

To Sydney Howard Gay.

Elmwood, June 16, 1846.

My dear Gay, — if [1] there be any disjoint-
edness in this letter, you must lay it to the fact
that I am officiating this morning as general nur-
seryman and babytender, and am consequently
obliged every now and then to ripple the otherwise
smooth current of my epistolary communications
with such dishevelled oratorical flourishes as "kitser,
kee—eetser!" "jigger jig, jigger jig!" and the
like accompanied with whatever extemporary hush-
money may be within grasp in the shape of spoons,
whistles, pieces of paper and rattles.   As I can
conceive of no severer punishment that could be
inflicted on certain authors than to be Robinson
Crusoed on some desolate island with no companion
but the offspring of their brain, so I do not know
of any blessing more absorbing of all the faculties,
demanding more presence of mind and more of that
eternal vigilance which is the price of liberty, but
which in this case fails to attain it, than that of
being islanded in a room eighteen feet square with
the "sole daughter of one's house and home."   Then,

---

[1] The curious reader may see here one of the little idiosyncrasies in which Lowell indulged throughout his life, though this is
one of the first instances I have noted.

besides these parental responsibilities, there are the *aliena negotia centum* which have in the present instance made a gap of three hours between this sentence and the last.   Added to all these is the metallic pen which I resisted manfully, but to which I have succumbed at last, and which, while it obliterates all distinctions of chirography, has, in conjunction with the other accoutrements of easy writing (such as Reviews and newspapers), hastened the decline and fall, and finally made complete shipwreck of the letterwriters, as well as of the foliomakers.   It is no longer ' the mob of *gentlemen* who write with ease,' but the very mob itself — that *profanum vulgus* whom Horace Naso (*sic*) would have us hate and keep at arm's length — can buy steel pens by the gross and proceed Master of arts *per saltum*.   We have got now to that pitch when uneducated men (self-educated they are called) are all the rage, and the only learned animals who continue to be popular are pigs.   The public will rush after a paper which they are told is edited by a practical printer, and is eager to shape its ideas after the model of men who have none.   We shall ere long see advertised " Easy lessons in Latin by a gentleman who can bring testimonials that he knows no more of the language than Mr. Senator Webster ; " " The High School Reader, being a selection of popular pieces for reading and declamation by a Lady, who is just learning the alphabet under the distinguished tuition of herself, and who is nearly mistress of that delightful *mélange* of literary miscellanies."   The injury to letters arising from

an author's losing that space for meditation which
was formerly afforded him by the wise necessity of
mending his pen is incalculable. Every one nowadays can write decently and nobody writes well.
" Painfulness " is obsolete as a thing as well as in
the capacity of a noun. No more Horace Wal-
poles, no more Baxters, and Whole Duties of
men!

But one would think that I had the whole summer before me for the writing of this letter. Let
me come a little nearer the matter in hand. I
wish a distinct understanding to exist between us
in regard to my contributions for the *Standard*.
When Mrs. Chapman first proposed that I should
become a contributor I told her frankly that it was
a duty for which (having commenced author very
early and got indurated in certain modes of authorship and life) I was totally unfitted. I was satisfied with the *Standard* as it was. The paper has
never been so good since I have seen it, and no
abolitionist could reasonably ask a better. I feared
that an uncoalescing partnership of several minds
might deprive the paper of that *unity* of conception
and purpose in which the main strength of every
understanding lies. This, however, I did not urge,
because I knew that a change was to be made at
any rate. At the same time I was not only willing
but desirous that my name should appear, because
I scorned to be indebted for any share of my modi-
cum of popularity to my abolitionism without in-
curring at the same time whatever odium might be
attached to a complete identification with a body

of heroic men and women whom not to love and
admire would prove me unworthy of either of those
sentiments, and whose superiors in all that consti-
tutes true manhood and womanhood I believe never
existed.   There were other considerations which
weighed heavily with me to decline the office altogether.   In the first place, I was sure that Mrs.
Chapman and Mr. Garrison greatly overrated my
popularity and the advantage which it would be to
the paper to have my name attached to it.   I am
not flattering myself (I have too good an opinion
of myself to do so), but judge from something Garrison said to me.   It is all nonsense.   However it
may be in that glorious Hereafter (toward which
no man who is good for anything can help casting
half an eye) the reputation of a poet who has a
high idea of his vocation, is resolved to be true to
that vocation and hates humbug, must be small in
his generation.   The thing matters nothing to me,
one way or the other, except when it chances to
take in those whom I respect, as in the present
case.   I am *teres atque rotundus*, a microcosm in
myself, my own author, public, critic, and posterity, and care for no other.   But we abolitionists
must get rid of a habit we have fallen into of affirm-
ing all the geese who come to us from the magic
circle of Respectability to be swans.   I said so
about Longfellow and I said so about myself.
What does a man more than his simple duty in
coming out for the truth ? and if we exhaust our
epithets of laudation at this stage of the business,
what shall we do if the man turns out to be a real

reformer, and does *more* than his duty? Beside, is it any sacrifice to be in the right? Has not being an abolitionist (as Emerson says of hell) its "infinite satisfactions" as well as those *infiniti guai* that Dante tells us of? To my mind

> "All other pleasures are not worth its pains."

In the next place (turn back a page or two and you will find that I have laid down a "firstly"), if I have any vocation, it is the making of verse. When I take my pen for that, the world opens itself ungrudgingly before me, everything seems clear and easy as it seems sinking to the bottom would be as one leans over the edge of his boat in one of those dear coves at Fresh Pond. But, when I do prose, it is *invitâ Minerva.* I feel as if I were wasting time and keeping back my message. My true place is to serve the cause as a poet. Then my heart leaps on before me into the conflict. I write to you frankly as becomes one who is to be your fellow-worker. I wish you to understand clearly my capabilities that you may not attribute that to lukewarmness or indolence which is truly but an obedience to my Demon. Thirdly (I believe it is thirdly), I have always been a very Quaker in following the Light and writing only when the Spirit moved. This is a tower of strength which one must march out of in working for a weekly newspaper, and every man owes it to himself, so long as he does the duty which he sees, to remain here impregnably intrenched.

Now, it seems to me that we contributors should

write just enough to allow you this privilege of
only writing when the wind sits fair. Having
stated the poetical *cons*, I will now state the plain
pros of the matter. I will help you as much as
I can and ought. I had rather give the cause
one good poem than a thousand indifferent prose
articles. I mean to send all the poems I write (on
whatever subject) first to the *Standard*, except such
arrows as I may deem it better to shoot from the
ambushment of the *Courier*, because the old Enemy offers me a fairer mark from that quarter. I
will endeavor also to be of service to you in your
literary selections.

I have told you what *I* expect to do. You
must tell me in return what *you* expect me to do.
I agree with you entirely in your notions as to the
imprint and the initials.[1] The paper must seem to
be unanimous. Garrison is point blank the other
way. But his vocation has not been so much to

---

[1] Mr. Gay had written: "I do not know how you feel about the
Imprint, but my own opinion is that there had better be either no
name, or only one there. Every one will know that yourself, Mrs.
Chapman and Quincy and Briggs and others contribute to its columns. The more we can make believe contribute to it the better,
and to put three or four names in the Imprint will seem to limit
the number. I wish that all its readers shall believe that a variety of people have had a hand in the making up of every number,
and not only those whose names are before them. For the same
reason I wish that the initial system shall be done with. The
readers will be prone to believe the best if they are not certain,
and if there are none of these 'small caps,' as the printers say, to
guide, they may sometimes be humbugged into eating my chaff
for your and others' wheat." Mr. Gay had his way at first, but
before long his readers' curiosity drove him into the use of initials
as signatures.

feel the pulse of the public as to startle it into a quicker heat, and if we who make the paper can't settle it, who shall? I have one or two suggestions to make, but shall only hint at them, hoping to see you at Dedham on the 14th prox? It seems to me eminently necessary that there should be an entire concert among us, and that, to this end, we should meet to exchange thoughts (those of us who are hereabout) and to wind each other up. We ought to know what each one's " beat " is, and what each is going to write.

Then, too, would it not be well to have a *Weekly Pasquil* (I do not call it *Punch* to avoid confusion), in which squibs and facetiæ of one kind or other may be garnered up? I am sure I come across enough comical thoughts in a week to make up a good share of any such corner, and Briggs and yourself and Quincy could help.

You will find a squib of mine in this week's *Courier*. I wish it to continue anonymous, for I wish Slavery to think it has as many enemies as possible. If I may judge from the number of persons who have asked me if I wrote it, I have struck the old hulk of the Public between wind and water. I suppose you will copy it, and if so I wish you would correct a misprint or two. . . . Give our best regards to your wife, and believe me, very truly your friend,

J. R. LOWELL.

I shall send you a poem next week.[1]

---

[1] See *Letters of James Russell Lowell*, i. 111–116. Copyright, 1893, by Harper & Brothers.

The "squib" to which Lowell refers in this letter was the first of the afterward famous "Biglow Papers," introduced by the rustic letter of Ezekiel Biglow to Mister Eddyter. The poem was the one beginning

> "Thrash away, you 'll *hev* to rattle
> On them kettle-drums o' yourn,"

and the stanzas themselves have the inspiriting dash and electrifying rat-tat-tat of this new recruiting-sergeant in the little army of anti-slavery reformers. Lowell himself felt that he had sounded a real summons in these verses, yet singularly enough it was more than a twelvemonth before he followed with another in the same vein. The poem was at once copied into the *Standard* before the corrections its author sent could be made, and the next week appeared the first of Lowell's prose contributions, a column and a half on Daniel Webster, whose intellectual strength made him the special mark of those men of New England who wished to turn all the artillery of native make against the great foe. Whittier's two poems "Ichabod" and "The Lost Occasion" express nobly the mingled love, pride, and deep anger with which the anti-slavery men regarded this strong nature. "Ichabod" was written after Webster's speech of 7 March, 1850, and Whittier may well have carried in his memory a sentence from Lowell's trenchant unsigned article: "Shall not the Recording Angel write *Ichabod* after the name of this man in the great book of Doom?"

For some unexplained reason, though the con-

nection was now made, for eighteen months after
this editorial article Lowell printed little in the
Standard save an occasional poem.   The real connection was not made till the spring of 1848.   In
the number of the paper for 6 April of that year
it was announced that for the ensuing volume the
Standard would be under the charge of the present
editor, Sydney Howard Gay, but with James Russell Lowell as corresponding editor.   His name
appeared thus on the headline of the paper and
continued to keep its place until 31 May, 1849,
when Edmund Quincy's name was bracketed with
it.   For a while Mr. Quincy's name took the second place, but as his contributions increased and
Lowell's diminished, they changed places in order,
and finally Lowell's name, though without any
public announcement, was dropped from the headline 27 May, 1852, many months after he had
practically ceased to contribute.

The definite arrangement which Lowell made
with the Executive Committee of the American
Anti-Slavery Society, who were the general man-
agers of the *Standard*, was effected in a personal
interview with Mr. Gay, who had come on to Dedham and there met Lowell.   The conditions were
simple and are rehearsed in a letter to Briggs,
26 March, 1848.   Lowell was to receive a salary
of $500 a year, and for this was to furnish a
weekly contribution, either in verse or prose, but
the verse was not to be restricted to direct attacks
on slavery, and in his prose he now and then went
outside the line of domestic politics, and occasion-

ally even took up a distinctly literary topic. " The Committee," writes Mr. Gay, " accepts your proviso of a termination to the arrangement whenever either party please, and accord to you any reasonable latitude in the choice of subjects that you may desire." It was plain from the outset that Lowell was not overconfident of his ability to make the agreement one of mutual satisfaction. He felt that in his independence of thought he was not likely always to be at one with his associates, yet he was so heartily in accord with them in the fundamental doctrine of opposition to slavery, morally and politically, that he was glad of the opportunity of taking an active part in the fight. And then he undoubtedly looked to some advantage from the stimulus he should receive from the necessity of a weekly contribution. " I did not like," he writes to Briggs, " to take pay for anti-slavery work, but as my abolitionism has cut me off from the most profitable sources of my literary emoluments, as the offer was unsolicited on my part, and as I wanted the money, I thought I had a right to take it. I have spent more than my income every year since I have been married, and that only for necessities. If I can once get clear, I think I can keep so. I do not agree with the abolitionists in their disunion and non-voting theories. They treat ideas as ignorant persons do cherries. They think them unwholesome unless they are swallowed stones and all."

The first number of the *Standard* under this new arrangement, that for 6 April, 1848, which contained the announcement, held as Lowell's initial contribution his "Ode to France," which no doubt he had written without regard to this publication, for it bears date "February, 1848," and indicates that in his study at Elmwood he was looking out on the large world, and was brooding over those great general ideas of freedom which were the intellectual and moral furniture of his being. He could exclaim : —

> " Since first I heard our North-wind blow,
> Since first I saw Atlantic throw
> On our grim rocks his thunderous snow,
>   I loved thee, Freedom: as a boy
> The rattle of thy shield at Marathon
>   Did with a Grecian joy
>   Through all my pulses run :
> But I have learned to love thee now
> Without the helm upon thy gleaming brow,
>   A maiden mild and undefiled,
> Like her who bore the world's redeeming child."

And in the next number of the paper he had an article on "The French Revolution of 1848," in which he wrote wittily of the flight of the "broker-king," and exultingly of the triumph of the idea of the people. "Louis Philippe," he wrote, "extinguished the last sparks of loyalty in France as effectually as if that had been the one object of his eighteen years' reign. He had made monarchy contemptible. He had been a stock-jobber, a family match-maker. The French had seen their royalty gradually

> ' melt,
> Thaw, and resolve itself into a *Jew.*'

During a long and peaceful reign, the king had in no way contrived to *grow on to* the people. He was in no sense of the word a Head to them. A nation can be loyal to a Man, or to the representative of an Idea. Louis Philippe was neither. When all the Royalty of France can be comfortably driven out of it in a street-cab, one would think the experiment of a Republic might be safely ventured upon. |To us the late events in Paris seem less a Revolution, than the quiet opening of a flower, [which,] before it can blossom, must detrude the capsule which has hitherto enveloped and compressed it." The article disclosed Lowell's eager faith in the French people as receptive and swift to appreciate and assimilate an idea. When in the summer the news came of mob violence, he wrote again, defending the workmen of Paris, and insisting upon it that the social order was to blame. " The great problem of the over-supply of labor," he wrote, " is not to be settled by a decimation of the laboring class, whether by gunpowder or starvation Society in a healthy condition would feel the loss of every pair of willing and useful hands thrust violently out of it. That these Parisian *ouvriers* were driven to rebellion by desperation is palpable. That they had ideas in their heads is plain from their conduct immediately after the Revolution. They were suffering then. It was they who had achieved the victory over the old order of things. In the then anarchistic state of the capital, rapine, had that been their object, was within easy reach. But the revolution of February was not the chaotic movement of men to whom any change was preferable to the wretched present.

Not so much subversion as subversion for the sake of organization was what they aimed at. The giant Labor did not merely turn over from one side to the other for an easier position. Rather he rose up

'Like blind Orion hungry for the morn.'

It was *light* which the people demanded. Social *order* was precisely the thing they wished for in the place of social chaos. Government was what they asked. They had learned by bitter experience that it was on the body of old King Log Laissez-faire that King Stork perched to devour them. *Let-alone* is good policy after you have once got your perfect system established to let alone. There is not in all history an instance of such heroic self-denial as that which was displayed by what it is the fashion to call the Mob of Paris during the few days immediately following the flight of the Orleans dynasty. What was the shield which the noble Lamartine held up between the Provisional Government and the people? Simply the Idea of the Republic! And this Idea was respected by starving men with arms in their hands."

The verses "To Lamartine," also, which appeared in August, illustrate the appeal which French idealism made to Lowell's mind. It is not surprising that the year 1848, which seemed at the time to witness the lifting of the lid from the Republican pot which was at the boiling point, should not only have quickened the pulse of lovers of freedom in America, but should have given

generous-minded men here a twinge of envy as
they contrasted the sanguine expectancy of Europe
with what they saw of the seared conscience of
America; and in the papers just quoted Lowell
turns fiercely upon the public expressions of sympathy with the ruling powers of Europe. It was
a natural transition from these reflections on the
movements in France to ask bitterly in his next
editorial article, "Shall we ever be Republicans?"
In this he speculates on the extraordinary lack of
agreement in the United States between names
and things, and finds slavery the opiate which has
made men's minds drowsy.

"The truth is," he declares, "that we have never
been more than nominal republicans. We have
never got over a certain shamefacedness at the dis-
respectability of our position. We feel as if when
we espoused Liberty we had contracted a *mésal-
liance*. The criticism of the traveller who looks at
us from a monarchical point of view exasperates
us. Instead of minding our own business we have
been pitifully anxious as to what would be thought
of us in Europe. We have had Europe in our
minds fifty times, where we have had God and
conscience once. Our literature has endeavored to
convince Europeans that we are as like them as
circumstances would admit. The men who have
the highest and boldest bearing among us are the
slaveholders. We are anxious to be acknowledged
as one of the great Powers of Christendom, for-
getful that all the fleets and navies in the world
are weak in comparison with one sentence in the

Declaration of Independence. When every other argument in favor of our infamous Mexican war has been exhausted, there was this still left — that it would make us more respected abroad. We are as afraid of our own principles as a raw recruit of his musket. As far as the outward machinery of our government is concerned, we are democratic only in our predilection for little men.

" When will men learn that the only true conservatism lies in growth and progress, that whatever has ceased growing has begun to die ? It is not the conservative, but the retarding element which resides in the pocket. It is droll to witness the fate of this conservatism when the ship of any state goes to pieces. It lashes itself firmly to the ponderous anchor it has provided for such an emergency, cuts all loose, and — goes to the bottom. There are a great many things to be done in this country, but the first is the abolition of slavery. If it were not so arrant a sin as it is, we should abolish it (if for no other reason) that it accustoms our public men to being cowards. We are astonished, under the present system, when a Northern representative gets so far as to surmise that his soul is his own, and make a hero of him forthwith. But we shall never have that inward fortunateness without which all outward prosperity is a cheat and delusion, till we have torn up this deadly upas, no matter with what dear and sacred things its pestilential roots may be entwined."

Lowell had said to Briggs that he was not at one with the Abolitionists who favored disunion, and with that sanity of political judgment which made it impossible for him to be a revolutionist even in theory, he saw not in politics and political institutions that finality which rests in an organic national life. Thus he never could be a blind partisan, and he was quick to see the shams and concealments which were hidden in the conventions of political terms. A clever English publicist once said that the Constitution forms a sort of false bottom to American political thinking, and Lowell, who was as ardent and sensitive an American as ever lived, played most amusingly in one of the earliest of these newspaper articles with the conceit of "The Sacred Parasol." He told Gay afterward that he wished he had put his paper into rhyme. If he had, he would doubtless have caught and held more attention by such a satire. Citing the marvellous incident reported by Father John de Peano Carpini of the people in the land of Kergis, who dwelt under ground because they could not endure the horrible noise made by the sun when it rose, he applied the parable to American politics, only it is the mode of thought that is subterranean, not the habit of living. "As we manage everything by Conventions, we get together and resolve that the sun has not risen, and so settle the matter, as far as we are concerned, definitively. Meanwhile, the sun of a new political truth got quietly above the horizon in our Declaration of Independence. Watchers upon the mountain tops had caught sight of a ray now and then before, but this was the first time that the heavenly light-

bringer had gained an objective existence in the
eyes of an entire people." This was all very well,
until the light began to penetrate dark places
which it was for the interest of certain people to
keep dark. "Fears in regard to *heliolites* became
now very common, and a parasol of some kind was
found necessary as a protection against this celes-
tial bombardment. A stout machine of parchment
was accordingly constructed, and, under the respectable name of a Constitution, was interposed
wherever there seemed to be danger from the hostile incursions of Light. Whenever this is spread,
a dim twilight, more perplexing than absolute
darkness, reigns everywhere beneath its shadow.
. . . It is amazing what importance anything, however simple, gains by being elevated into a symbol.
Mahomet's green breeches were doubtless in themselves common things enough and would perhaps
have found an indifferent market in Brattle or
Chatham Street. They might have hung stretched
upon a pole at the door of one of those second-
hand repositories without ever finding a customer
or exciting any feeling but of wonder at the un-
couthness of their cut. But lengthen the pole a
little, and so raise the cast-off garment into a ban-
ner or symbol, and it becomes at once full of inspiration, and perhaps makes a Western General
Taylor of the very tailor who cut and stitched it
and had tossed it over carelessly a hundred times.
. . . In the same way this contrivance of ours,
though the work of our own hands, has acquired a
superstitious potency in our eyes. The vitality of

the state has been transferred from the citizens to this. Were a sacrilegious assault made upon it, our whole body politic would collapse at once. Gradually men are beginning to believe that, like the famous *ancile* at Rome, it fell down from heaven, and it is possible that it may have been brought thence by a distinguished personage who once made the descent. Meanwhile our Goddess of Liberty is never allowed to go abroad without the holy parasol over her head to prevent her from being tanned, since any darkening of complexion might be productive of serious inconvenience in the neighborhood of the Capitol." With this grave banter Lowell goes on to instance cases where the Sacred Parasol has caused a shifting of relations in the twilight created by it, and warns people of the danger they would be in if exposed to the direct rays of the Sun of Righteousness.

The article shows the kind of reënforcement which Lowell brought to the anti-slavery camp. Edmund Quincy had something of the same wit and irony, but he had also a greater love of detail and busied himself over current incidents with the eagerness of a political detective, running down fugitives from divine justice with an ardor which was always heightened by the complexities of the case. Lowell, though he did not neglect to use incidents for the illustration of his argument, never got far away from the elemental principles for which his wit and sense of justice and love of freedom stood. He played with his subject often, but it was the play of a cat with his captive — one stroke of the paw, when the time came, and the mouse was dead.

Meanwhile the little band of the faithful, for whom the *Anti-Slavery Standard* was a weekly rally, read with delight the incisive editorial articles, and though they were not always supplied with downright arguments from this source, they had, what they scarcely got otherwise in the midst of their tremendous seriousness, the opportunity to rub their hands with glee over a telling rapier thrust, and also to have their horizon suddenly enlarged by the historical and literary comparisons which were swept into range by this active-minded scout.

The grim earnest in which Mr. Gay was working, in preparing for this weekly bombardment, left him little leisure for sitting down and admiring the mechanism of his guns, and Lowell in his retirement at Elmwood was more or less conscious of a certain doubt whether he was not firing blank cartridges. "You see," he wrote, "that I have fallen into the fault which I told you I should be in danger of, viz., dealing too much in generalities. The truth is, I see so few papers except what are on our side that I cannot write a controversial article. I intend to review Webster's speech and to write an article on the Presidential nomination. Perhaps they will be more to the purpose. Meanwhile, how can you expect a man to work with any spirit if he never hears of his employer? Why don't you write me and say frankly how you are satisfied or dissatisfied, and what you want?" Gay

wrote later : " You may be sure I shall write you
fast enough when you write what you ought not ;
until I do you may be sure that I — so far as that
is of any consequence — am pleased. I hear your
articles spoken of highly from all quarters, and
have heard only one criticism from one or two
persons, — that they seemed to be written rather
hastily. But that I believe is the way you write
everything. It is a bad way to get into, though,
and newspaper writing is a great temptation to it."

The political doctrines which Lowell advocated
were naturally not those of expediency, but of
downright frankness and honesty. It is true that
he and his associates had the great advantage, in
proclaiming principles, of being quite unable to
carry them out successfully at the polls. Such a
position reënforces candor. Just as the Gold Democrats in the political contest of 1896 could draw
up the most admirable platform that has been seen
for many years, since they were out in the open,
and were neither on the defensive nor preparing to
carry their candidates into office, so the Abolitionists in 1848 felt under no obligation to support
either Taylor or Cass, and could speak their minds
freely concerning both. But Lowell, in the article which he wrote on " The Nominations for the
Presidency," characteristically struck that note of
independence in politics which was a cardinal
point in his political creed and was to be exempli-
fied forcibly his life through, both in speech and
conduct. In this he was not illustrating a principle which he maintained, so much as he was living

a natural life.   Independence was a fundamental note in his nature.

"The word NO," he wrote, "is the shibboleth of politicians.   There is some malformation or deficiency in their vocal organs which either prevents their uttering it at all, or gives it so thick a pronunciation as to be unintelligible.   A mouth filled with the national pudding, or watering in the expectation of it, is wholly incompetent to this perplexing monosyllable.   One might imagine that America had been colonized by a tribe of those nondescript African animals, the Aye Ayes.   As Pius Ninth has not yet lost his popularity in this country by issuing a bull against slavery, our youth, who are always ready to hurrah for anything, might be practised in the formation of the refractory negative by being encouraged to shout *Viva Pio Nono*.[1]

"If present indications are to be relied upon, no very general defection from the ranks of either party will result from the nominations.   Politicians, who have so long been accustomed to weigh the expediency of any measure by its chance of success, are unable to perceive that there is a kind of victory in simple resistance.   It is a great deal to conquer only the habit of slavish obedience to party.   The great obstacle is the reluctance of politicians to assume moral rather than political grounds."[2]

---

[1] A little of this jest is preserved in Parson Wilbur's note to the second *Biglow paper*, as published in book form.

[2] In his address on "The Place of the Independent in Politics,"

It was, after all, a man of letters and not a journalist who was engaged on these weekly diatribes,
and Lowell showed his instinctive sense of literary
art not only in the abundance of allusion and in
the use of such special forms as irony, but even
now and then in the very structure of his essays,
for essays they were rather than editorial articles,
for the most part. Thus, taking his suggestion
in topic from an attempt at running away slaves
from the District of Columbia, he composes an Imaginary Conversation between Mr. Calhoun, Mr.
Foote, and General Cass. There is an amusing,
faint reflection of Landor in the manner of the
piece, and the three personages are decidedly more
discriminated in character than his old men of
straw, Philip and John, so that the reader really
seems to hear these worthies discoursing together,
and not struggling against the betrayal of the master of the show, who is shifting his voice from one
to the other. To be sure, no one would mistake
the delicious irony of Lowell's Mr. Foote for the
grave and pious language of the real Mr. Foote,
but the imitation is given with an air of seriousness. "It is a sentiment of the Bible," Mr. Foote
is made to say, "that riches have the wings of
the morning and fly to the uttermost parts of the
earth. But the South labors under this greater
misfortune, that her property is endowed with legs

delivered forty years later, Lowell pithily says: "A moral purpose multiplies us (Independents) by ten, as it multiplied the early
Abolitionists. They emancipated the negro; and we mean to
emancipate the respectable white man."

of a kind of brute instinct (understanding I will not call it) to use them in a northerly direction. It is a crowning mercy that God has taken away the wings from our wealth. The elder patriarchs were doubtless deemed unworthy of this providential interference. It was reserved for Christians and Democrats. The legs we can generally manage, but it would have been inconvenient to be continually clipping the wings, not to mention possible damage to the stock. For these and other comforts make us duly thankful!

"MR. CASS.

" My friend Louis Philippe — ah, I had forgotten : I should have said my late friend.

"MR. CALHOUN.

" The unfortunate are never the friends of the wise man.

"MR. CASS.

" I was about to say that the Count de Neuilly has often remarked to me that we were fortunate in having so conservative an element as 'persons held to service or labor' (I believe I do not venture beyond safe Constitutional ground) mingled in a just proportion with our otherwise too rapidly progressive institutions. There is no duty of a good statesman, he said, at once so difficult and so necessary as that of keeping steadily behind his age. But, however much satisfaction a sound politician who adheres to this theory may reap in the purity of his own conscience, he will find that the dust incident to such a position will sometimes so choke him as to prevent his giving an intelligible answer to the often perplexing questions of his constituents. Yet I know not whether in such exigencies a cough be not the safest, as it is the readiest reply. It is an oracle susceptible of any retrospective interpretation.

"MR. CALHOUN.

" A politician who renders himself intelligible has put a rope round his own neck, and it would be strange indeed if his opponents should be unable to find a suitable tree. The present Revolutionary Government of France has taken many long strides towards the edge of that precipice which overhangs social and political chaos, but none longer than in bringing Government face to face with the people. That government is the most stable which is the most complicated and the most expensive. Men admire most what they do not understand, and cling tightest to what they have paid or are paying most for. They love to see money spent liberally by other people, and have no idea that every time Uncle Sam unbuttons his pocket, he has previously put his hand into their own. I have great fears for France. The Provisional Government talks too much and too well, — above all things it talks too clearly. In that wild enthusiasm generated by the turmoil of great and sudden social changes, and by contact with the magnetism of excited masses of men, sentiments are often uttered, which, however striking and beautiful they might be if

their application were restricted to the Utopias of
poetry, are dangerous in their tendencies and results if once brought into contact with the realities
of life. Despotisms profited more than the Cath-
olic Church by shutting up Christ in the sepul-
chre of a dead language. A prudent and far-see-
ing man will confine his more inspired thoughts to
the solitude of his closet. If once let loose, it is
impossible to recall these winged messengers to
the safer perch of his finger. He may keep an
aviary of angels if he will, but he must be careful not to leave the door open. They have an
unaccountable predilection for entering the hut of
the slave, and for seating themselves beside the
hearth of the laborer. Mr. Jefferson,[1] by embody-
ing some hasty expressions in the Declaration of
Independence, introduced explosive matter into
our system."

And so the conversation goes on touching upon
current topics, all having some bearing on the
great underlying theme. One sees the three men
moving over the ice, cautiously, and not daring to
try its firmness by stamping on it, Mr. Calhoun
alone maintaining a rigidity of posture as if he

[1] There is a reference to Jefferson in a letter written ten years
later, which is interesting as one of the rare apprizements by
Lowell of American public men. "I have run through Randall's
Jefferson with the ends of my fingers — a perfect chaos of biography — but enough to confirm me in the belief that Jefferson
was the first *American* man. I doubt if we have produced a better thinker or writer. His style is admirable in general, warmed
with just enough enthusiasm for eloquence, not too much for conviction." — J. R. L. to C. E. Norton, 11 October, 1848.

had satisfied himself that his theory of the probable
thickness of the ice was irrefutable.

Lowell complained to Gay that their position
was so purely destructive as to require them to
look at everything from a point of criticism, and
that this became wearisome. In saying this, he
was thinking probably of the general attitude
which was by necessity taken by a small knot of
political and moral agitators employing their en-
gines against a strongly intrenched evil. Criticism,
however, in its more comprehensive sense, was the
weapon which he most naturally used, but he
turned his critical inquiry rather upon men than
upon institutions, or even upon political measures.
In this Imaginary Conversation, for example, the
public men satirized were examined for their mental
and moral characteristics. Through his studies in
literature and history, with his insight as a poet
and man of imagination, and his habit of holding
up before his mind fundamental ideas such as truth
and freedom, Lowell was chiefly interested in the
characters of public men ; in applying his criticism to Foote, Cass, Calhoun, Clay, Webster, and
other of his contemporaries, though he was mainly
testing them by their attitude toward slavery, he
was constantly measuring them by great and permanent standards. The larger the man, the more
thoroughly interested was he in penetrating the
man's words and deeds, and seeking to come at
the bottom facts of his nature.

I have already referred to the early occasion he
took, in his connection with the *Standard*, to try

his judgment upon Webster, and it is interesting
to observe that no other statesman of the time was
so constantly the subject of his criticism.   In common with others, he watched with eagerness the
course of Webster in connection with the Whig
nomination for the presidency in 1848, when the
disappointment of the Massachusetts senator was
so little disguised.   " What Will Mr. Webster
Do?" was the title of the article which he published
in the *Standard* after General Taylor had been
nominated — that nomination " not fit to be made."
Lowell never had the modern journalist's faculty
for jumping at once into the centre of his subject.
Like his own " musing organist," he is very apt to
" begin doubtfully and far away," but he is also
pretty sure to strike a note at the outset which has,
it turns out, a real relation to the theme he means
to play.   Thus in this article he begins with the
reflection : " It is astonishing to see how fond men
are of company.   We demand a select society even
upon the fence, and will not jump on this side or
that till we have made as accurate a prospective
census as possible ; " and so on for several para-
graphs of acute and amusing variations, noting
especially the disposition to set expediency in the
place of principle, when looking out for the majority with whom we wish to side.   " After all," he
goes on, " even in estimating expediencies, we are
loath to trust ourselves.   We desire rather the
judgment of this or that notable person, and dare
not so much as write *Honesty is the best policy*, or
any other prudent morality, till he has set us a

copy at the top of the page.   In Massachusetts
just now there are we know not how many people
waiting for Mr. Webster's action on the recent
nomination for the Presidency, and no doubt there
is hardly a village in the country which has not its
little coterie of self-dispossessed politicians expecting in like manner the moment when the decision
of some person, whose stomach does the thinking
for theirs, shall allow them to take sides.

"'What will Mr. Webster do?' asks Smith.
'Greatest man of the age!' says Brown.   'Of any
age,' adds Jones triumphantly.   Meanwhile the
greatest mind of any age is sulking at Marshfield.
It has had its rattle taken away from it.   It has
been told that nominations were not good for it.
It has not been allowed to climb up the back of the
Presidential chair.   We have a fancy that a truly
great mind can move the world as well from a three-
legged stool in a garret as from the easiest cushion
in the White House.   Where the great mind is,
there is the President's house, whether at Wood's
Hole or Washington.

"We would not be understood as detracting in
the least from Mr. Webster's reputation as a man
of great power.   He has hitherto given evidence of
a great force, it seems to us, rather than of a great
intellect.   But it is a force working without results.
It is like a steam-engine [1] which is connected by no
band with the machinery which it ought to turn.
A great intellect leaves behind it something more
than a great reputation.   The earth is in some way

[1] "A steam-engine in breeches," was Carlyle's characterization.

the better for its having taken flesh upon itself.
We cannot find that Mr. Webster has communicated an impulse to any of the great ideas which it
is the destiny of the nineteenth century to incar-
nate in action. His energies have been absorbed
by Tariff and Constitution and Party — dry bones
into which the touch of no prophet could send
life. . . .

"'What will Mr. Webster do?' This is of more
importance to him than to the great principle which
is beginning to winnow the old parties. This, having God on its side, can do very well without Mr.
Webster — but can he do as well without it? The
truth of that principle will not be affected by his
taking one side or the other. But *occasio celeris*,
and the great man is always the man of the occasion. He mounts and guides that mad steed whose
neck is clothed with thunder, and whose fierce *ha!
ha!* at the sound of the trumpets appals weaker
spirits. Two or three years ago we spoke of one
occasion which Mr. Webster allowed to slip away
from him. That was the annexation of Texas. Another is offered him now. We do not believe that
party ever got what was meant for mankind. Mr.
Webster has now once more an opportunity of
showing which he was meant for. If party be large
enough to hold him, then mankind can afford to let
him go. Nevertheless, it is sad to imagine him
still grinding for the Philistines. We cannot help
thinking that his first appearance as Samson grasping the pillars of the idol temple would draw a
fuller house than Mr. Van Buren in the same
character. . . .

"Let us concede to Mr. Webster's worshippers that he has heretofore given proof enough of a great intellect, and let us demand of him now that he make use of, perhaps, his last chance to become a great *Man*. Of what profit are the hands of a giant in the picking up of pins? Let him leave Banks and Tariffs to more slender fingers. If ever a man was intended for a shepherd of the people, Daniel Webster is. The people are fast awakening to great principles: what they want is a great man to concentrate and intensify their diffuse enthusiasm. And it is not every sort of greatness that will serve for the occasion. Webster, if he would only let himself go, has every qualification for a popular leader. The use of such a man would be that of a conductor to gather, from every part of the cloud of popular indignation, the scattered electricity which would waste itself in heat lightnings, and grasping it into one huge thunderbolt, let it fall like the messenger of an angry god among the triflers in the Capitol.

"Let Mr. Webster give over at last the futile task of sowing the barren seashore of the present, and devote himself to the Future, the only legitimate seed-field of great minds. Slimmer and glibber men will slip through the labyrinth of politics more easily than he. He will always be outstripped and outwitted. Politics are in their nature transitory. He who writes his name on them, be the letters never so large, writes it on the sand. The next wind of shifting opinion puffs it out forever. It is never too late to do a wise or great action. We

do not yet wholly despair of hearing the voice of
our Daniel reading the *Mene*, *Mene*, written on the
wall of our political fabric."

The Buffalo Convention indorsed the nomination
of Martin Van Buren, by the Barnburners, or anti-
slavery wing of the Democratic party, with the result that the disaffected Whigs came to the support
of General Taylor, and Webster rather tardily
came forward and cast in his influence on that side.
Lowell had been watching for his action, and at
once wrote one of his bantering yet serious articles.

"Mr. Webster," he said, "with the tan of the
Richmond October sun not yet out of his face, is
shocked beyond measure at Mr. Van Buren's
former pro-slavery attitude. Sitting upon the
fence at Marshfield, he tells his neighbors that,
should he and Mr. Van Buren meet upon the same
political platform, they could not look at each
other without laughing. If Mr. Webster's face
looks as black as it is said to have done just after
the Philadelphia nomination, we think it the last
thing in the world that any one would venture
even a smile at. Mr. Webster finds fault with
Mr. Van Buren because Northern Democratic
Senators voted in favor of the annexation of
Texas. But where was Mr. Webster himself? If
he foresaw that Texas would be a Trojan horse,
why did he not say so? If people would not come
to hear him in Faneuil Hall, could he not have
gathered his friends and neighbors together at
Marshfield, as he did last week? It is perfectly
clear now by actual demonstration, as it was clear

then to persons who thought about the matter, that
if Mr. Webster had put himself at the head of the
opposers of annexation, Texas would never have
been annexed, and he would have been the next
President of the United States. The effect of the
Free Soil movement, led by men with not a tithe
of his influence, upon the Compromise Bill, puts
this beyond a question. Where was the Wilmot
Proviso then? At the Springfield Convention a
year ago, Mr. Webster laid claim to this as 'his
thunder.' In the Marshfield speech he dates its
origin as far back as 1787. A precocious Cyclops,
truly, to be forging thunderbolts in his fifth year!
If Mr. Webster should live till 1852, and his retrospective anti-slavery feeling go on increasing at its
present ratio, he will tell us that he established the
Liberator in 1831."

Quite at the end of Lowell's stated contributions
to the *Standard* came the longest of his articles in
the form of a running comment on Webster's fate-
ful seventh of March speech, and in his comment
he pronounced that judgment which was inevitable
from an anti-slavery prophet. " It has been characterized," he says, " like most of Mr. Webster's
speeches, as a 'masterly effort.' Some of them
have been masterly successes, but this we sincerely
hope and believe *was* an effort. . . . It is the plea
of a lawyer and an advocate, but not of a statesman. It is not even the plea of an advocate on
the side which he was retained to argue. We
have heard enough of Democratic defalcations :
here is a great Whig defalcation which dwarfs

them all, for it is not money which has disappeared in this instance, but professions, pledges, principles. Men do not defend themselves in advance against accusations of inconsistency unless they feel an uncomfortable sense that there is some justice in the charge. This feeling pervades a great part of Mr. Webster's speech like a blush." He uses a fine scorn in dissecting Mr. Webster's specious plea that slavery is nowhere directly prohibited in the teachings of the New Testament, and quietly asks if incest is anywhere forbidden there. " But if," he adds, " Mr. Webster were really in search of a scriptural prohibition of slavery, we think he might find it in that commandment which forbids us to covet anything that is our neighbor's. For if we may not do that, then *a fortiori* we may not covet our neighbor himself. . . . Mr. Webster, we have said, avoids carefully all the moral points of the argument. He falls in with the common assumption that this is a question of political preponderance between the North and the South. . . . It is not a question between the North and the South. It is a struggle between the South (we had almost said Calhoun) and the spirit of the nineteenth century after Christ. . . . Is slavery the only thing whose sensitiveness is to be respected? Freedom has been thought by some to have her finer feelings also." And he closes the discussion of the speech in these words : —

" If Mr. Webster's speech should not find any one to confute it in the Senate, — a hard task, for assumptions and tergiversations are not easily re-

plied to, — it will not be without answers abundant
and conclusive. It will be answered by every generous instinct of the human heart, by every principle which a New Englander has imbibed in the
Church, the Schoolhouse, or the Home, but especially by those inextinguishable sentiments which
move men's hatred of treachery and contempt for
the traitor."

The agreement which Lowell had with the
Standard left him at liberty to send either prose
or poetry, and as his prose had not necessarily a
direct reference to the anti-slavery contest, so his
poetry was to be independent of any polemic consideration. It was Lowell the writer whom Gay
wished most to attach to the paper for the added
weight and influence he would bring, and Lowell
in making and holding to his agreement was not
indifferent to the gentle stimulus which a regular
engagement afforded. He was to send something
on Friday if possible, on Saturday at any rate,
of each week, and when the end of the week came,
a sudden suggestion might turn him away from a
half-finished article to let loose a poem in its place.
The first five " Biglow Papers " were published in
the *Courier*, the last four in the *Standard*, where
also appeared, early in the connection, that poem
entitled " Freedom," which holds the essence of
Lowell's thought on this large subject, and is the
best expression of the attitude of his mind as he
entered with a certain sense of special enlistment
upon the direct business of a crusade against slavery. The suggestion came from the revolution in

France which swept Louis Philippe from his
throne, and from that light blaze of revolutionary
fire which for a moment kindled hopes in Germany
and Italy. During this time appeared also several
poems which reflected with varying lights the
thought that stirred in him at the new birth, as
it seemed, with which humanity was travailing.
Such are the apologue of " Ambrose," that grim
poem " The Sower," " Bibliolatres," " A Parable,"
but here also were " Beaver Brook," first called
" The Mill," occasionally a poem like " Eurydice "
which had been lying unprinted in his portfolio,
and a few bits of rhymed satire which were thrown
off by him on the spur of the moment, and were
too careless in manner to be worth his gathering
later into his volumes.

The active members of the anti-slavery society
who controlled the policy of the *Standard* were
divided in their judgment of the value of Lowell's
contributions. Those who like Mr. Gay himself
were thoroughly in earnest, but held their minds
open on other sides than the north-north-east, regarded Lowell as an important acquisition. His
fame was growing, and he could have found a ready
market for his wares if he had chosen to turn them
to the best commercial account, but he cheerfully
gave his time and thought to a paper which was
always in an impecunious condition, so that the editor found it hard enough to pay the very moderate
stipend agreed upon. Lowell, as we have seen,
hated to be paid for his services to the anti-slavery
cause, and never complained of the inadequacy of

his salary; but he took a rational view of the
case, and accepted what the paper could give, not
measuring his own contributions by the meagre
standard of his pay. Nor did he show any sensitiveness when his work came under editorial stric-
ture. The intensity of feeling which possessed the
anti-slavery men who were in the thick of the fight
made them abnormally critical of those who seemed
in any way to hold back, and when Lowell wrote a
long review, with hearty praise, of a new volume of
Whittier's poetry, signing it with his initials, Mr.
Gay did not scruple to prefix an editorial note, in
which he denounced Whittier for his course in
1840, when he refused to follow the lead of those
abolitionists who insisted upon the acceptance of
women delegates at the London convention. The
quarrel then aroused led to a break in the unity
of the anti-slavery group. " Older abolitionists,"
wrote Gay, "cannot forget what Lowell cannot be
aware of, that in the struggle of 1840, which was
a struggle of life and death to the anti-slavery
cause, Whittier the Quaker was found side by side
with the men who would have sacrificed that cause
to crush, according even to their own acknowledgment, the right of woman to plead publicly in be-
half of the slave." Lowell took the matter quietly
enough: " I could not very well say less, and you
could not say more," was his comment.

Yet how emphatically Mr. Gay valued Lowell's
contributions appears from all the letters of that
anxious and harassed editor. Near the close of
the connection, he wrote to Lowell: " I expected

much good for the paper when I proposed that you
should lighten my editorial labor, but it has received, I know, far more benefit than I looked for,
great as that was. The influence of the *Standard*
— leaving myself out of the question — since it was
established has been very great, and it would also,
I am sure, have been very famous had its aim been
other than it was. No small amount of energy and
intellect have been bestowed upon it, and its nurs-
ing fathers and mothers have taken good care of its
being. But of this I am sure, and nobody else is
in a position to know it so well as I — that of all
the good things ever done for it, no one so good
ever was done, as making you its joint editor. Its
influence through you has been felt where it never
was before. Through you it has a reputation which
in all its previous existence it had failed to gain.
A respect and regard is accorded to it because of
your efforts, which no other person ever had, and
no other person probably would ever have gained
for it."

But the *Standard* was not Mr. Gay's paper to
do with as he would, and there was a section of the
committee in control that was impatient of a contributor who was not as they were, fighting away
on foot, with stout oak staves in their hands, but
was flying about as a sort of light-horse contingent,
and sometimes seemed out of sight and yet not in
the enemy's country. "There is a small class,"
Mr. Gay wrote, — "Stephen Foster is a good
representative of it, — who did not consider you
worth much, and many of whom confess they do

not understand what you would be at." The portrait which Lowell had drawn of Stephen Foster in his letter to Mr. McKim is likely to help the reader understand that he might possibly even feel contempt for Lowell's indirect method of attacking slavery.

> " Hard by, as calm as summer even,
> Smiles the reviled and pelted Stephen,
> The unappeasable Boanerges
> To all the Churches and the Clergies.
>
> . . . .
>
> A man with caoutchouc endurance,
> A perfect gem for life insurance,
> A kind of maddened John the Baptist,
> To whom the harshest word comes aptest,
> Who, struck by stone or brick ill-starred,
> Hurls back an epithet as hard,
> Which, deadlier than stone or brick,
> Has a propensity to stick.
> His oratory is like the scream
> Of the iron-horse's frenzied steam
> Which warns the world to leave wide space
> For the black engine's swerveless race."

Lowell himself was under no illusions. He was warmly attached to Gay, and he had a keen intellectual admiration for Edmund Quincy. He respected to the full his several associates, but he knew well that, though he identified himself cordially with the small knot of earnest men and women who cried aloud and spared not, his temperament, his ideals, and his humor forbade him to shut himself up within the bounds they set themselves. Despite the independence he claimed and that was granted him, he could not escape the sense of his restrictions. "I told you and the Executive Committee honestly before I began," he wrote Gay, "that they were setting me about a business for which I was not fitted. I feel as if the whole of them were looking over my shoulder whenever I sit down to write, and it quite paralyzes me." And yet ten days later he could send his poem, " The Mill," better known as " Beaver Brook," and write, " I am just in time for the mail now, and I positively admire myself that I can sit down and write a poem to the *Standard's* order so resolutely."

At the end of his first year's engagement Lowell began to receive intimations that the paper was in a hard way financially. " I am very sorry to see," he writes the editor, " that the *Standard* is raised on so insecure a staff. I did not expect, (and so told the Executive Committee) that my writing for it would increase the circulation, but, I say again, as I said before, that they ought to be entirely satisfied with *you*. Not only is your own editorial work done with spirit and vigor, but your selections are such as to render the paper one of the most interesting I see. But they ought to do something themselves. Phillips and Quincy could do a great deal if they would. They can't expect two persons to give the paper an infinite variety, nor me to devote myself wholly to it. I have continued to write after my year was up, but I have had no intimation from the Committee whether they wished my services any longer or not. I am very willing to continue, for if I were to give up this engagement, I must find some other, in order to make the two ends meet."

It then transpired that there had been a warm discussion in the Committee over the continuance of the arrangement, and Gay and his friends had at last effected a compromise by which the salary of $500 was to be divided between Lowell and Quincy, Lowell being required to contribute every other week only.   Lowell accepted the situation philosophically, and doubtless felt some relief. " All through the year," he wrote to Gay, " I have felt that I worked under a disadvantage. I have missed that inspiration (or call it magnetism) which flows into one from a thoroughly sympathetic audience.   Properly speaking, I have never had it as an author, for I have never been popular. But then I have never needed it, because I wrote to please myself and not to please the people : whereas, in writing for the *Standard*, I have felt that I ought in some degree to admit the whole Executive Committee into my workshop, and defer as much as possible to the opinion of persons whose opinion (however valuable on a point of morals) would not probably weigh a pin with me on an æsthetic question.   I have felt that I ought to work in my own way, and yet I have also felt that I ought to *try* to work in *their* way, so that I have failed of working in either.   Nevertheless, I think that the Executive Committee would have found it hard to get some two or three of the poems I have furnished from any other quarter."   The entire letter, which is printed by Mr. Norton,[1] is interesting as further defining Lowell's attitude

[1] *Letters*, i. 157, 21 May, 1849.

toward his associates in the anti-slavery cause, and
his separation from them on some of the crucial
points. But it is clear that the whole situation was
complicated for him by the pecuniary embarrassment under which he labored. He was ready, if it
would relieve the situation, to release the Committee altogether, but he was willing to write once a
fortnight if they *wished* him to do so. "To tell
the truth," he says, "I need money more this year
than last. My father has just resigned a quarter
part of his salary,[1] and a large part of the household expenses must devolve upon me. But I have
resolved to turn as much of our land as I can into
money, and invest it, though I confess I should
prefer to leave it as it is, and where I am sure it
would be safe for Mab and the rest."

At the end of his second year the engagement
was ended, though, largely out of friendship for

[1] Dr. Lowell's course in this matter was characteristic of his
fine sense of honor. Previous to the ordination of his colleague,
Dr. Bartol, 1 March, 1837, he received from the West Church
Society a salary of $2000 a year. At a meeting of the proprie-
tors held 22 April, 1849, a letter was read from Dr. Lowell, in
which he says: "It was always a favorite object with me, in the
event of the settlement of a colleague pastor, to resign the whole
of my salary, or at most, to retain only a small portion of it, that
you might have less hesitation in calling upon me for the services
I might be able to render you." It was with great reluctance, he
added, that he then came to the conclusion it was his duty to ac-
cede to the request of the proprietors and retain all the salary he
had been accustomed to receive; now he could do so no longer,
and he insisted respectfully on an arrangement by which he
should resign a quarter of his salary, "with the purpose at no distant day, if Providence permit, of resigning a further sum." In
1854 Dr. Lowell resigned the whole of his salary, but the Society
declined to accept the proposal.

Gay, Lowell contributed occasionally, and his name indeed was kept at the head of the paper, bracketed with that of Mr. Quincy, for another year. He laughed, by the way, at the designation "corresponding editor." "It has always seemed to me to be nonsense. There can, in the nature of the thing, be no such person as a *corresponding* editor. Moreover, in this particular case, my unhappy genius will keep seeing the double sense in the word *corresponding*, and suggesting that E. Q. and I correspond in very few particulars, — meaning no offence to either of us. 'Contributor' would be the fitting word."

The connection with the *Standard* had not altered Lowell's position in politics. It found him independent, and left him so. He was no less a reformer at the end than he was at the beginning, but he was confirmed in his belief that the world must be healed by degrees; and as he was a disbeliever in the short cut to emancipation by way of disunion, so he was at once a firm believer in radical reform, but skeptical of ultimate success through the rooting out of individual evils. He found himself among people who were sure of their panaceas. He himself in the first flush of his restless desire for activity had been disposed, under the influence of the woman he loved, to attack the evil of intemperance by the method of total abstinence, but his zeal was short-lived. He appears never to have accepted woman suffrage as the solution of the problem of society, and it is doubtful if at any time he would have given his adhesion to the

mode of immediate emancipation if he had been
called on to discuss it. His imagination and his
sense of humor both prevented him from being a
thick and thin reformer, and he refused to allow
his hatred of slavery to be complicated with practical measures for the reform of various other evils
which troubled society. It was because he saw in
slavery in the United States the arch foe of freedom and the insidious corrupter of national life
that he concentrated his reforming energy upon
this evil. He has said of Wordsworth that "fortunately he gave up politics that he might devote
himself to his own noble calling, to which politics
are subordinate ; " but it might be said with equal
truth of Lowell that he never gave up poetry, and
that when he was writing every week, or every
other week, for the *Standard*, whether in verse or
in prose, he was dominated by an imagination
which kept steadily before his eyes great principles and doctrines which found in the anti-slavery
movement an illustration but not an exclusive end.
It is not surprising, therefore, that he should have
seemed to others, and sometimes to himself, not to
see the enemy just in front of him.

Nevertheless, the experience was worth much to
him. It resulted, as it might not except for this
stimulus, in the "Biglow Papers," and it also demonstrated more clearly than ever the supremacy
of the literary function with him, since he never
laid it aside under the strong provocation which his
journalistic work incited, and maintained from first
to last the integrity of his spirit. The conserva-

tism which underlay and indeed supported his radicalism was confirmed by his experience, and it issued moreover in a large comprehensiveness, so that he came out of the ranks not only with a greater sympathy with his comrades,[1] but with a larger toleration for the men he attacked. "At this minute," he writes to Gay, "the song of the bobolink comes rippling through my opening window and preaches peace. Two months ago the same missionary was in his South Carolina pulpit, and can I think that he chose another text, or delivered another sermon there? Hath not a slaveholder hands, organs, dimensions, senses, affections, passions? fed with the same food, hurt with the same weapons, subject to the same diseases, healed by the same means, warmed and cooled by the same summer and winter as an abolitionist? If you pinch them, do they not bleed? If you tickle them, do they not laugh? If you poison them, do they not die? If you wrong them, shall they not revenge? Nay, I will go a step farther, and ask if all this do not apply to parsons also? Even *they* are human."

[1] "I do not blame Foster or Philbrick or Jackson for not being satisfied with me; but, on the other hand, I thank God that he has gradually taught me to be quite satisfied with *them*." — *Letters*, i. 157.

CHAPTER V

A FABLE FOR CRITICS, THE BIGLOW PAPERS, AND THE VISION OF SIR LAUNFAL

1847–1848

IT was while he was most busily engaged in contributing to the *Standard* his weekly poems, criticisms, and editorial articles, that Lowell wrote and published a group of books, varied in subject and treatment, dashed off each and all with an eager abandonment to the intellectual excitement which produced them, and read by a later generation as capital illustrations not only of their author's spontaneity, but also of the permanent direction of his nature. It is not unfair to suppose that the steady application to work in connection with a cause which appealed to moral enthusiasm aroused in a mind like Lowell's an exhilaration of temper very provocative of creation. The poems which he sent, one after the other, in a continuous flight, were witnesses to this activity of imagination, and the very tension of his mind kept him in a state of excitement, so that his diversions took the form of intellectual amusement. Two or three numbers of the " Biglow Papers " had appeared, when Lowell wrote his friend Briggs that he was at work on a satirical poem, but apparently he did not disclose its exact character, though he intimated at the beginning that he meant to give the poem to his friend. In point of fact, Lowell appears to have written at full speed five or six hundred lines of "A Fable for Critics" in October, 1847, and then to have been so busily engaged in getting ready his new volume of "Poems," which appeared at the end of the year, that he laid it aside. "I have been waiting with a good deal of impatience," Briggs writes, 7 November, 1847, "for the manuscript of the satirical poem which you promised to send me. As I have not seen anything advertised which sounds like you I am half afraid that you are not going to publish it. But you must be convinced from the great popularity that Hosea's efforts have received that the sale of the poem will be large and profitable."

In his reply, 13 November, Lowell says : " My satire remains just as it was ; about six hundred lines I think are written. I left it because I wished to finish it in one mood of mind, and not to get that and my serious poems in the new volume entangled. It is a rambling, disjointed affair, and I may alter the form of it, but if I can get it read I know it will take. I intend to give it some serial title and continue it at intervals. . . . I shall send you my satire in manuscript when it is finished. Meanwhile, here is a taste and I want your opinion. Here is Emerson. I think it good. — There, I have given you three or four specimen bricks — what think you of the house? . . . Remember that my satire is a secret. Read the extract to

Page." Mr. Briggs was delighted with what was shown him, and longed for more. "The characteristics of Alcott," he says, "I could not judge of, although they are most happily expressed, as I have known nothing about him; but the character of Emerson was the best thing of the kind I have read." He returns to the subject on Christmas day, but is still ignorant of Lowell's intention as to the disposition of the manuscript. "I think that the book would be a very popular one, but still, it strikes me that your subjects are too localized to be widely understood; but they would have all the merit of fictions at least, and your method would make them universally acceptable."

But now Lowell gives his friend a more explicit statement of his intention as to the publication of his satire. The volume of poems was out of the way, and on the last day of 1847 he writes as follows : "I have not time left to say much more than happy New Year! I have been hard at work copying my satire that I might get it (what was finished of it, at least) to you by New Year's day as a present. As it is, I can only send the first part. It was all written with one impulse, and was the work of not a great many hours; but it was written in good spirits (*con amore*, as Leupp said he used to smoke), and therefore seems to me to have a hearty and easy swing about it that is pleasant. But I was interrupted midway by being obliged to get ready the copy for my volume, and I have never been able to weld my present mood upon the old, without making an ugly swelling at the joint.

"I wish you to understand that I make you a New Year's gift, not of the manuscript, but of the thing itself. I wish you to get it printed (if you think the sale will warrant it) for your own benefit. At the same time I am desirous of retaining my copyright, in order that if circumstances render it desirable, I may still possess a control over it. Therefore, if you think it would repay publishing (I have no doubt of it, or I should not offer it to you), I wish you would enter the copyright in your own name and then make a transfer to me 'in consideration of etc.'

"Now I know that you are as proud as — you ought to be, but if the proceeds of the sale would be of service to you, you have no right to refuse them. I don't make you a pecuniary present, though I trust you would not hesitate to accept one from me, if you needed it, and I could raise the money, but I give you something which I have made myself, and made on purpose for you.

"I know nothing about your circumstances. If beloved W. P. needs it most, let him have it, and I know that you would consider it the best gift I could make you. I will not consent to that disposal of it, however, unless he need it most. In case the proceeds amount to anything handsome (for it may be popular) and you intend them for W. P., let it be done in this way, which would please him and me too, and nobody but myself would be the gainer. Do you in that case sit to Page for your portrait — the said effigies to belong to your humble servant.

"I am making as particular directions as if I were drawing my will, but I have a sort of presentiment (which I never had in regard to anything else) that this little bit of pleasantry will *take*. Perhaps I have said too much of the Centurion.[1] But it was only the comicality of his *character* that attracted me, — for the man himself personally never entered my head.   But the sketch is clever? — I want your opinion on what I have sent immediately."[2]

Mr. Briggs replied at once, accepting the gift in the spirit in which it was given, delighting in the poem, and proposing to arrange immediately for its publication by Putnam.   He was confident, as was Page, that the book would be a great hit, and promptly provided for the disposition of the profits.   "One third," he wrote, "should be invested for Queen Mab, to be given her on her eighteenth birthday; one third to be disposed of in the same manner for my little angel; and the other third to be given to Page, for which he should paint your portrait for me and mine for you.   This would be making the best disposition of the fund that I could devise, and I think will not be displeasing to you.   If the profits should be small, I will divide them equally between the little ones. It will be something quite new for two young ladies to receive their marriage portions from the profits of an American poem."

[1] Cornelius Matthews.

[2] The greater part of this letter will be found in *Letters of James Russell Lowell*, i. 120.   Copyright by Harper & Brothers, 1893.

Lowell was highly entertained by this proposal. " I could not help laughing," he wrote, " as I read your proposed disposition of the expected finances. To look at you in the character of Alnaschar was something so novel as to be quite captivating to my imagination. Not that I have any fear that you will kick over the basket, but I am afraid the contents will hardly be so attractive to the public as to allow the proceeds of the sale to be divided into three. It is really quite a triumph to be able to laugh at my practical friend. However, I will not impoverish your future, but will let you enjoy it as long as it lasts. . . . I have now, in addition to what I sent you, and exclusive of Emerson, etc., about a hundred lines written, chiefly about Willis and Longfellow. But in your arrangements with the printer, you must reckon on allowing me at least a month. I cannot write unless in the mood."

It was when about half the poem had been written that Lowell began his constant work for the *Standard*, and he was impatient to finish the poem, yet found it hard to get into the right mood. "I want to get my windows open," he wrote to Briggs, 26 March, 1848, "and to write in the fresh air. I ought not to have sent you any part of it till I had finished it entirely. I feel a sense of responsibility which hinders my pen from running along as it ought in such a theme. I wish the last half to be as jolly and unconstrained as the first. If you had not praised what I sent you, I dare say you would have had the whole of it ere this. Praise is the only thing that can make me feel any doubt of myself." And then, recurring to Briggs's air castle to be built with the proceeds : " As to your plan for dividing the profits I will have nothing to do with it. I wish they might be a thousand dollars with all my heart, but I do not see that they will be more than enough to buy something for my little niece there in New York. If I had not thought it the only poem I ever wrote on which there was like to be *some* immediate profit, I should never have given it to you at all. In making it a present to you, I was giving myself a *douceur*, and the greater the sale the larger the bribe to myself. A part of the condition is that if it make a loss — I pay it. If this be not agreed to, the bargain is null, and I never will finish it. . . . Now that I *have* let you into the secret of the ' Fable ' before it was finished, I hope you will write and give me a spur. I suppose you did not wish to say anything about it till after it became yours. But I wish to be dunned. Tell me whether its being published at any particular time will make any difference, etc., etc., and make any suggestions. I think I shall say nothing about Margaret Fuller (though she offer so fair a target), because she has done me an ill-natured turn.[1] I shall revenge myself amply upon her by writing

[1] The reference apparently is to Miss Fuller's criticism of Lowell three years previously, in which she said : " His interest in the moral questions of the day has supplied the want of vitality in himself ; his great facility at versification has enabled him to fill the ear with a copious stream of pleasant sound. But his verse is stereotyped : his thoughts sound no depth, and posterity will not remember him." — *Papers on Literature and Art*, p. 308.

better. She is a very foolish, conceited woman, who has got together a great deal of information, but not enough *knowledge* to save her from being ill-tempered. However, the temptation may be too strong for me. It certainly would have been if she had never said anything about me. Even Maria thinks I ought to give her a line or two." Briggs begged him not to leave out Miss Fuller, " she will accuse you of doing it to spite her."

The spring months went by with occasional dashes at the "Fable" and on 12 May, Lowell wrote to his friend : " I have begun upon the 'Fable' again fairly, and am making some headway. I think with what I sent you (which I believe was about 500 lines) it will make something over a thousand. I have done since I sent the first half, Willis, Longfellow, Bryant, Miss Fuller, and Mrs. Child. In Longfellow's case I have attempted no characterization. The same (in a degree) may be said of S. M. F. With her I have been perfectly good humored, but I have a fancy that what I say will stick uncomfortably. It will make you laugh. So will L. M. C. After S. M. F. I make a short digression on bores in general which has some drollery in it. Willis I think good. Bryant is funny, and as far as I could make it immitigably just. Indeed I have endeavored to be so in all. I am glad I did B. before I got your letter.[1] The only verses I shall

---

[1] Briggs did not like Bryant, and in this he was abetted by Page, to whom Bryant at this time was sitting. Page was angry because, in the brief notice of Lowell's *Poems* which Bryant

add regarding him are some complimentary ones
which I left for a happier mood after I had written
the comic part.   I steal from him, indeed !   If he
knew me he would not say so.   When I steal I
shall go to a specie vault, not to a till.   Does he
think that he invented the past, and has a pre-
scriptive title to it ?   Do not think I am provoked.
I am simply amused.   If he had *riled* me, I might
have knocked him into a cocked hat in my satire.
But that, on second thoughts, would be no revenge,
for it might make him President, a cocked hat being now the chief qualification.[1]   It would be more
severe to knock him into the middle of next week,
as that is in the future, and he has such a partial-
ity toward the past."

In the passage on bores, which follows the lines
on Margaret Fuller, Lowell explains that —

" These sketches I made (not to be too explicit)
From two honest fellows who made me a visit," —

but he is explicit enough regarding them in the
same letter to Mr. Briggs : " I had a horrible visi-
tation the other evening from Mr. ——, of Philadelphia, accompanied by Messrs. —— and ——, of
Boston.   After their departure, I wrote the ' digression on bores' which I mentioned above.   ——,
I believe, likes my poetry, but likes his own too
well to appreciate anybody's else.   He is about to
start a magazine and has issued a prospectus of

wrote, he commended only the " Morning Glory," which was Mrs.
Lowell's, and because Bryant intimated that Lowell's " To the
Past " was suggested by a poem of his own with the same title.

[1] This was the year of General Taylor's nomination.

the very most prodigious description. One would think it to have been written with a quill plucked from the wing of ' our country's bird.' He wished to have a portrait and memoir of me in his first number. I escaped from the more immediate crucifixion, however, on the ground that I had no sketch of myself that would answer his purpose. As his project may fail after the first number, I may get off altogether. I have sometimes given offence by answering such applications with a smile, so I have changed my tactics, and give assent. . . . I hope to finish the ' Fable ' next week."

On 24 July, Lowell wrote to Gay, who was in the secret, that he had finished the " Fable," and shortly after he made a visit to New York, but it was not till near the end of August that he sent the last instalment of copy. The proof followed, and Lowell took occasion to make at least one omission, due apparently to better knowledge which led him to revise his judgment. He was too late, apparently, for another correction, for he wrote to Briggs, 4 October, asking him to strike out the four lines relating to Miss Fuller, beginning

" There is one thing she owns in her own single right,"

which still stand. The poem was printed from type, so that as each sheet was printed, and the type distributed, it was not possible, as in the case of electrotype plates, to make corrections up to the last moment before printing the entire book. In the same letter he writes : —

" I send half the proof to-day — t' other to-morrow with Irving and Judd. I am *druv like all possessed*. I am keeping up with the printers with Wilbur's Notes, Glossary, Index, and Introduction. I have two sets of hands to satiate, one on the body of the book, one on the extremities.

"I wish to see title-page and preface. Also, be sure and have a written acknowledgment from G. P. P. that the copyright remains with *you*. Then send me a transfer of it for value received. I will endorse in such a way that it shall remain to you and yours in case anything happen to me. Don't think my precaution indelicate. I only wish to provide against accidents. Let Putnam take out copyright and let it stand in your name as far as he and the rest of the world are concerned. I am anxious about it (I need scarcely say) solely on these two accounts, — that it may never fall into strangers' hands, and that it may never be taken from you. More to-morrow."

Two days later he wrote to Briggs, "I am, you see, as good as my word and better. For, as I was copying the other verses this morning, I thought I might as well throw you in Holmes to boot. Let the new passage begin thus, —

"Here, 'Forgive me, Apollo,' I cried, 'while I pour' &c., &c.

Please make the alteration and put in marks of quotation at the beginning of each new paragraph if I have omitted them. Also in this line if it runs as I think it does,

" 'So, compared to you moderns, is old Melesigines,'

insert ' sounds ' instead of ' is.'

" I wish you would do up a copy with ' author's and so forths,' *dated New York*, and put it into Ticknor's first box directed to Dr. O. W. Holmes, Boston, and also one directed to Professor Felton, Cambridge, in Ticknor's or Nichols's as it may chance. . . .

" Print the title-page thus : —

" ' Reader, walk up ' etc., as far as ' ruinous rate ' in large italics in old-fashioned style in an inverted cone

A

down to   Fable for Critics   in very large caps. Then the rest in small caps properly broken up so as to conceal the fact of the rhyme.[1]

" You will like the tribute to our Massachusetts. It is clearly the best passage in the poem, and you will see how adroitly it comes back to the *theme*, the general comic and satiric tone, of the rest."

The date on the rhymed title-page was antici-

[1] In a letter to me about the *Fable* written in 1890, Lowell says : " Mr. Putnam, I believe, never discovered that the title-page was in metre, nor that it was in rhyme either. Mr. Norton told me the other day that he had a copy of some later edition (after Putnam had changed his place of business), in which the imprint was ' G. P. Putnam, Astor (or something) Place.' I don't remember whether I knew of it at the time, but had I known, I should have let it pass as adding to the humor of the book." The first title-page ended

SET FORTH IN
October, the 31st day, in the year '48
G. P. PUTNAM, BROADWAY.

pated a little, for the book was advertised for 20
October, and delivered on the 25th. A thousand copies had been printed from type and were
quickly disposed of. The little book was then
stereotyped and a second edition issued the first of
the New Year, with the new preface which is still
attached to the poem. In February it had gone
to a third edition, but at the end of November,
1849, it had not sold beyond three thousand copies,
though a fourth edition was then talked of. It is
to be feared that Mr. Briggs's golden eggs were
addled.

It will be remembered that in December, 1846,
Lowell wrote the amusing lines to James Miller
McKim, editor of the *Pennsylvania Freeman*,
which were printed in that paper, and are included
among his collected poems under the heading " Letter from Boston." In the same measure as that
used in " A Fable for Critics," Lowell made rapid
sketches of the conspicuous anti-slavery people as
seen at the bazaar just held in Faneuil Hall. The
success of the squib very likely suggested to him
the fun of playing the same game with the literati
of the day. Both poems, indeed, may have taken a
hint from Leigh Hunt's " The Feast of the Poets," [1]
which had been brought afresh to Lowell's notice,
if not disclosed to him for the first time, by the
little volume " Rimini and other Poems by Leigh
Hunt," issued by Ticknor in 1844. The measure
is the same. Phœbus Apollo also introduces the

[1] Hunt's poem again doubtless owed its being to Lord Byron's
English Bards and Scotch Reviewers.

poets, though Hunt's scheme is more deliberate
than Lowell's, and there is the same disposition to
make use of unexpected rhymes.   Hunt used his
sauciness upon his contemporaries, Spencer, Rogers, Montgomery, Crabbe, Hayley, Gifford, Scott,
Campbell, Moore, Southey, Coleridge, Wordsworth,
Landor, and Rose.   The reader can easily pick out
the names here which have well outlived Hunt's
mockery, and those which were as well known to
Hunt's contemporaries as are some in the "Fable"
to Lowell's.   Hunt, to be sure, confined himself to
poets and poetasters, while Lowell drew his examples from the more conspicuous writers in the
United States, whether of prose or of verse.

There was little mystery about the authorship of
the "Fable."   Lowell did not put his name on the
title-page, but he wrote himself all over the book;
and though the publication was anonymous, he
made no objection to the disclosure to Putnam, and
apparently was careless about confining the knowledge to Briggs, Gay, and Page.   Longfellow records in his diary under 15 June, 1848, "Passed
an hour or two with Lowell, who read to me his
satire on American authors; full of fun, and with
very true portraits, as seen from that side."   It
does not appear if Lowell read to his guest what he
had recently written about him in the satire.   And
Dr. Holmes, to whom a copy of the book, as we
have seen, was sent with the "author's and so
forths," acknowledged it in a letter to Lowell, in
which he characterizes it as "capital — crammed
full and rammed down hard — powder (lots of it)

— shot — slugs — bullets — very little wadding,
and that is gun-cotton — all crowded into a rusty
looking blunderbuss barrel as it were, — capped
with a percussion preface, — and cocked with a
title-page as apropos as a wink to a joke." [1]

Clever as are the portraits, — some of the lines
are bitten in with a little acid, — and though there
are but few of the authors characterized who have
not even a more secure place to-day than then, the
" Fable " can scarcely be said ever to have had or
retained much vogue as a whole. In the excitement of writing his crackling lines Lowell believed
himself to be making a hit, but hardly had the ink
dried than he saw it for what it was, intellectual
effervescence that made one hilarious for the moment. " It seems bald and poor enough now, the
Lord knows," he wrote between the first and second editions. Forty years afterward, however, on

---

[1] Morse's *Life and Letters of Oliver Wendell Holmes*, ii. 107. In
an unfinished letter to Dr. Holmes written from Madrid in 1878,
Lowell refers to a recent criticism of Holmes's poems, in which the
characterization in the *Fable* was quoted. " I thought the young
fellow who wrote it had some sense, especially as he quoted something I said of you in my impudence thirty years ago. It is an
awful thought, but these who then were passing out of the bald-
ness of infancy are now entering upon that of middle age, and here
we both are as if nothing had happened. And probably precious
little has happened, — I mean of any great account. The more
one reads of history the more one sees mankind doing the same
foolish things over again with admirable gravity and then contemplating themselves with the satisfaction of Jack Horner. I remember when I was writing the *Fable for Critics* and used to walk
up and down the front walk at Elmwood, I paused to watch the
ant-hills, and in the seemingly aimless and yet ceaseless activity of
their citizens thought I saw a very close paraphrase of the life of
men."

recalling it, he said it was the first popular thing he had written. He never was quite easy as to his treatment of Bryant: " I am quite sensible now," he wrote in 1855, " that I did not do Mr. Bryant justice in the ' Fable.' But there was no personal feeling in what I said, though I have regretted what I *did* say because it might seem personal." And as late as 1887 he characterized his poem written for Bryant's birthday as a kind of palinode to what he had said of him in the " Fable," " which has something of youth's infallibility in it, or at any rate of youth's irresponsibility." Aside from this slight uneasiness, Lowell does not appear to have repented of any of his judgments, nor did he ever revise the poem for subsequent editions. No doubt, the disregard of the poem has been due largely to the ephemeral nature of much of the jocoseness. The puns, good and bad, with which it is sprinkled, are so many notices of " good for this time only," and the petty personalities and trivial bits of satire lower the average of the whole. The " Fable " must be taken for just what it was to the author and his friends, a piece of high spirits with which to make sport: the salt that savors it is to be found in the few masterly characterizations and criticisms.

And yet, turning away from this *jeu d'esprit* as a piece of literature, and looking at it as a reflection of Lowell's mind in a very ardent passage of his life, we may justly regard with strong interest so frank an expression, not merely of his likes and dislikes, but of the underlying principle of criticism

which was native to him and found abundant illustration from the days of the *Pioneer* to the later
days of the *North American Review.* His impatience of yard-stick criticism and of a timid waiting
upon foreign judgment, so hotly uttered in his rapid
lines, sprang from the intuitive perception and the
independence of spirit which lie at the basis of all
his own criticism.   This intuitive perception was
indeed that of a man who often formed hasty impressions and was not without personal prejudice,
but it was at least a first-hand judgment, and not
the composite result of other men's opinions, and
it came from a mind through which the wind of a
free nature was always blowing.   The lightning
flashes which disclose the inherent and lasting qualities of Emerson, Hawthorne, Cooper, Holmes,
Whittier, Bryant, Longfellow are all witnesses to
the penetration and clear intelligence which Lowell
possessed.   It must not be forgotten that Lowell,
himself only just past the period of youth, was writing of men whose reputation is secure enough now,
but who were at that time not wholly discriminated
by the general public from a number of mediocri-
ties who crowded about them, and there is an even-
handed justice in the poem which not unfitly is put
into the mouth of that court of last resort, Phœbus
Apollo himself.

The independence which goes along with the in-
tuition is simply the integrity of a nature which is
not given to the concealment of its judgments. As
he laughingly said of himself later, he was very
cock-sure of himself at this time.   In after years,

when he was speaking in his own voice from a more
historic platform, he might choose his phrases more
deliberately, but none the less did he speak his
mind out. There was confidence in himself first
and last, but the impetuous, almost reckless utterance of his youth, when he saw things clearly as
youth does when it is conscious of breathing the air
of freedom and bathing in the light of truth, yielded
only to the temper which maturity brings and was
more moderate and charitable in expression because
it had the larger vision. When one considers the
eagerness with which Lowell vented himself in the
months of his close connection with the *Anti-Slavery Standard*, one is not surprised that in a book
which is at once a defence of criticism and a swift
survey of the whole field of American letters as it
lay under the eye of this knight-errant of freedom
and truth, Lowell should have displayed, with little reserve, the frankness and impetuosity of his
nature. It is only after a closer inspection that
one discovers also how sound and how generous is
his judgment.

How much satire gains from moral earnestness
and a righteous scorn is easily seen in the book
which followed close on the heels of " A Fable for
Critics," and with its pungency weakened the impression which might otherwise have been created
by its companion in literature. We have already
seen that the first number of the " Biglow Papers "
appeared in the *Courier* of Boston in June, 1846,
and that Lowell reckoned on producing a greater

effect by withholding his name. He told Gay that he might very likely continue to fire from this masked battery while he was openly keeping up with others a fusillade in the *Standard*. In point of fact the first five numbers were printed in the *Courier*, but when the fifth was printed, Lowell was at the beginning of his real connection with the *Standard*, and the remaining four were printed in that paper.

The series, thus begun in the *Courier* in June, 1846, was closed in the *Standard* in September, 1848.[1] Although Lowell did not sign his name to any of the numbers either in the *Courier* or in the *Standard*, the authorship was a very open secret indeed. Still, he had the pleasure which sprang from the dramatic assumption, and he took good care not to confuse the personalities in the little comedy, by thrusting his own real figure on the stage. As he wrote forty years later: "I had great fun out of it. I have often wished that I could have had a literary *nom de plume* and kept my own to myself. I should n't have cared a doit what happened to him."

A dozen years later, on the eve of the war for the Union, Mr. Hughes, who was introducing the book to the English public, wanted Lowell to write an historical introduction. In declining to do this,[2]

---

[1] The Bibliographical Note in the Appendix gives the dates of the successive numbers. See Appendix C.

[2] When he was supervising the final *Riverside* edition of his writings, he gladly accepted the services of a graduate student at Harvard, now Professor of Law in Western Reserve University, Mr. Frank Beverly Williams, who prepared a series of notes.

he gave a brief and clear statement of his political position at the time of writing the "Biglow Papers." "I believed our war with Mexico (though we had as just ground for it as a strong nation ever has against a weak one) to be essentially a war of false pretences, and that it would result in widening the boundaries and so prolonging the life of slavery. Believing that it is the manifest destiny of the English race to occupy this whole continent, and to display there that practical understanding in matters of government and colonization which no other race has given such proof of possessing since the Romans, I hated to see a noble hope evaporated into a lying phrase to sweeten the foul breath of demagogues. Leaving the sin of it to God, I believed and still believe that slavery is the Achilles heel of our polity: that it is a temporary and false supremacy of the white races, sure to destroy that supremacy at last, because an enslaved people always prove themselves of more enduring fibre than their enslavers, as not suffering from the social vices sure to be engendered by oppression in the governing class. Against these and many other things I thought all honest men should protest. I was born and bred in the country, and the dialect was homely to me. I tried my first 'Biglow Paper' in a newspaper and found that it had a great run. So I wrote the others from time to time during the year which followed, always very rapidly, and sometimes (as with 'What Mr. Robinson thinks') at one sitting."

The cleverness of the refrain in this last named

poem started it on a hilarious career, and it is perhaps only in one of Gilbert's topical songs that we
can match the success of a collocation of words,
where the quaintness of turn keeps a barren phrase
perennially amusing.   It was with an echo of it in
his mind no doubt that when he had just done
reading the proofs of the entire volume, Lowell
snapped his whip in like fashion in a poem for the
Standard, which he never reprinted, but which is
interesting from the diversity shown in the handling of a single theme.

In the fall of 1848, Harrison Gray Otis, writing in advocacy of the election of Zachary Taylor,
referred to an incident in 1831, when, as Mayor
of Boston, he answered an application from the
Governors of Virginia and Georgia for information
respecting the persons responsible for *The Liberator*. "Some time afterward," he says, "it was
reported to me by the city officers that they had
ferreted out the paper and its editor : that his office
was an obscure hole, his only visible auxiliary a
negro boy, and his supporters a very few insignificant persons of all colors."   Lowell saw the letter
in one of the newspapers of the day, clipped out
this sentence, pasted it on a sheet of paper, and
wrote below it, with the title "the day of small
things," the notable lines which in his collected
poems bear the heading "To W. L. Garrison."
The poem was published in the *Standard*, 19 October, 1848, but the incident evidently made a
strong impression on him, especially when he considered what had taken place in seventeen years ;

for immediately afterward he wrote again, and in
the number for 26 October, appeared

THE EX-MAYOR'S CRUMB OF CONSOLATION.

A PATHETIC BALLAD.[1]

" Two Governors once a letter writ
    To the Mayor of a distant city,
And told him a paper was published in it,
That was telling the truth, and 't was therefore fit
That the same should be crushed as dead as a nit
    By an Aldermanic Committee :
      ' Don't say so ? ' says Otis,
      ' I 'll enquire if so 't is :
Dreadful ! telling the truth ?   What a pity !

" ' It can't be the Atlas, that 's perfectly clear,
    And of course it is n't the Advertiser,
'T is out of the Transcript's appropriate sphere,
The Post is above suspicion : oh dear,
To think of such accidents happening here !
    I hoped that our people were wiser.
      While we 're going,' says Otis,
      ' *Faustissimis votis,*
How very annoying such flies are ! '

" So, without more ado, he enquired all round
    Among people of wealth and standing ;
But wealth looked scornful, and standing frowned ;
At last in a garret with smoke imbrowned,
The conspirators all together he found, —
    One man with a colored boy banding ;
      ' 'Pon my word,' says Otis,
      ' Decidedly low 't is,'
As he groped for the stairs on the landing.

" So he wrote to the Governors back agen,
    And told them 't was something unworthy of mention ;

[1] Mr. Otis died October 28. " Only think of H. G. O ! " wrote
Lowell to Gay early in November; " I would not have squibbed
him if I had known he was sick, but I never hear anything."

That 't was only a single man with a pen,
And a font of type in a sort of den,
A person unknown to Aldermen,
   And, of course, beneath attention ;
     ' And therefore,' wrote Otis,
      Annuentibus totis,
' There 's no reason for apprehension.'

" But one man with a pen is a terrible thing,
   With a head and heart behind it,
And this one man's words had an ominous ring,
That somehow in people's ears would cling ; —
   ' But the mob 's uncorrupted : they 've eggs to fling ;
   So 't is hardly worth while to mind it ;
     As for freedom,' says Otis,
     ' I 've given her notice
To leave town, in writing, and underlined it.'

" But the one man's helper grew into a sect,
   That laughed at all efforts to check or scare it,
Old parties before it were scattered and wrecked,
And respectable folks knew not what to expect ; —
   ' 'T is some consolation, at least to reflect
   And will help us, I think, to bear it,
     That all this,' says Otis,
     ' Though by no means *in votis,*
Began with one man and a boy in a garret.' "

Lowell himself, in the Introduction which he wrote to the Second Series, bears witness to the popularity of the " Biglow Papers " while they were still uncollected. " Very far," he says, " from being a popular author under my own name, so far indeed as to be almost unread, I found the verses of my pseudonym copied everywhere : I saw them pinned up in workshops : I heard them quoted and their authorship debated." It was, it may be said, no new thing to seek to arrest the public attention with the vernacular applied to public affairs. Major Jack Downing and Sam Slick had been notable exemplars, and they had many imitators ; but party politics, or even local characteristics, may give rise to the merely idle jest of satire ; the reader who laughed over the racy narrative of the unlettered Ezekiel, and then took up Hosea's poem and caught the gust of Yankee wrath and humor blown fresh in his face, knew that he was in with the appearance of something new in American literature.

After the first heat, Lowell began to distrust his mode a little. " As for Hosea," he writes to Briggs, " I am sorry that I began by making him such a detestable speller. There is no fun in bad spelling of itself, but only where the misspelling suggests something else which is droll *per se*. You see I am getting him out of it gradually. I mean to altogether. Parson Wilbur is about to propose a subscription for fitting him for college, and has already commenced his education." [1] He dropped this intention, however, and the later numbers of the series show no marked departure from the general scheme of Yankee spelling. There is no doubt, though, that when it came to a revision of the papers for final book publication, Lowell did make an attempt to introduce some sort of consistency or effectiveness in the form. He groaned over the labor involved, and confessed that he

[1] Writing forty years later in excuse of a petty solecism, he said : " I think it must have been written when I was fresh from the last *Biglow Papers*. When my soul enters Mr. Biglow's person, she divests herself for the time of all conventional speech, and for some time after she leaves it is apt to forget herself."

made a great many alterations in spelling even
after the pages had been stereotyped. "It is the
hardest book to print," he wrote Mr. Gay, "that
ever I had anything to do with, and, what with
corrections and Mr. Wilbur's annotations, keeps
me more employed than I care to be."

The labor was partly of his own making, but
after all was consequent chiefly upon the sense of
art which led the author to do much more than
simply collect and reprint what he had written
currente calamo in the *Courier* and *Standard*.
The great popularity attained by the successive
numbers showed him that he had hit the mark,
but also the conception of the whole grew in his
mind, and he seized the opportunity which reprinting afforded, to shape his satire and give it a
body, by filling out the characters who constituted
his *dramatis personæ*. "When I came to collect [the papers] and publish them in a volume,"
he wrote in 1859 to Mr. Hughes, in the letter already quoted, "I conceived my parson-editor with
his pedantry and verbosity, his amiable vanity
and superiority to the verses he was editing, as a
fitting artistic background and foil. It gave me
the chance, too, of glancing obliquely at many
things which were beyond the horizon of my other
characters. I was told afterwards that my Parson
Wilbur was only Jedediah Cleishbotham over
again, and I dare say it may be so; but I drew
him from the life as well as I could, and for the
authentic reasons I have mentioned."

There was a slight undercurrent of reference

to his own father in this characterization. "My father," he wrote Hughes, "was as proud of his pedigree as a Talbot or Stanley could be, and Parson Wilbur's genealogical mania was a private joke between us." [1]

So thoroughly did he think himself into the artistic conception of the book that he even proposed at one time to put Jaalam on the title-page as place of publication, and to have it "printed on brownish paper with those little head and tail pieces which used to adorn our earlier publications — such as hives, scrolls, urns, and the like." This external fitness he did not secure, but he elaborated a system of notes, glossary, and index, letting the fun lurk in every part, and completed the effect by the notices of an independent press, which must have made the actual writers of book notices hesitate a little before they dropped into their customary machine-made manner when treating of this special work. The burlesque of Carlyle in one of these is especially clever. In supplying all this apparatus he drew a little on his prose papers in

[1] He had the ill luck which not infrequently attends the writers of fiction, to make use of an actual name in one of his inventions, and received this protest from the Rev. H. Wilbur : —

"Unknown Sir, I believe there is no other clergyman in New England besides myself of the same name you sometimes associate with your writings. Perhaps with the scintillations of your genius my name would be more likely to descend to posterity than from writings or labours of my own. But if your edification could be as well promoted under the ministry of Parson Smith or some *fictitious* name not likely to be associated with individuality as with the *old Parson* you will much oblige yours very respectfully."

the *Standard*, but it is doubtful if most readers get beyond the verse, or do more than glance at the drollery which lies *perdu* in the prose equipment, so much swifter is the flight of the arrows of satire when they are barbed with rhyme.

The success of the book was immediate. The first edition of 1500 was gone in a week, and the author could say with satisfaction that "the book was actually out of print before a second edition could be struck off from the plates." In later years the book was apt to fill him with a kind of amused astonishment. The unstinted praise which Hughes gave to the "Biglow Papers," quotations from which were always on his tongue's end, drew from Lowell the expression : "I was astonished to find what a heap of wisdom was accumulated in those admirable volumes." It is not strange that, in looking back from the tranquil temper of older years, Lowell should be struck with the high spirits, the tension of feeling, and the abandon of utterance which characterize this work; but when he was in the thick of the fight a second time he was more impressed by the moral earnestness which underlay all this free lancing. "The success of my experiment," he wrote, in the Introduction to the Second Series, "soon began not only to astonish me, but to make me feel the responsibility of knowing that I held in my hand a weapon instead of the mere fencing stick I had supposed. . . . If I put on the cap and bells, and made myself one of the court fools of King Demos, it was less to make his Majesty laugh than to win a passage to his royal ears

for certain serious things which I had deeply at
heart."

The force which Lowell displayed in this satire
made his book at once a powerful ally of a sentiment which heretofore had been crassly ridiculed ;
it turned the tables and put Anti-slavery, which had
been fighting sturdily on foot with pikes, into the
saddle, and gave it a flashing sabre. For Lowell
himself it won an accolade from King Demos. He
rose up a knight, and thenceforth possessed a freedom which was a freedom of nature, not a simple
badge of service in a single cause. His patriotism
and moral fervor found other vents in later life, and
he never sheathed the sword which he had drawn
from the scabbard ; but it is significant of the sta-
bility of his genius that he was not misled into a
limitation of his powers by the sudden distinction
which came to him. For, though we naturally
think first of the political significance of the " Biglow Papers," the book, in its fullest meaning, is an
expression of Lowell's personality, and has in it
the essence of New England. The character of the
race from which its author sprang is preserved in
its vernacular and in the characters of the *dramatis personœ*. Not unwittingly, but in the full consciousness of his own inheritance, Lowell became
the spokesman of a racy people, whose moral force
had a certain acrid quality, and, when thrown to
the winds, as in the person of Birdofredom Sawin,
was replaced by an insolent shrewdness. Nor is
the exemplification of New England less complete
for that infusion of homely sentiment and genuine

poetic sensibility which underlie and penetrate the sturdy moral force.

The "Biglow Papers" threw "A Fable for Critics" into the shade. It was nearly through the press when the "Fable" was published, and Briggs, who kept a close watch of his friend's production, wrote: "I am pretty confident that the 'Fable' will suit the market for which it is intended, unless it should be killed by Hosea, who will help to divert public attention from his own kind." It is to be suspected that Lowell himself felt the strong contrast which lay in the two works when he was driving them through the press side by side, and rather lost interest in the ebullition of an hour, as he threw himself with an almost exhausted energy into a book which carried at its heart a flame of passionate scorn. The only passage in "A Fable for Critics" which he dwelt upon with genuine delight was his apostrophe to Massachusetts, and that is almost out of key with the rest of the poem. But a third book was shortly to follow and to divide with the other two the popularity which fell to Lowell as a writer.

It does not appear just when "The Vision of Sir Launfal" was written, but in a letter to Briggs, dated 1 February, 1848, Lowell speaks of it as "a sort of story, and more likely to be popular than what I write generally. Maria thinks very highly of it. I shall probably publish it by myself next summer." But it was not till the "Biglow Papers" were off his hands that Lowell took steps to print the book, which was published 17 December, 1848. It was not long after that he went to Watertown for the wedding of Mrs. Lowell's sister with Dr. Estes Howe, and the next day he wrote to Briggs: " I walked to Watertown over the snow with the new moon before me and a sky exactly like that in Page's evening landscape. Orion was rising behind me, and as I stood on the hill just before you enter the village, the stillness of the fields around me was delicious, broken only by the tinkle of a little brook which runs too swiftly for Frost to catch it. My picture of the brook in 'Sir Launfal' was drawn from it. But why do I send you this description — like the bones of a chicken I had picked ? Simply because I was so happy as I stood there, and felt so sure of doing something that would justify my friends. But why do I not say that I *have* done something ? I believe I have done better than the world knows yet, but the past seems so little compared with the future." And then referring to a recent notice of him which intimated that he was well to do, he says : " I wish I might be for a day or two. I should like such an income as Billy Lee desired, who, when some one asked his idea of a competence, replied, 'A million a minute, and your expenses paid !' But I am richer than he thinks for. I am the first poet who has endeavored to express the American Idea, and I shall be popular by and by. Only I suppose I must be dead first. But I do not want anything more than I have."

It is not very likely that Lowell was thinking

specifically of " Sir Launfal " when he wrote this.
It is more likely that he would have named " Prometheus," " Columbus," or " Freedom " if he had
been asked to name names ; and yet it is not straining language too far to say that when he took up an
Arthurian story he had a different attitude toward
the whole cycle of legends from that of Tennyson
who, a half dozen years before, had begun to revive
the legends for the pleasure of English-reading
people.   The exuberance of the poet as he carols of
June in the prelude to Part First is an expression
of the joyous spring which was in the veins of the
young American, glad in the sense of freedom and
hope.   As Tennyson threw into his retelling of
Arthurian romance a moral sense, so Lowell, also
a moralist in his poetic apprehension, made a parable of his tale, and, in the broadest interpretation
of democracy, sang of the levelling of all ranks in
a common divine humanity.   There is a subterranean passage connecting the " Biglow Papers " with
" Sir Launfal " ; it is the holy zeal which attacks
slavery issuing in this fable of a beautiful charity,
Christendom in the guise of a beggar.

The invention is a very simple one, and appears
to have been suggested by Tennyson's " Sir Gala-
had," but the verses in the poem which linger longest in the mind are not those connected with the
fable, but rather the full-throated burst of song in
praise of June.   Indeed, one might seriously maintain from Lowell's verse that there was an especial
affinity which he held with this month.   Witness
the joyous rush of pleasure with which " Under

the Willows "[1] is begun, and the light-heartedness
with which Hosea Biglow leaves the half-catalogue
manner rehearsing the movement of Spring in
" Sunthin' in the Pastoral Line," and leaps almost vociferously into the warm, generous air of
June, when " all comes crowdin' in."   The poem
entitled " Al Fresco " is but a variation on the
same theme ; when he first published it, save the
opening stanza, in the *Anti-Slavery Standard,* he
gave it the title of " A Day in June."   And when,
compelled to lie indoors, he found a compensation
in Calderon singing to him like a nightingale, it
was still a wistful look he cast on his catbird that
joined with the oriole and the cuckoo to call him
out of doors, and he sighed to think that he could
not like them be a pipe for June to play on. " The
Nightingale in the Study " was written when he
sought in illness for something that would seclude
him from himself; but the three poems of 1848
were the outcome of a nature so tingling with vitality that expression was its necessity, and spontaneity the law of its being.   Literature, freedom,
and nature in turn appealed to the young enthusiast ; the visions he saw stirred him, in the quiet
of Elmwood, to eager, impetuous delivery ; and his
natural voice was a singing one.

[1] He intended first to call this " A June Idyll."

CHAPTER VI

WHEN, in the spring of 1845, the Lowells returned to Cambridge from Philadelphia, where they
had spent the first four months of their married
life, it was to share the family home of Elmwood
for the next six years. Lowell's father retired in
the summer of 1845 from active charge of the West
Parish in Boston, but retained his interest in various societies which gave him partial occupation,
leaving him leisure for the indulgence of his taste
for reading and for the pleasures of gardening and
small farming. His mother, whose malady slowly
but steadily increased, was under watchful care.
She was taken to various health resorts in hopes of
recovery, and spent a part of her last years under
more constant treatment at an asylum for the men-
tally deranged. Miss Rebecca Lowell had charge
of the little household, and now and then went on
journeys with her father or mother or both, leaving
the young couple to themselves. As one child after
another came into the circle, the grandfather found
a solace for the sorrow which lay heavily upon him,
and his letters, when he was on one of his journeys, were filled with affectionate messages for his

new daughter and her children, mingled with careful charges to his son concerning the well-being of the cattle, small and large, and the proper harvesting of the little crops.

Mrs. Lowell's family lived near by in Watertown, and one by one her sisters married, one of them coming to Cambridge to live. The society of the college town was open, and it was in these early years that Lowell formed one of a whist club, which, with but slight variation in membership, continued its meetings to the end of his life, and the simple records of which were kept by Lowell. Its most constant members were Mr. John Holmes, a younger brother of Dr. Oliver Wendell Holmes, Mr. John Bartlett, who was for a while a bookseller in Cambridge, and afterward until his retirement a member of the publishing firm of Little, Brown & Co. of Boston, and best known by his handbook of " Familiar Quotations " and his elaborate " Concordance to Shakespeare," and finally Dr. Estes Howe, who married Mrs. Lowell's sister.

Lowell was much given to concealing in his verse or prose little allusions which might be passed over by readers unaware of what lay beneath, but would be taken as a whispered aside by his friends. Thus in a " Preliminary Note to the Second Edition " of " A Fable for Critics," he says: " I can walk with the Doctor, get facts from the Don, or draw out the Lambish quintessence of John, and feel nothing more than a half comic sorrow, to think that they all [1] will be lying to-

---

[1] That is, the hostile criticisms of his book.

morrow tossed carelessly up on the waste-paper shelves, and forgotten by all but their half dozen selves."

In the summer of 1846 the sickness of little Blanche took the family suddenly to Stockbridge in the Berkshire Hills, whence Lowell wrote to Carter : "Stockbridge is without exception the quietest place I was ever in, and the office of postmaster here one of the most congenial to my taste and habits of any I ever saw or heard of. The postmaster has no regular hours whatever. Even if engaged in sorting the mail, he will run out and lock the door behind him, to play with his grandchildren. I do not believe that in the cabinet of any postmaster-general there is a more unique specimen. He is a gray-bearded old gentleman of between sixty and seventy, wears the loose calico gown so much in vogue among the country clergy, and feels continually that he is an important limb of the great body politic. I do not mean that he is vain. There is too profound a responsibility attached to his office to allow of so light and unworthy a passion. There is a solemn, half-melancholy grandeur about him, a foreboding, perchance, of that change of administration which may lop him from the parent tree, — a Montezuma-like dread of that mysterious stranger into whose hands his sceptre must pass. In purchasing a couple of steel pens or a few cigars of him (for he keeps a small variety store) you feel that the parcel is done up and handed over the counter by one of the potent hands of government itself. . . . We have

found Stockbridge an exceedingly pleasant place
and have made many agreeable acquaintances.
Blanche is a favorite throughout the village and
knows everybody."

Longfellow, who was near by in Pittsfield at this
time, notes in his Diary, 16 August: " In the afternoon Lowell came with his wife from Lenox to see
us.   He looks as hale as a young farmer ; she very
pale and fragile.   They are driving about the country and go southward to Great Barrington and the
region of the Bash Bish."

The illness of Blanche which led her parents to
take her into the country was slight and temporary.
The child grew in beauty and winning grace, and
endeared herself to her father in a manner which
left its signs long afterward.   Early in March,
1847, however, when she was vigorous and gave
promise of a hearty life, she was seized suddenly
with a malady consequent upon too rapid teething,
and after a week's sickness died.   " In the fourteen months she was with us (for which God be
thanked)," Lowell wrote to Briggs, " she showed
no trace of any evil tendency, and it is wonderful
how in so brief a space she could have twined her
little life round so many hearts.   Wherever she
went everybody loved her.   My poor father loved
her so that he almost broke his heart in endeavoring to console Maria when it was at last decided
the dear child was not to be spared to us."   After
Blanche was buried, her father took her tiny shoes,
the only ones she had ever worn, and hung them in
his chamber.   There they stayed till his own death.

"The Changeling" preserves in poetry the experience of the father in this first great sorrow of his life, and "The First Snow-Fall" intimates the consolation which was shortly to be brought, for in September the second child, Mabel, was born.

The literary product of 1847 was inconsiderable. A few poems appeared, and Lowell even contemplated trying his hand at a tragedy founded on the Conquest of Mexico, — the first conquest, as one of his friends slyly remarks, — suggested no doubt by Prescott's history, which had appeared four years earlier, and had just been followed by the "Conquest of Peru." He made some progress with the tragedy, and even purposed offering it in competition for the large prize promised by Forrest for a good acting tragedy, but no line of it appears to have been preserved. He contributed also two or three articles to the *North American Review*, and in the fall of the year he set about the collection of such poems as he had written since his previous volume appeared. In the midst of this work he wrote to his friend Carter, then in the little village of Pepperell, and his letter reflects pleasantly the attitude he always took toward New England country life, as well as shows the wistfulness of his regard for his lost child.

"There are pleasanter ways of looking at a country village like Pepperell," he writes to his somewhat discontented correspondent; "there are good studies both within doors and without, and either picture will be new to you. Talk to the men about farming, and you will find yourself in good

society at once. Inquire of the women about the
mysteries of cheese — and butter-making, and you
will be more entertained than with the Georgics.
At first, you find yourself in a false relation with
them. You touch at no points and bristle repel-
lingly at all. They flounder in their conversation
and seek shelter in the weather or the price of
pork, because they consider themselves under a
painful necessity to entertain you. They can't
converse because they try — effort being the un-
timely grave of all true interchange of natures.
They make a well where there should be a fountain. Get them upon any common ground, and
you will find there is genuine stuff in them. The
essence of good society is simply a community in
habits of thought and topics of interest. When
we approach each other naturally, we meet easily
and gracefully; if we hurry too much we are apt
to come together with an unpleasant bump.

" Who knows how much domestic interest was
involved in that question the goodwife asked you
about Mr. Praisegod's servant ? Perhaps she has
a son, or a daughter betrothed to a neighbor's
son, who thinks of beginning life (as many of the
farmers' children in our country towns do) by entering into service in the city. Perhaps she wished
and yet did not dare to ask of the temptations he
would be exposed to. I love our Yankees with all
their sharp angles.

" Maria is and has been remarkably well ever
since the birth of our little darling, if I may call
her so when Blanche still holds the first place in

our hearts. Little Miss Mabel thrives wonder-
fully. She is, I think, as good a child as her little
sister — though I tremble to trace any likeness
between the two. She certainly has not Blanche's
noble and thoughtful eyes, which were noticeable
even when she was first born. But some of her
ways are very like her sister's. Those who have
seen her say that she is a very beautiful child."

Toward the end of the year the volume of poems
pressed hard upon him. "I should have written
to you," he writes to Briggs, 13 November, 1847,
"at any rate just to say that I loved you still and
to ask how you did, had I not been most prepos-
terously busy with the printers. I had calculated
in a loose way that I had ' copy ' enough prepared
to make as large a volume as I intended mine
should be, but about three weeks ago the printers
overtook me, and since then we have been neck
and neck for something like a hundred pages —
thirty page heats. It was only yesterday that I
won the cup. Everybody has a notion that it is of
advantage to be out before Christmas; and though
I feel a sort of contempt for a demand so adven-
titiously created, and do not wish anybody to buy
my book but those who buy to read, yet it is one
of these little points which we find it convenient to
yield in life, and not the less readily because it
will be for our advantage not to be obstinate. I
have a foolish kind of pride in these particulars.
I had rather, for example, that you should have
copied into the *Mirror* a column of abuse than
those exaggerated commendations of my Louisville

friend. I do not know whether it is a common feeling or not, but I can never get to consider myself as anything more than a boy. My temperament is so youthful, that whenever I am addressed (I mean by mere acquaintances) as if my opinion were worth anything, I can hardly help laughing. I cannot but think to myself with an inward laugh: ' My good friend, you would be as mad as a hornet with me, if you knew that I was only a boy of twelve behind a bearded vizor.' This feeling is so strong that I have got into a way of looking on the Poet Lowell as an altogether different personage from myself, and feel a little offended when my friends confound the two."

The volume of poems to which Lowell refers in this letter came out just before Christmas, 1847. It· bore the words " Second Series " on the title-page, being coupled in the author's mind with the Poems issued four years previous. It is in the main a collection of the poems which Lowell in the past four years had scattered through papers and magazines, though he omitted several which had appeared in print, one or two of which indeed he went back and picked up on issuing his next collection a score of years later. He did not draw on his Biglow poems, reserving them for a volume by themselves, and he omitted several that were in a similar vein. There was perhaps no single poem in the new series which struck a deeper note than is to be found in one or two of the poems in the earlier collection, yet the art of the second series is firmer than that of the first, and the book as a

whole is distinctly more even and more free from
the mere sentimentalism which marks the previous
volume.   Scattered through it are a few of the
more serious of his anti-slavery poems, as if for a
testimony ; but he does not retain the violent, not
to say turgid, songs which he had thrown out upon
occasions of public excitement.

There is one poem among the few contributed
directly to the volume, which is familiar to lovers of
Lowell himself rather than of Lowell the poet, if
we may take his own discrimination, and it is most
likely that it was written under conditions referred
to in the letter just quoted.   " An Indian-Summer
Reverie," which fills sixteen pages of the little volume, near its close, bears the marks of rapid writing.   It is easy to believe that Lowell, coming
away from the printing-office, where he had learned
that the printers needed at once more copy, paused
near the willows, and in the warm, hazy November
afternoon let his mind drift idly over the scene
and blend with it reflections on his own life.   The
poet, by virtue of his gift, is always young, and yet
when young is the most retrospective of men.   Not
yet thirty, Lowell could remember his youth, and
helped by the autumn that was in the air, could
see nature and man and his own full life through
a medium which has the mistiness and the color of
the Indian Summer.   There are poetic lines and
phrases in the poem, and more than all the veil of
the season hangs tremulously over the whole, so
that one is gently stirred by the poetic feeling of
the rambling verses ; yet, after all, the most endur-

ing impression is of the young man himself in that
still hour of his life, when he was conscious, not so
much of a reform to which he must put his hand,
as of the love of beauty, and of the vague melancholy which mingles with beauty in the soul of a
susceptible poet. The river winding through the
marshes, the distant sound of the ploughman, the
near chatter of the chipmunk, the individual trees,
each living its own life, the march of the seasons
flinging lights and shadows over the broad scene,
the pictures of human life associated with his own
experience, the hurried survey of his village years
— all these pictures float before his vision; and
then, with an abruptness which is like the choking
of the singer's voice with tears, there wells up the
thought of the little life which held as in one
precious drop the love and faith of his heart. Mr.
Briggs, in a letter written upon receiving the volume, says: " I have just laid it aside with my eyes
full of tears after reading 'The Changeling,' which
appears to me the greatest poem in the collection,
and I think that it will be so regarded by and by,
a good many years hence, when I shall be wholly
forgotten and you will only be known by the free
thoughts you will leave behind you." Mr. Briggs
had himself lost a child, and his grief had been
commemorated by Lowell; this same letter an-
nounces the birth of a daughter. One's personal
experience often colors if it does not obscure one's
critical judgment; but in taking account of Lowell's
life and its expression, we may not overlook the
fact that up to this time certainly he was singu-

larly ingenuous in making poetry, not simply a
vehicle for the conveyance of large emotions gen-
eralized from personal experience, but a precipita-
tion of his most intimate emotions.   His love, his
tender feelings for his friends, his generous and
ardent hopes for humanity, his passion for freedom
and truth, all lay at the depths of his being; but
they rose to the surface perpetually in his poems
and his letters, and he had scarcely learned to hold
them in check by that hard mundane wisdom which
comes to most through the attrition of daily living.

Thus far Lowell had looked out on life pretty
steadily from the sheltered privacy of a happy
home, and he was not immediately to change his
surroundings; but a certain induration was now to
be effected which can scarcely be said to have
arrested his spontaneity, but may fairly be looked
upon as leading him to regard himself more as
others regarded him, as no longer a " boy of twelve
behind a bearded vizor," but as grown up and become a man of the world.   For it was not long
after this that the relation into which he had entered with the *National Anti-Slavery Standard*,
and which had undergone a sort of suspension as we
have seen, became a very close and exacting one.

The seclusion of his life satisfied Lowell; he was
an infrequent visitor to Boston even, and made
but few journeys.   Now and then he went to New
York, and, as we have seen, once to Stockbridge.
To Canada also he made one journey; but it is
clear from the circumstances attending these flit-
tings that the Lowells had no money to spend on

luxuries. They could live simply and without much outlay of cash at Elmwood, but travelling meant hoarding first, and in those early married years the young couple was not often out of debt. Even a trip to New York had to be postponed again and again on this account. Mr. Gay's drafts in payment of account for contributions to the *Standard* were irregular and always seemed to come just in the nick of time.

" I thought to see you this week," Lowell wrote to Gay, 8 June, 1848, when acknowledging one of these raven-flights, — " but cannot come yet. I cannot come without any money, and leave my wife with $62\frac{1}{2}$ cents, such being the budget brought in by my secretary of the treasury this week. . . . I am expecting some money daily — I always am — I always have been, and yet have never been fairly out of debt since I entered college." And again, writing to the same, 26 February, 1849, " The truth is, that I have just been able to keep my head above water ; but there is a hole in my life-preserver, and what wind I can raise from your quarter comes just in season to make up for leakage and save me from total submersion. Since the day after I received your remittance for December, I have literally not had a copper, except a small sum which I borrowed. It was all spent before I got it. So is the last one, too. As long as I have money I don't think anything about it, except to fancy my present stock inexhaustible and capable of buying up the world." A few days later, on receiving the draft which his half-humorous letter called for, he wrote in the same strain: " I am not very often down in the mouth: but sometimes, at the end of the year, when I have done a tolerable share of work, and have nothing to show for it, I feel as if I had rather be a spruce clerk on India wharf than a man of letters. Regularly I look forward to New Year, and think that I shall begin the next January out of debt, and as regularly I am disappointed."

Yet all this time, with his frugal living and his vain effort to be even with the world, he could not refrain from obeying his generous impulses. His gift of " A Fable for Critics " to Briggs illustrates this spirit, and a passage in one of his letters shows the secret giver who is perhaps a little more lovable in the eyes of the Lord than the cheerful public one. Mr. Briggs had written to him 16 November, 1849: " On Monday evening Page and I were at Willis's house, and in the course of a conversation about Poe, Willis mentioned that you had written him a very pleasant letter about Poe, and enclosed something really handsome for Mrs. Clemm. 'I could not help thinking,' said Willis, 'that if Lowell had known what Poe wrote to me about him just previous to his death, he would hardly have been so liberal.'" " What a contemptible idea of me Willis must have," Lowell replied, " to think that anything Poe might say of me would make any difference in my feeling pity for his poor mother-in-law. I confess it does not raise my opinion of Willis. I knew before as well as I know now, that Poe must have been abusing me,

for he knew that ever since his conduct toward
you about the *Broadway Journal* I had thought
meanly of him. I think Willis would hardly care
to see some letters of Poe to me in which *he* is
spoken of. My 'pleasant letter' to W. was about
ten lines, rather less than more I fancy, and my
'generous donation' was five dollars! I particularly requested of him that it should be anonymous,
which I think a good principle, as it guards us
against giving from any unworthy motive. That
Willis should publish it at the street corners only
proves the truth of Swift's axiom that any man
may gain the reputation of generosity by £20 a
year spent judiciously."

When Hawthorne lost his place in the Salem
Custom House, Lowell with other of his friends
made active effort to set him on his feet. He wrote
to Mr. Duyckinck, 13 January, 1850: "Perhaps
you know that Hawthorne was last spring turned
out of an office which he held in the Salem Custom
House, and which was his sole support. He is
now, I learn, very poor, and some money has just
been raised for him by his friends in this neighborhood. Could not something be also done in New
York? I know that you appreciate him, and that
you will be glad to do anything in your power. I
take it for granted that you know personally all
those who would be most likely to give. I write
also to Mr. O'Sullivan, who is a friend of Hawthorne's, but am ignorant whether he is now in
New York. Of course Hawthorne is entirely ignorant that anything of the kind is going on, and

it would be better that ' a bird in the air ' should
seem to have carried the news to New York, and
that if anything be raised, it should go thence,
directly, as a spontaneous gift."

The money which Lowell and others collected
for Hawthorne was sent in the most anonymous
fashion through Mr. George S. Hillard, and Hawthorne acknowledged the gift in a letter which
moves one by its mingling of gratitude and humili-
ation. " I read your letter," he writes to Hillard,
" in the vestibule of the post office [at Salem] ;
and it drew — what my troubles never have — the
water to my eyes ; so that I was glad of the sharply
cold west wind that blew into them as I came
homeward, and gave them an excuse for being red
and bleared.

" There was much that was very sweet — and
something too that was very bitter — mingled with
that same moisture. It is sweet to be remembered
and cared for by one's friends — some of whom
know me for what I am, while others, perhaps,
know me only through a generous faith — sweet to
think that they deem me worth upholding in my
poor work through life. And it is bitter, nevertheless, to need their support. It is something
else besides pride that teaches me that ill-success
in life is really and justly a matter of shame. I
am ashamed of it, and I ought to be. The fault
of a failure is attributable — in a great degree at
least — to the man who fails. I should apply this
truth in judging of other men ; and it behooves
me not to shun its point or edge in taking it home

to my *own* heart.   Nobody has a right to live in
the world, unless he be strong and able, and applies his ability to good purpose.

" The money, dear Hillard, will smooth my path
for a long time to come. The only way in which
a man can retain his self-respect, while availing
himself of the generosity of his friends, is by making it an incitement to his utmost exertions, so
that he may not need their help again.   I shall
look upon it so — nor will shun any drudgery that
my hand shall find to do, if thereby I may win
bread."

Nearly four years later, when Hawthorne had
leapt into fame and prosperity after the publication of " The Scarlet Letter," he wrote again to
Hillard from Liverpool : " I herewith send you a
draft on Ticknor for the sum (with interest included) which was so kindly given me by unknown friends, through you, about four years ago.
I have always hoped and intended to do this,
from the first moment when I made up my mind
to accept the money.   It would not have been
right to speak of this purpose, before it was in my
power to accomplish it ; but it has never been out
of my mind for a single day, nor hardly, I think,
for a single working hour.   I am most happy that
this loan (as I may fairly call it, at this moment)
can now be repaid without the risk on my part of
leaving my wife and children utterly destitute.   I
should have done it sooner ; but I felt that it would
be selfish to purchase the great satisfaction for
myself, at any fresh risk to them.   We are not

rich, nor are we ever likely to be ; but the miserable pinch is over.

"The friends who were so generous to me must not suppose that I have not felt deeply grateful, nor that my delight at relieving myself from this pecuniary obligation is of any ungracious kind. I have been grateful all along, and am more so now than ever. This act of kindness did me an unspeakable amount of good ; for it came when I most needed to be assured that anybody thought it worth while to keep me from sinking. And it did me even greater good than this, in making me sensible of the need of sterner efforts than my former ones, in order to establish a right for myself to live and be comfortable. For it is my creed (and was so even at that wretched time) that a man has no claim upon his fellow creatures, beyond bread and water, and a grave, unless he can win it by his own strength or skill. But so much the kinder were those unknown friends whom I thank again with all my heart." [1]

Aside from his modest salary from the *Standard*, Lowell's income from his writings was meagre enough. In publishing his volumes of poetry, he appears to have been largely if not entirely at the expense of manufacture, and in the imperfectly organized condition of the book market at that time, he had himself to supervise arrangements for selling his volume of poems in New York. There

---

[1] These letters from Hawthorne were first printed in the London *Athenæum*, 10, 17 August, 1889, and have since been included in vol. xvii. of the *Old Manse Edition* of Hawthorne's writings.

are one or two hints that, after his release from
contributing to the *Standard*, he contemplated
some new editorial position, perhaps even meditated
a fresh periodical venture. At any rate, his friend
Briggs remonstrated with him, in a letter written
15 March, 1849 : " Don't, my dear friend, think
of selling yourself to a weekly or monthly periodical of any kind, except as a contributor *deo vo-
lente*. The drudgery of editorship would destroy
you, and bring you no profit. Make up your mind
resolutely to refuse any offers, let them be never
so tempting. In a mere pecuniary point of view,
it would be more profitable for you to sell your
writings where you could procure the best pay for
them; they will be worth more and more as your
wants grow." And in December, 1850, Emerson,
who was enlisting Hawthorne's interest in a new
magazine projected by Mr. George Bradburn,
" that impossible problem of a New England magazine," as he calls it, writes : " I told him to go to
Lowell, who had been for a year meditating the
like project."

It is possible that there was some plan for turning the *Massachusetts Quarterly Review* into a
brisker and more distinctly literary journal. At
any rate, Lowell, writing to Emerson 19 February,
1850, says : " The plan seems a little more forward.
I have seen Parker, who is as placable as the raven
down of darkness, and not unwilling to shift his
Old Man of the sea to other shoulders. Longfellow
also is toward, and talks in a quite Californian
manner of raising funds by voluntary subscription."

The *Massachusetts Quarterly*, which had been
started in 1847 as an organ of more progressive
thought than the *North American Review*, was
under the management of Theodore Parker, and
Lowell was evidently a welcome though not constant contributor, as this letter to the editor intimates : —

ELMWOOD, July 28, [1848].

MY DEAR SIR : — Do *you* know where parsons
go to who don't believe in original sin? I think
that your experience as an editor will bring you
nearer orthodoxy by convincing you of the total
depravity of contributors. I have no doubt that
the plague of booksellers was sent to punish authors
for their sins toward editors.

Your note was so illegible that I was unable to
make out that part of it in which you reproached
me for my remissness. I shall choose rather to
treasure it as containing I know not what commendations of my promptitude and punctuality. I
will have it framed and glazed and exhibit it to
editors inquiring my qualifications, as the enthusiastic testimony of the Rev. Theo. Parker, and fearlessly defy all detection.

I assure you that it is not my fault that I did
not send the enclosed [1] earlier. I have suffered all
this summer with a severe pain in the head, which
has entirely crippled me for a great part of the
time. It is what people call a *fullness* in the head,
but its effect is to produce an entire emptiness.

As it is, I am reluctant to send the article.

[1] An article on Landor.

I hardly know what is in it myself, but I am quite conscious that it is disjointed and wholly incomplete. I found it impossible to concentrate my mind upon it so as to give it any unity or entireness. Believe the writing it has worried me more than the not receiving it worried you.

I send it as to a man in a strait to whom *anything* will be useful. I throw it *quasi lignum naufrago*. If I had one of the cedarn columns of the temple, I would cast it overboard to you; but having only a shapeless log, I give you that, as being as useful to a drowning man as if it were already made into a Mercury.

I have, you see, given directions to the printer to copy "The Hamadryad." My copy is a borrowed one, and if you own one I should be obliged to you if you would send it to the printing-office, as your warning about not smutching, etc., would probably have more weight with your printers than mine. If you have no copy please let me know through the P. O. and I will send the one I have, as I have obtained permission to do.

I should like to see the proofs, and as I am going to New York on Monday next to be absent a week, I should like to have them sent to me there to the care of S. H. Gay, 142 Nassau St., if it should be necessary to print before I return. If there is too much hurry, will you be good enough to look at them yourself.

If the article seem too short for a Review, you are welcome to insert it among your literary notices, or to return it.

I must thank you before I close my note for the pleasure I received in reading a recent sermon of yours which I saw in the *Chronotype.* You have not so much mounted the pulpit as lifted it up to you.

Very truly your Eumenides-driven contributor,

J. R. L.[1]

The most substantial magazine in his own neighborhood was the *North American Review*, and to that, in his early period, Lowell contributed but half a dozen articles. It is partly characteristic of the manner of the heavy reviewing of the day, and wholly characteristic of Lowell, that in each of these cases quite two thirds of the article is taken up with prolegomena. Before he could settle down to an examination of "The New Timon," he must needs analyze at great length the quality of Pope, who had served as a sort of pattern : it is interesting, by the way, to note that in the last paragraph of his review, he guesses the book to have been written by Bulwer. So in reviewing Disraeli's "Tancred," he despatches the book itself somewhat summarily after a dozen pages of witty reflections on novel-writing. A review of Browning is more definitely an examination of this poet, with large extracts from "Luria," though it has the inevitable long introduction on poetry in

[1] In a note to T. W. Higginson, who proposed an article in the *Atlantic* on Parker, Lowell wrote 28 June, 1860 : " I think that folks have confounded (as they commonly do) *force* with *power* in estimating him, and so have overrated him."

general; but its appreciation and discriminating judgment of Browning at a time when " Sordello," " Paracelsus," and " Bells and Pomegranates " were the only poems and collection by which to measure him, indicate surely how direct and at first hand were Lowell's critical appraisals. " Above all," he says, after a glowing rehearsal of the contents of " Bells and Pomegranates," " his personages are not mere mouthpieces for the author's idiosyncrasies. We take leave of Mr. Browning at the end of ' Sordello,' and except in some shorter lyrics see no more of him. His men and women *are* men and women, and not Mr. Browning masquerading in different colored dominoes : " and in the same article occurs a passage which might lead one to think Lowell was musing over his own qualities : " Wit makes other men laugh, and that only once. It may be repeated indefinitely to new audiences and produce the same result. Humor makes the humorist himself laugh. He is a part of his humor, and it can never be repeated without loss."

In the more substantial literary criticism of his maturity Lowell occupied himself mainly with the great names of world literature, but at this time he was especially intent on his contemporaries in America and England, and he was keenly alive to manifestations of spirit which gave evidence of transcending the bounds of local reputation. In a review of Longfellow's " Kavanagh " he made the book really only a peg from which to hang a long disquisition upon nationality in literature, a subject which, it will be remembered, receives considerable

attention in the book. Lowell's own conclusion
is that " Nationality is only a less narrow form of
provincialism, a sublimer sort of clownishness and
ill manners."

It was with the heartiest good - will that he
welcomed Thoreau's " Week on the Concord and
Merrimack Rivers," just after the publication of
that book. As in his other reviews of this period, he must needs preface his consideration of
the book itself with some general remarks on
travellers, which he liked well enough to preserve
in his " Leaves from my Journal in Italy and Elsewhere," published in " Fireside Travels ; " but the
main part of his article is a generous appreciation
of Thoreau's faculty of insight into the things of
nature. " A graduate of Cambridge, — the fields
and woods, the axe, the hoe, and the rake have since
admitted him *ad eundem.* Mark how his imaginative sympathy goes beneath the crust, deeper down
than that of Burns, and needs no plough to turn
up the object of its muse." He makes, however, a
clear distinction between Thoreau the observer and
man of reflection and Thoreau the bookman. " As
long as he continues an honest Boswell, his book is
delightful ; but sometimes he serves his two rivers
as Hazlitt did Northcote, and makes them run
Thoreau or Emerson, or, indeed, anything but their
own transparent element. What, for instance, have
Concord and Merrimack to do with Boodh, themselves professors of an elder and to them wholly
sufficient religion, namely, the willing subjects of
watery laws, to seek their ocean ? We have digres-

sions on Boodh, on Anacreon (with translations
hardly so good as Cowley), on Perseus, on Friendship, and we know not what. We come upon them
like snags, jolting us headforemost out of our
places as we are rowing placidly up stream, or
drifting down. Mr. Thoreau becomes so absorbed
in these discussions that he seems, as it were, to
catch a crab, and disappears uncomfortably from
his seat at the bow-oar. We could forgive them
all, especially that on Books, and that on Friendship (which is worthy of one who has so long com-
merced with Nature and with Emerson), we could
welcome them all, were they put by themselves at
the end of the book. But as it is, they are out of
proportion and out of place, and mar our Merri-
macking dreadfully. We were bid to a river-party,
not to be preached at. They thrust themselves
obtrusively out of the narrative, like those quarries
of red glass which the Bowery dandies (emulous of
Sisyphus) push laboriously before them as breast-
pins." He finds fault with Thoreau for some of
his verse, but regards with admiration his prose.
" The style is compact, and the language has an
antique purity like wine grown colorless with age."
Lowell expressed the same admiration for Thoreau's style when he wrote again about him a dozen
years later, after re-reading his books, but his
point of view had by that time changed, and he
was more concerned to look into Thoreau's philosophy of life.

The article on Landor, written at this time, was
quite exclusively an examination of the genius of a

writer for whom he had long had a great admiration; and inasmuch as he had himself tried the form of conversation, it is worth while to note the excellent judgment he passes on Landor's art. "Of his 'Imaginary Conversations' we may generally say that they would be better defined as dialogues between the imaginations of the persons introduced than between the persons themselves. There is a something in all men and women who deserve the much-abused title of *individuals*, which we call their character, something finer than the man or woman, and yet which *is* the man or woman nevertheless. We feel it in whatever they say or do, but it is better than their speech or deed, and can be conceived of apart from these. It is his own conceptions of the characters of different personages that Landor brings in as interlocutors. Between Shakespeare's historical and ideal personages we perceive no difference in point of reality. They are alike historical to us. We allow him to substitute his Richard for the Richard of history, and we suspect that those are few who doubt whether Caliban ever existed. Whatever Hamlet and Cæsar say we feel to be theirs, though we know it to be Shakespeare's. Whatever Landor puts into the mouth of Pericles and Michael Angelo and Tell, we know to be his, though we can conceive that it might have been theirs. Don Quixote would never have attacked any puppets of his. The hand which jerked the wires, and the mouth which uttered the speeches would have been too clearly visible." Here again it is interesting to take up

the reminiscences of Landor and of his own early
acquaintance with his writings, which he printed in
1888, when introducing a group of Landor's letters ;
for the comparison shows that though his enthusiasm for this writer had somewhat abated with
years, the general tone of his judgment was the
same.

The article on Landor was a deferred one. It
was to have been written for the June number of
the *Massachusetts Quarterly Review*, but did not
appear till December. His child's sickness and
work on the " Biglow Papers " drove other things
out of his head. Indeed, as he wrote rapidly when
he was moved to write at all, so he was afflicted
with obstinate inertia when ideas did not come
spontaneously. " I am again a delinquent," he
wrote to Gay, 25 November, 1848, — " and this
time I am ashamed to say, out of pure laziness and
having nothing to write about. But my next article
I intend to write on Tuesday, so that you will be
sure of it in time. Do forgive me this once more,
and forgive also (if you can) the stupidity of my
contribution. I feel like a squeezed turnip on which
the experiment of extracting blood has been tried.
I am haunted, like Barnaby Rudge's father, with
the sound of a *Bell*, not having sent anything yet
to that horrible annual.[1] Upon my word I am
almost crazy with it. I have not an idea in my
head, and believe firmly that I never shall have
one again. And I obtained a reprieve ending a
week ago last Friday ! "

[1] *The Liberty Bell.*

But if he groaned thus over writing for publication, he was lavish of criticism and what might
be called material for literature, when writing to
his friends.   The letters which Mr. Norton prints,
dated in this period, abound in felicitous comment
on men and incidents, and even a postscript will
sometimes ramble on into the dimensions almost of
a separate letter.   After indulging in a long epistle
to Mr. Briggs, dated 12 May, 1848, he suddenly
remembers that he means to send some poems of his
wife's for a collection which Griswold was making
of the writings of the female poets of America ; and
after some lively comments on her contemporaries,
he takes note of articles recently written by Briggs,
and falls into a strain which he has disclosed elsewhere in somewhat similar terms : " You are wrong
and N. P. W. is right (as I think) in the main, in
what he says about American Society.   There is as
striking a want of external as of internal culture
among our men.   We ought to have produced the
finest race of *gentlemen* in the world.   But Europeans have laughed us into a nation of snobs.   We
are ashamed of our institutions.   Our literature
aims to convince Europe that America is as conservative and respectable as herself.   I have often
remarked that educated Americans have the least
dignified bearing of any cultivated people.   They
all stoop in the shoulders, intellectually as well as
physically.   A nation of freemen, we alone of all
others have the gait of slaves.   The great power of
the English aristocracy lies in their polish.   That
impresses the great middle class, who have a sort of

dim conception of its value. A man gains in *power*
as he gains in ease. It is a great advantage to him
to be cultivated in all parts of his nature. Among
scholars, R. W. E. has as fine a manner, as much
poise, as I ever saw. Yet I have seen him quite
dethroned by a pure man of the world. His face
degenerated into a puzzled state. I go so far as to
believe that all great men have felt the importance
of the outward and visible impression they should
produce. Socrates was as wise as Plato, indeed he
was Plato's master, but Plato dressed better, and
has the greater name. Pericles was the first gentleman of Greece, — not the George IV. though,
exactly. Remember Cæsar's laurel-wig.

" I might multiply instances, but I wish to have
room to say how much I have been pleased with
Thackeray's ' Vanity Fair.' He has not Dickens's
talents as a caricaturist, but he draws with more
truth. Dickens can take a character to pieces and
make us laugh immoderately at the comic parts of
it — or he takes only the comic part, as boys take
the honey-bag of the bee, destroying the whole in-
sect to get at it. But Thackeray can put a character
together. He has more constructive power. D. is
a satirizer, T. a satirist. I don't think D. ever made
anything equal to Becky Sharp. Rawdon Craw-
ley, too, is admirable ; so in truth are all the characters in their way, except Amelia, who is nothing
in particular.

" I liked ' Wuthering Heights,' too, as you did,
though not so much. There is great power in it, but
it is like looking at nature through a crooked pane

of glass. Some English journalist has nicknamed
the author Salvator Rosa, and our journalists of
course all repeat it. But it is nonsense. For it
is not wildness and rudeness that the author is
remarkable for, but delicacy. A character may be
distorted without being wild or rude. Unnatural
causes may crook a violet as well as an oak. Ro-
chester is a truly refined character, and his rough-
ness and coarseness are only the shields (scabs, as
it were) over his finer nature. My sheet ends our
conversation."

There is a picture of the Lowells at home at this
time, drawn by Miss Fredrika Bremer. Lowell
had reviewed her writings in their English dress
— it was his first contribution to the *North American*, — and on her coming to America a meeting
occurred, which resulted in a friendly visit paid
by Miss Bremer to Elmwood. The form in which
she recorded her impressions of travel was in letters home, afterward gathered into a book. It
was on 15 December, 1849, that she wrote : —

"The whole family assembles every day for
morning and evening prayer around the venerable old man ; and he it is who blesses every meal.
His prayers, which are always extempore, are full
of the true and inward life, and I felt them as a
pleasant, refreshing dew upon my head, and seldom
arose from my knees with dry eyes. With him
live his youngest son, the poet, and his wife ; such
a handsome and happy young couple as one can
hardly imagine. He is full of life and youthful
ardor, she as gentle, as delicate, and as fair as a

lily, and one of the most lovable women that I
have seen in this country, because her beauty is
full of soul and grace, as is everything which she
does or says. This young couple belong to the
class of those of whom one can be quite sure; one
could not for an hour, nay, not for half an hour, be
doubtful about them. She, like him, has a poetical tendency, and has also written anonymously
some poems, remarkable for their deep and tender
feeling, especially maternal, but her mind has more
philosophical depth than his. Singularly enough,
I did not discern in him that deeply earnest spirit
which charmed me in many of his poems. He
seems to me occasionally to be brilliant, witty,
gay, especially in the evening, when he has what
he calls his 'evening fever,' and his talk is then
like an incessant play of fireworks. I find him
very agreeable and amiable; he seems to have
many friends, mostly young men. . . . There is a
trace of beauty and taste in everything she [Mrs.
L.] touches, whether of mind or body; and above
all she beautifies life. . . . Pity it is that this
much-loved young wife seems to have delicate
lungs. Her low, weak voice tells of this. [Madame
Lowell was plainly not at home.] Maria reads
her husband's poetry charmingly well." [1]

Near the close of 1849 Lowell reissued in two
volumes, under the imprint of W. D. Ticknor &
Co., the two series which had appeared in 1843

[1] *The Homes of the New World: Impressions of America.* By
Fredrika Bremer. New York: Harper & Bros. 1853. Vol. i.
pp. 130, 131.

and 1847, and thus registered himself, as it were,
among the regular vine-growers on the slopes of
Parnassus. Moreover, with his former products
thus formally garnered, he began to please himself
with the prospect of some more thoroughgoing
piece of poetical composition. He was practically
clear of his regular engagement with the *Standard*, and his " Biglow Papers " had given him the
opportunity to free his mind in an exhilarating
fashion on the supreme question of the hour.
There was something of a rebound from this in
" The Vision of Sir Launfal," but the free use of
the Yankee vernacular with the immediate popularity which it secured must have set him thinking of the possibility of using this form in some
freer and more genuinely poetic fashion. The little
pastoral, " The Courtin'," published in a fragmentary form, was an experiment in this direction at
once highly successful, and accordingly we find
him writing to Mr. Briggs on the eve of the publication of his two volumes of Poems: " I think
you will find my poems improved in the new edition. I have not altered much, but I have left out
the poorest and put others in their places. My
next volume, I think, will show an advance. It is
to be called ' The Nooning.' Now guess what it
will be. The name suggests pleasant thoughts,
does it not? But I shall not tell you anything
about it yet, and you must not mention it." And
a few weeks later, with the project still high in his
mind, he wrote to the same correspondent: " Maria
invented the title for me, and is it not a pleasant

one? I am going to bring together a party of half
a dozen old friends at Elmwood. They go down
to the river and bathe, and then one proposes that
they shall go up into a great willow-tree (which
stands at the end of the causey near our house,
and has seats in it) to take their nooning. There
they agree that each shall tell a story or recite a
poem of some sort. In the tree they find a coun-
tryman already resting himself, who enters into
the plan and tells a humorous tale, with touches of
Yankee character and habits in it. *I* am to read
my poem of the 'Voyage of Leif' to Vinland, in
which I mean to bring my hero straight into Boston Bay, as befits a Bay-state poet. Two of my
poems are already written — one 'The Fountain of
Youth' (no connection with any other firm), and
the other an 'Address to the Muse' by the Transcendentalist of the party. I guess I am safe in
saying that the first of these two is the best thing
I have done yet. But you shall judge when you
see it. But 'Leif's Voyage' is to be far better."
The scheme thus formed intended clearly a group
of poems lightly tied together: indeed the plan,
always a favorite one, was carried out on very
nearly the same lines by Mr. Longfellow in his
"Tales of a Wayside Inn" a dozen years later,
and it is not impossible that Lowell, who had been
interrupted in his plan, was still more reluctant to
complete it, when it would have so much the air
of being a copy of his neighbor's design. At any
rate, the *disjecta membra* of the poem found publication in a straggling fashion. Writing to Mr.

J. B. Thayer, in reply to an inquiry about the poem, years after, Lowell says : " ' The June Idyl ' [renamed ' Under the Willows '] (written in '51 or '52) is a part of what I had written as the induction to it. The description of spring in one of the ' Biglow Papers ' is another fragment of the same, tagged with rhyme for the nonce. So is a passage in ' Mason and Slidell,' beginning ' Oh strange new world.' The ' Voyage to Vinland,' the ' Pictures from Appledore,' and ' Fitz-Adam's Story ' were written for the ' Nooning ' as originally planned. So, you see, I had made some progress. Perhaps it will come by and by — not in the shape I meant at first, for something broke my life in two, and I cannot piece it together again. Besides, the Muse asks *all* of a man, and for many years I have been unable to give myself up as I would." To this list should be added " Fragments of an Unfinished Poem," which was printed in the author's final Riverside edition, when he had abandoned all thought of completing the " Nooning."

That Lowell was conscious of his vocation by this time, and that with the publication of his collected poems he was entering upon a new, resolute course of poetic action, is clear from a few pregnant sentences in a letter to Briggs, dated 23 January, 1850 : " My poems hitherto have been a true record of my life, and I mean that they shall continue to be. . . . I begin to feel that I must enter on a new year of my apprenticeship. My poems have thus far had a regular and natural sequence. First, Love and the mere happiness of

existence beginning to be conscious of itself, then
Freedom — both being the sides which Beauty presented to me — and now I am going to try more
wholly after Beauty herself. Next, if I live, I
shall present Life as I have seen it. In the
'Nooning' I shall have not even a glance towards
Reform. If the poems I have already written are
good for anything they are perennial, and it is
tedious as well as foolish to repeat one's self. I
have preached sermons enow, and now I am going
to come down out of the pulpit and *go about
among my parish*. I shall turn my barrel over
and read my old discourses ; it will be time to
write new ones when my hearers have sucked all
the meaning out of those old ones. Certainly I
shall not grind for any Philistines, whether Reformers or Conservatives. I find that Reform
cannot take up the whole of me, and I am quite
sure that eyes were given us to look about us with
sometimes, and not to be always looking forward.
If some of my good red-hot friends were to see
this they would call me a backslider, but there are
other directions in which one may get away from
people besides the rearward one. . . . I am not
certain that my next appearance will not be in a
pamphlet on the Hungarian question in answer to
the *North American Review*. But I shall not
write anything if I can help it. I am tired of controversy, and, though I have cut out the oars with
which to row up my friend Bowen, yet I have
enough to do, and, besides, am not so well as usual,
being troubled in my head as I was summer before

last. I should like to play for a year, and after I
have written and printed the ' Nooning ' I mean to
take a nooning and lie under the trees looking at
the skies."

The Hungarian movement interested both Lowell
and his sister, Mrs. Putnam, deeply. Lowell had
printed in the *Standard* his verses to Kossuth,
and Mrs. Putnam had written vigorously in the
Christian Examiner. Robert Carter also printed
a series of papers on the subject in the *Boston
Atlas*, which were reprinted in a pamphlet. Lowell did not write the pamphlet he meditated, but a
year later he wrote seven columns in the *Boston
Daily Advertiser*, in defence of his sister against
Professor Bowen's attack. " It was the severest
job I ever undertook," he wrote Gay. " I believe
I was longer at work in actual hours than in writing all Hosea Biglow and the ' Fable for Critics.' "
He had displayed his interest previously by a stirring appeal for funds in aid of the Hungarian
exiles.[1]

And now came three events to the little household at Elmwood that wrought a change in the life
of Lowell and his wife. The first was the death of
their third child, Rose, 2 February, 1850, after a
half-year's life only. The loss brought vividly to
remembrance the experience which had entered so
deeply into their lives when the first-born, Blanche,
was taken away. " For Rose," Lowell writes to
Gay, " I would have no funeral; my father only
made a prayer, and then I walked up alone to

[1] See *Boston Courier*, 3 January, 1850.

Mount Auburn and saw her body laid by her sister's. She was a very lovely child — we think the loveliest of our three. She was more like Blanche than Mabel, and her disease was the same. Her illness lasted a week, but I never had any hope, so that she died to me the first day the doctor came. She was very beautiful — fair, with large dark gray eyes and fine features. Her smile was especially charming, and she was full of smiles till her sickness began. Dear little child! she had never spoken, only smiled."

Again death came that way, and on 30 March, 1850, Lowell's mother died. The cloud which had for years hung over her had deepened, and her death was looked upon as a release, for whether at home or in seclusion she was alike separated from her family. As Lowell wrote : —

> " We can touch thee, still we are no nearer;
> Gather round thee, still thou art alone;
> The wide chasm of reason is between us;
> Thou confutest kindness with a moan;
> We can speak to thee, and thou canst answer,
> Like two prisoners through a wall of stone." [1]

The third event was the birth of the fourth child and only son, Walter. Gay had lately lost a boy, and Lowell's announcement to him of this birth was tempered by the fact. " I should have written you a note the other day," he writes, 3 January, 1851, " to let you know that we have a son, only I could not somehow make up my mind to it. It pained me to think of the associations which such

[1] " The Darkened Mind."

news would revive in you. Yet I had rather you should hear it from me than from any one else. . . . The boy is a nice little fellow, and said (by his mother) to look like me. He was born on the 22d December, and I am doubting whether to name him Pilgrim Father or no. I have offered Maria her choice between that name and Larkin, which last I think would go uncommonly well with Lowell. She has not yet made up her mind.

" But now for the tragic part of it. Just after we had got him cleverly born on the 22d, there springs me up an Antiquary (like a Jack in a box) and asserts that the Pilgrims landed on the 21st, that eleven days were added instead of ten in allowing for O. S., and that there is no use in disputing about it. But I appeal to any sensible person (I have no reference to antiquaries) whether, as applied to Larkin, this decision be not of the nature of an *ex post facto* law, by which he, the said Larkin, ought not of right to be concluded. What was he to know of it in his retirement, with no access to reading-rooms or newspapers ? Inheriting from his father a taste for anniversaries, no doubt he laid his plans with deliberation, and is he now to give up his birthright for a mess of antiquarian pottage ? Had proper notice been given, he would surely have bestirred himself to have arrived a day earlier. On the whole I shall advise Larkin to contest the point. For my part, I shall stick to the 22d, though it upset the whole Gregorian calendar, which to me, indeed, smacks a little too strongly of the Scarlet Woman. Would

Mrs. Charles Lowell

not the Pilgrim Fathers have sworn to the 22d, if they had known that ever a Pope of Rome would go for the 21st? Surely the Babe Unborn should not suffer for the want of accurate astronomical knowledge in them of old time. That other mythological character, the Oldest Inhabitant, should rather be held responsible as approaching nearer to a contemporaneousness with the guilty. However, till this matter is settled, I shall keep it to myself whether the 21st or the 22d were the day of his kindly nativity." [1]

Lowell had been longing for a holiday; Mrs. Lowell's health, never robust, gave him now new cause of solicitude; the death of his mother severed one special cord that would tie him to his home, and thus, in the spring of 1851, it was decided to carry out a design formed more than once before, and spend a year at least in Europe. The Lowells tried to persuade the Gays to accompany them, but without success. "We are going," Lowell wrote to Gay, "in a fine ship which will sail from Boston on the 1st July. She was built for a packet, has fine accommodations, and will land us at Genoa — a very fit spot for us New-Worlders to land at and make our first discovery of the Old.

> À Castilla y à Leon
> (To Yankees also be it known)

[1] Whether or no this started Mr. Gay on an historical investigation, he did inquire into the matter; for thirty years later he published in the *Atlantic* for November, 1881, an article entitled, "When did the Pilgrim Fathers land at Plymouth?" in which he established to his own satisfaction that the first landing was neither on the 21st or 22d, but on the 4th of January, 1621.

Nuevo Mundo dió Colon :
And so we Western men owe a
Kind of debt to Genoa.

Also people can live like princes (only more re-
spectably) in Italy on fifteen hundred a year. We
are going to travel on our own land. That is, we
shall spend at the rate of about ten acres a year,
selling our birthrights as we go along for messes
of European pottage. Well, Raphael and the rest
of them are worth it. My plan is to sit down in
Florence (where, at least, the coral and bells and
the gutta-percha dogs will be cheaper) till I have
cut my eye (talian) teeth. *Tuscany* must be a
good place for that. Then I shall be able to travel
about without being too monstrously cheated."

CHAPTER VII

FIFTEEN MONTHS IN EUROPE

1851–1852

MR. AND MRS. LOWELL, their two children, a nurse, and a goat sailed from Boston, Saturday, 12 July, 1851, in the barque Sultana, Watson, master, which went to the Mediterranean and dropped the little party at Malta. " We had a very good run from land to land," Lowell wrote his father a few days before reaching Malta, " making the light at Cape St. Vincent on the night of the seventeenth day out. I stayed upon deck until we could see the light, — the cape we did not see at all, nor any land till the next morning. Then we saw the coast of Spain very dim and blue, — only the outline of a mountain and some high land here and there. The day before we made land we had a tolerably good specimen of a gale of wind, enough at any rate to get up so much sea that we were in danger of having our lee quarter boat washed away, the keel of which hangs above the level of the poop deck. As it was we lost the covering of one of our port-holes, which was knocked out by the water which was swashing about on the lower deck.

" I was the only one of the party at table that day, and there was an amount of vivacity among

the dishes such as I never saw before. I took my
soup by the process of absorption, the whole of it
having suddenly leaped out of my plate into my
lap. The table was literally at an angle of 45° all
the time, with occasional eccentricities of the hori-
zontal and the perpendicular, every change of level
(or dip rather) being accomplished with a sudden
jerk, which gave us a fine opportunity for studying the force of projectiles. Imagine the Captain,
the First Mate, and myself at every one of these
sudden hiccoughs (as it were) of the vessel, each
endeavoring to think that he has six hands and
finding too late that he has only two, during which
interval between doubt and certainty, I have seen
the contents of three dishes, A B C, change places,
A taking the empty space left by B, B in like
manner ejecting C, and C very naturally, having
nowhere else to go, is thrown loose upon society
and leads a nomadic life, first upon the tablecloth,
then upon the seat, then upon the floor, every new
position being a degradation, until at last it finds
precarious lodging in one of the lee staterooms.
You find your legs in a permanent condition of
drunkenness, and that without any of the previous
exhilaration. The surface of the country is such as
I never saw described in any geographical work;
the only thing at all approaching it which I have
met with was the state of affairs during the great
earthquake at Lisbon. You have just completed
your arrangements for descending an inclined
plane, when you find yourself climbing an almost
perpendicular precipice, the surface of which being,

by a curious freak of nature, of painted floor-cloth, renders your foothold quite precarious.   It is like nothing but a nightmare.

" Mabel was very sick, and her only comfort was to lie in my berth and take ' strange food ' (which she immediately returned again) through a spoon which opens in a very mysterious and interesting manner out of the handle of a knife which John Holmes gave me the day we sailed.[1] However, she was up again the next day, and has continued most devoted in her attendance at table, not to speak of little supernumerary lunches of crackers and toast which she contrives to extract from the compassion of the steward or cook.   The galley is a favorite place of resort for her, to which she retires as one would to a summer-house, and where, inhaling the fumes from a cooking-stove of a very warm temperament, she converses with the cook (as well as I can learn) on cosmography, and picks up little separate bits of geography like disjointed fragments of several different dissected maps.   With what extraordinary and thrilling narratives she repays him I can only guess, but I heard her this morning assuring Mary that she had seen two rats, one red and the other blue, running about the cabin.   Indeed, her theories on the subject of

[1] In another letter written on shipboard, Lowell refers to the gift thus : " I held it in especial esteem because it was given in a way so characteristic of John, who sidled up to me as if he were asking a favor instead of doing one, and having slipped it into my hand in a particularly let-not-your-right-hand-know-what-your-left-hand-doeth kind of manner, instantly vanished and remained absconded for half an hour."

natural history correspond with that era of the
science when Goldsmith wrote his ' Animated Nature.' She cultivates her vocal powers by singing
'Jeannette and Jeannot' with extraordinary vigor,
and with a total irrecognition of the original air,
which may arise from some hereditary contempt of
the French. She assists regularly at ' 'bouting
ship,' as she calls it, standing at the wheel with
admirable gravity. The Captain always takes the
wheel and issues the orders when the ship is put
about, and as this ceremony has taken place pretty
regularly every few hours for the last eight days,
Mabel has acquired all the requisite phrases. At
intervals during the day, a shrill voice may be
heard crying out, ' 'Bout ship!' ' Mainsail ha-u-l!'
'Tacks and sheets!' ' Let go and ha-u-ll,' the
whole prefixed by an exceedingly emphatic ' Ha-a-
a-rd a lee !! ' There is no part of the vessel except
the hold and the rigging which she has not repeatedly inspected. With all the sailors she is on
intimate terms, and employs them at odd hours in
the manufacture of various articles of furniture.
. . . Nannie has been a constant source of interest
and amusement to Mabel, who climbs up to visit
her every day fifty times at least, and gives her
little handfuls of hay and oats which Nannie seems
to eat with a particular relish."

The humorous account of the chief mate which
occurs in the section " In the Mediterranean," in
" Leaves from my Journal," is taken from a full
and lively letter written by Lowell a few days later
on shipboard to his brother-in-law, Dr. Estes Howe.

By that time they were off Tunis. " Perhaps the
finest thing we have seen," he writes to Dr. Howe,
"was the first view of the African coast, which was
Cape Espartel in Morocco. There were five mountains in the background, the highest being as tall
as the Catskills, but the outlines much sharper and
grander. They were heaped together as we saw
the Adirondacks from Burlington. We were a
whole day and half the night in beating through
the Straits of Gibraltar, and had very fine views of
the shores on both sides. The little Spanish town
of Tarifa had a great charm for me, lying under a
mountain opposite the Moorish coast, with its now
useless walls all around it. The fires of the char-
coal burners on the mountains were exceedingly
picturesque, especially at night, when they gave to
some dozen peaks on both sides the aspect of vol-
canoes. Apes Hill, opposite the rock of Gibraltar,
is higher and more peculiar in its forms than the
rock itself. In some views it is almost a perfect
cone, and again, some of the lower peaks, when you
can catch their individual outlines, are pyramidal.
After getting through the Straits, we kept along
the Spanish coast, with very light winds and a new
moon, as far as Cape de Gat. We were four days
in making these 150 miles (we ran 280 miles in
one day on the Atlantic). All along there were
noble mountains, with here and there a little white
town sprinkled along their bases on the edge of the
water like the grains of rice which the girl dropped
in the fairy tale. Sometimes you see larger buildings on the slope of the mountain, which seem to

be convents. All are white except the watch-tow-
ers, which you see now and then on points, and
these are commonly of a soft brown, the color of
the stone. The hues of the mountains at sunset
and just after were exquisite. The nearer ones
were of a deep purple, and I now understand what
was meant by the Mediterranean atmosphere." . . .

The travellers made a brief halt at Malta,
whence they took steamer to Naples, and from
there went by rail to Florence. There they stayed,
living in the Via Maggio, from the 26th of August
to the 30th of October. Neither in his letters nor
in the sketches which he afterward published
under the title of "Leaves from my Journal in
Italy and Elsewhere" can one find more than a
slight record of Lowell's sojourn in a city which
was especially endeared to him by that study of
Dante which had been his real introduction to the
great world. "I liked my Florentine better than
my Roman walks," he said ; "apart from any difference in the men, I had a far deeper emotion
when I stood on the *Sasso di Dante*, than at Horace's Sabine farm, or by the tomb of Virgil ;"[1] for
he found it harder "to bridge over the gulf of
Paganism than of centuries," and the marked individuality of mediæval Italian towns attracted
him all the more for their being modern and Christian. In Florence there was an added pleasure in
the companionship of Mr. and Mrs. Frank Shaw,
and in the society of William Page.

In a letter to Mr. John Holmes, written from

[1] *Leaves from my Journal, Works,* i. 213.

Rome half a year later, Lowell writes : " Once when I was in Florence, Page and Shaw and I took a walk out of the city to see a famous *Cenacolo* of Andrea del Sarto in the refectory of a suppressed convent, about a mile and a half outside the Porta Santa Croce. We took a roundabout course among the hills, going first to Galileo's tower, and then to that of the old Church of San Miniato which Michelangelo defended. Thence we descended steeply toward the Arno, crossed it by a ferry-boat, and then found ourselves opposite a *trattoria*. It was a warm October day, and we unanimously turned in at the open door. There were three rooms, one upstairs, where one might dine 'more obscurely and courageously,' the kitchen, and the room in which we were. As I sat upon the corner of the bench, I looked out through some grape-trailers which hung waving over the door, and saw first the Arno, then, beyond it a hill on which stood a villa with a garden laid out in squares with huge walls of box and a clump of tall black cypresses in the middle, then, to the right of this, the ruined tower of San Miniato, and beyond it that from which Milton had doubtless watched the moon rising 'o'er the top of Fesole.' This was my landscape. Behind me was the kitchen. The cook in his white linen cap was stirring alternately a huge cauldron of soup and a pan of sausages, which exploded into sudden flame now and then, as if by spontaneous combustion. A woman wound up at short intervals a jack which turned three or four chickens before the fire, and attended a kind of lake of hot fat in which countless tiny fishes darted, squirmed, and turned topsy-turvy in a way so much more active and with an expression of so much more enjoyment than is wont to characterize living fish, that you would have said they had now for the first time found their element, and were created to revel in boiling oil. The wine sold here was the produce of the vineyard which you could see behind and on each side of the little *trattoria*. We had a large loaf of bread, and something like a quart and a half of pure cool wine for nine of our cents. During the whole time I was in Florence, though I never saw any one drink water, I also never saw a single drunken man, except some Austrian soldiers, and only four of these — two of them officers. In Rome, also, drunkenness is exceedingly rare, but less so, I think, than in Florence. Here you see everywhere the sign, *Spaccio d' Acqua Vitœ*. In Florence I never remember to have seen spirits advertised for sale, except by those who dealt in the wants of the *Forestieri*."

Just before leaving the city for Rome, Lowell was filled with consternation at a letter received from home, telling him that his father had been stricken with paralysis. His first impulse was to take his family to Rome and then return at once to America, but a little reflection showed him how useless this would be. "I should never have left home," he wrote his father from Pisa, where they had halted on their way to Leghorn, "if I had not thought that you wished it, or rather wished that we should have been abroad and got back. I hope to find a letter awaiting us at Rome. But at any rate we shall come home as soon as we can. I hardly know what I am writing, for I have just got word from Mr. Black at Leghorn, saying that our places are engaged on board the steamer for Civita Vecchia, and that we must be there as soon as possible in the morning. I am going on in the early train, leaving Maria to come at one o'clock with a servant from the hotel. It is now between nine and ten, and the rain still falls heavily. I fear a bad day to-morrow, and what with that and thinking about you and home, my mind is confused. I find nothing abroad which, after being seen, would tempt me away from Elmwood again. I enjoy the Art here, but I shall equally enjoy it there in the retrospect. I wish some of the buildings were on the other side of the water, but I suppose we should be more contented not to see them if they were."

The voyage by steamer to Civita Vecchia was a very rough one, occupying five days instead of the eleven hours in which it sometimes was made. A letter from Dr. Howe was received a few days after the Lowells reached Rome, which gave more exact account of Dr. Lowell's illness and left little hope of anything like permanent restoration. "Had it been possible," Lowell replied to his brother-in-law, "I should have come home at once. But I could neither leave Maria here, nor safely expose her to the inclemencies of a winter passage across the Atlantic. There is nothing for it, but to hope and pray. But the thought that I have no right

to be here casts a deeper shadow over everything
in the dreary city of ruin and of an activity that is
more sad than ruin itself. The dear Elmwood that
has always looked so sunny in my memory comes
now between me and the sun, and the long shadow
of its eclipse follows and falls upon me everywhere.
It is a wonderful satisfaction to me now to feel that
that dear Father and I have been so much at one
and have been sources of so much happiness to
each other for so many years."

The entrance into Rome is thus described in a
letter to Miss Maria Fay : —

" It has been raining fast, but as we approach
Rome, winding up and down among the hills and
hollows of the Campagna between high stone walls,
the clouds break and the moon shines out with supreme clearness. The tall reeds which lean over
the road here and there glisten like steel, wet as
they still are with the rain. The orange-trees have
all silver leaves, and even the dark laurels and
cypresses glitter. It is like an enchanted garden
of the Arabian Nights. Presently we overtake
other lumbering diligences (we are *posting* and
have done the thirty-five miles from Civita Vecchia
in ten hours), and rattling through the gate are
stopped by cocked-hatted officials, who demand
passports. Opposite are the high walls of the In-
quisition. We are in Rome. One ought to have
a sensation, and one has. It is that of chill. One
climbs stiffly down from the coupé, and stamps
about with short-skirted and long-booted postilions
whose huge spurs are clanking in every direction.

Very soon we, being armed with a *lascia passare*, — there are three coach loads of us, — drive off, leaving four other loads behind still wrangling and jangling with the cocked hats. As we rattle away, the light from the window of the *uffizio di polizia* gleams upon the musket of a blue overcoated French soldier marching to and fro on guard. Five minutes more rattle and the Dome glistens silverly in the moonlight, and the Titanic colonnade marches solemnly by us in ranks without end. Then a glimpse of feathery fountains, a turn to the right, a strip of gloomy street, a sudden turn to the left, and we are on the bridge of St. Angelo. Bernini's angels polk gayly on their pedestals with the emblems of the Passion in their arms, and by wringing your neck you may see behind you on the left the huge castle refusing to be comforted by the moonlight, with its triumphant archangel just alighting on its summit. Another sharp turn to the left, and you are in a black slit of street again, which at last, after half a mile of unsavoriness, becomes the Corso, the main street of modern Rome. And everything thus far is palpably modern, especially the Hotel d'Angleterre, at which we presently alight. Next day we remove to lodgings already engaged for us by F. Boott, near the Pincio, in the highest part of the city. Here we manage to be comfortable through a month of never-ceasing rain. Then it clears, and we have a month of cloudless sunshine, with roses blooming in the gardens and daisies in the fields. To-day is the first rainy day, and I devote it to you."

The Lowells had their quarters at Capo le Case,
No. 68, on the third *piano*, and were surrounded
by a few English and American friends. Mr. and
Mrs. Story were not in Rome when they first arrived, but joined them in about a fortnight, when
the rains had ceased at last and so permitted walks
in the Campagna. The first part of their stay had
been dreary enough, and drew from Lowell the
whimsical remark: " Sometimes as I look from the
Pincian, I think that the best thing about [mod-
ern Rome] is that the hills look like Brighton."
And Mrs. Lowell draws a humorous picture of her
husband, and their half homesick feelings, when
she writes: " Through Mr. Black we have the
English journals and papers, and it really gives
me a little home feeling when I see a bundle of
Examiners and *Athenæums* brought in just as
they used to be from Mr. Wells's, and see James
selecting his cigar with particular satisfaction and
giving the fire an express arrangement, and then
drawing up his chair to it and putting his feet on
the fender, beginning to read."

The anxiety, also, which Lowell felt over his
father's illness benumbed his faculties and made
him restless ; but with fair weather, better news
came, and the travellers gave themselves up more
unreservedly to the pleasures which the great city
afforded them. But Rome does not thrill one from
the start. It takes time for its ancient hands to
get that clutch which at last never loosens, and
Lowell at first seemed somewhat unaffected. " I
like," he wrote to his father, just before Christmas,

" to walk about in the fine sunshine and get unexpected and unguide-booked glimpses of fine scenery, but systematic sight-seeing is very irksome to
me.   Though we have been in Rome now nearly
as long as we were in Florence, I have not learned
to like it as well.   We were able to enjoy Florence
sincerely and without any reproaches, because we
had not heard of your illness.   Then, too, the
churches here are nearly all alike.   Going to see
them is like standing to watch a procession of
monks, — the same thing over and over again, and
when you have seen one you have seen all.   There
is a kind of clumsy magnificence about them, like
that of an elephant with his castle on his back and
his gilded trappings, and the heaviness somehow
weighs on one.   There is no spring and soar in
their architecture as in that of the Lombard
churches I have seen.   The Roman columns standing here and there look gentleman-like beside
them, and reproach them with their tawdry *purve-
nuism*.   The finest interior in Rome is that of the
Sta. Maria degli Angeli, which Michelangelo made
out of a single room in the baths of Diocletian.
Even the *size* of St. Peter's seems inconsiderable in
a city where the Coliseum still stands in crater-like
ruin, and where one may trace the foundations of
a palace large enough almost for a city. . . . Yesterday I walked out upon the Campagna, but by a
different gate from my favorite San Sebastiano.
Leaving the Porta del Popolo, we followed the
road as far as the Ponte Molle, then turned to
the right on the hither bank of the Tiber, which

we followed as far as the confluence of the Tiber and Anio, where was once the city of Antemnæ. As it had been destroyed by Romulus, however, there was nothing to be seen of the old Sabine stronghold except the flatiron-shaped bluff on which it stood, the natural height and steepness of which, aided no doubt by art, must have made the storming of it no very agreeable diversion. The view from the top is very beautiful, and it is a good place to study the Campagna scenery from, — I mean the Campagna in a state of nature. Below us flowed the swift and dirty Tiber, and the yet swifter and dirtier Anio. In front the Campagna wallowed away as far as the line of snow-streaked mountains which wall it in. Herds of cattle and of horses dotted it here and there, the gray cows looking like sheep in the distance to an eye used always to expect red in kine. Sometimes a sort of square tower rose, lonely and with no sign of life about it. Looking more carefully, however, it would turn out to be no tower at all; but only the cottage of a shepherd perched high above the inundation of malaria on the top of some ruinous tomb. Add malaria and the idea of desolation to an Illinois prairie, and you have the Campagna. Where Antemnæ had stood there now rose a conical wigwam built wholly of thatch, surmounted by a cross, at the door of which stood a woman in scarlet bodice and multitudinous petticoat, with a little girl ditto, ditto, but smaller. Seeing us get out a pocket spyglass, a boy of about eighteen years contrived to muster energy enough to come out and stare at us. He was dressed in sheepskin breeches with the wool on, short wide jacket, red waistcoat, and hat turned up at the side, and would have looked extremely well in a landscape — but nowhere else. A smaller boy came up with more impetuosity — fat, rosy - cheeked, Puck-like, and with eyes that looked as if their normal condition was that of being close-shut, but which once opened to the width necessary to take in the extraordinary apparition of three *forestieri* at once, would require some maternal aid to get back again. Large hawks were sliding over the air above us, and there was no sound except the sharp whistle of a peasant attending a drove of horses in the pasture below. Jemmy will like to know that the horses are belled here (I mean in the fields) as cows are with us, only that the bells are large enough for a town school. To-night I am going to make the *giro* of the churches to see the ceremonies with which Christmas is ushered in. First an illumination at Santa Maria Maggiore and the cradle of the Saviour carried in procession at ten o'clock, then mass at midnight in the San Luigi dei Francesi, then mass at St. Peter's at three o'clock A. M. I have not seen a ceremony of the church yet that was impressive, and hope to be better pleased to-night."

How he spent his Christmas is told in a letter to Miss Fay : —

"Let me tell you about Christmas week, first premising that I go to church ceremonies here merely that I may see for myself that they are not worth seeing.   Otherwise they are great bores and fitter for children.   The chief quality of the music is its interminableness, made up of rises and falls, and of the ceremonies generally you may take a yard anywhere as of printed cotton, certain that in figure and quality it will be precisely like what has gone before, and what will follow after.   On Christmas eve the *Presepio*, a piece of the manger in which the Saviour was cradled, was carried in procession at the church of Santa Maria Maggiore. Torches were stuck in the ground for nearly a quarter of a mile from the church, and ghostly dragoons in their long white cloaks (like Leonora's lover) appeared and vanished at intervals in the uncertain light.   The interior of the church is fine, but completely ruined by the trumpery hangings put up for the occasion.   There were ambassadors' boxes, as at the opera, and rows of raised seats on each side near the high altar, for such ladies as chose to come in black, with black veils upon their heads.   I stood among the undistinguished faithful, and it being a fast, there was such a smell as if Wethersfield had been first deluged and then cooked by subterranean fires.   I stood wedged between some very strong devotees (who must have squandered the savings of a year in a garlic debauch) in abject terror lest my head should be colonized from some of the overpopulated districts around me.

"At the end of the church I could dimly see the Pope, with a mitre on and off at intervals.   There was endless Gregorian chanting, then comparative

silence, with sudden epidemics among the crowd of
standing painfully on tiptoe to stare at nothing;
then more endless Gregorian chantings, more epidemics, and a faint suspicion of frankincense
among the garlic; then something incomprehensible
performed in dumb show by what seemed automaton candles, then an exceedingly slim procession
with the *Presepio*, which I could not see for the
simple reason that it was inclosed in a silver case.
At this point the Hallelujahs of the choir were
fine. Having now fairly bagged my spectacle, I
crowded my way out at the risk of my ribs (for
stone doorways are not elastic), and went home to
smoke a cigar preparatory to a midnight excursion
to San Luigi dei Francesi, where, according to
rumor, there was to be fine music. Here I found
more sight-seeing Inglesi, more garlic, more popu-
lous neighbors, more endless Gregorian chanting,
more automaton candles, and at midnight a clash
of music from a French band, not so good as our
Brigade Band at home.

"Christmas day, went to St. Peter's to hear
mass celebrated by the Pope in person. Here
were all kinds of antique costumes, — gentlemen in
black velvet doublets with slashed sleeves and
ruffs, other gentlemen in crimson ditto ditto, officers of the Swiss Guard in inlaid corselets, and
privates of ditto in a kind of striped red and yellow barber's pole uniform invented by Michelangelo, cardinals, bishops, ambassadors, etc., but
not nearly so large a crowd as I expected. The
music was good, and the whole ended by the Pope's

being carried through the Basilica blessing the people at intervals as he went along. I stood quite near and had a good view of his face. He looks like a fatter Edward Everett. This is one of the greatest ceremonies of the year. After it was over I stood in the piazza watching the equipages of the cardinals. Speaking of cardinals: I was walking the other day with an English friend, and we saw a cardinal coming toward us accompanied by his confessor and two footmen. Behind followed his carriage with a cocked-hatted coachman and another footman. Should we bow? He was old enough to deserve it, cardinal or not, so we bowed. Never did man get such percentage for an investment. First came off his Eminence's hat. At a respectful interval came that of the confessor, at another respectful interval those of the coachman and footmen. It was like a detachment of the allied army marching on Dunsinane with a *bough*.

" I have spoken rather disrespectfully of the music here, but I have heard good since I came. On New Year's day the Jesuits have a great celebration in the church of the Gesu. I took a two hours' slice of it in the afternoon. The music was exceedingly fine, a remarkably well-trained choir accompanied by the finest organ in Rome. The soprano was a boy with a voice that, with my eyes shut, I could not have distinguished from that of a woman. We are having also, every Tuesday, concerts by the St. Peter's choir, with music of Palestrina, Guglielmi, Mozart, etc.

The music of Palestrina has a special charm for me, reminding me more than any I ever heard of the æolian harp with its dainty unexpectedness. . . .

"In its modern architecture Rome does not please me so much as Florence, Pisa, Lucca, or Siena, on all of which the religion and politics of the Middle Ages have stamped themselves ineffaceably. The characteristic of Roman architecture is ostentation, not splendor, much less grace. Of course I am speaking generally — there are exceptions. But even in size the Roman remains dwarf all modern attempts. . . . There is something epic in the gray procession of aqueduct arches across the Campagna. They seem almost like the building of Nature, and are worthy of men whose eyes were toned to the proportions of an amphitheatre of mountains and of a city which received tribute from the entire world. Exceeding beautiful are the mountains which sentinel Rome, — the purple Alban mount, the gray-peaked Monte Gennaro, the hoary Lionessa, and farther off the blue island-like Soracte.

"In art also Rome is wondrously rich, especially in sculpture. For the study of painting I have seen no gallery like that of the Uffizi at Florence. And let me advise you, my dear Maria, to see all the Titians (of which there are many and good) in England. To me he is the greatest of the painters. This has one quality and that has another, but he combines more than any. I would rather be the owner of his 'Sacred and Profane Love' in the Borghese collection than of any single picture in Rome.[1]

"What do I *do?* I walk out upon the Campagna, I go to churches and galleries inadvertently (for I will not convert Italy into a monster exhibition), and I walk upon the Pincio. Here one may see all the Fashion and the Title of Rome. Here one may meet magnificent wet-nurses, bareheaded and red-bodiced, and insignificant princesses Paris-bonneted and corseted. Here one may see ermine mantles with so many tails that they remind you of the Arabian Nights. Here one may see the neat, clean-shirted, short-whiskered, always-conceited Englishman, feeling himself quite a Luther if he have struggled into a wide-awake hat; or the other Englishman with years of careful shaving showing unconquerably through the newly-assumed beard which he wears as unconsciously as Mrs. Todd might the Bloomer costume for the first time. Here you may see the American, every inch of him, from his hat to his boots, looking anxious not to commit itself. Here you may see all the foreign children in Rome, and among them Mabel, seeming as if her whole diet were *capers,* and that they had gradually penetrated and inspired her whole constitution. I have seen no pair of legs there which compared with hers either for size or for untamable activity. Here you may see the worst riding you can possibly imagine: Italians emulating the English style of rising in the stirrups and

[1] It was more than thirty years later that Lowell wrote the significant poem suggested by this picture.

bumping forlornly in every direction; French officers, reminding one of the proverb of setting a
beggar on horseback, and John Bulls, with superfluous eyeglass wedged in the left eye, chins run
out over white chokers, and a general upward
tendency of all the features as who should say,
'Regard me attentively but awfully; I am on intimate terms with Lord Fitzpollywog.' On Saturday evenings we are 'at home.' We have tea,
cake, and friends. . . . The evening before last I
went to a musical party at Mrs. Rich's. You
know what an English musical party is. Your
average Englishman enjoys nothing beyond 'God
save the Queen,' and that because he can either
beat time or swell the chorus with his own private
contribution of discord. But I saw here the dogged
resolution of the people who have conquered America and India. There was no shrinking under long
variations on the pianoforte, and I could well imagine a roast beef and plum-pudding basis under
the solid indifference which outlasted a half-hour's
fiddling. Miss Fanny Erskine, a niece of our hostess, sang well, especially in German, and Emiliani
is really a fine artist with the violin."

In an earlier letter to Dr. Howe, Lowell had
said: "I begin to think myself too old to travel.
As to men, — as I used to say at home, — the average of human nature to the square foot is very
much the same everywhere; and as to buildings
and such like monuments, I bring to them neither
the mind nor the eye of twenty. In almost all
such I find myself more interested, as they are

exponents and illustrations of the spiritual and
political life and progress of the people who built
them. The relations of races to the physical world
do not excite me to study and observation (only
to be fruitfully pursued on the spot) in any proportion to the interest I feel in those relations to
the moral advance of mankind, which one may as
easily trace at home, in their history and literature,
as here. But of Rome hereafter. I feel as if I
should continue a stranger and foreigner during
my whole six months' residence here." A month
or so later he revised a little of this judgment in a
letter to his father, in which he wrote : " You need
not be afraid of our getting attached to Europe. I
find the modes of life here more agreeable to me in
some respects, but nothing can replace Elmwood.
In regard to our coming home, the exact time will
depend entirely on the accounts we get of your
health. I do not wish to have the money we have
spent thrown away, for I see no chance of our ever
coming hither again, and so I wish to do everything as thoroughly as I can. I have profited already, I think, in the study of art. I make it a
rule now on entering a gallery to endeavor to make
out the painters of such pictures as I like by the
internal characteristics of the works themselves.
After I have made up my mind, I look at my catalogue. I find this an exceedingly good practice.
Of all the more prominent painters, I can now distinguish the style and motive almost at a glance.
Sometimes I make a particular study of a particular artist, if any gallery is especially rich in his

works. Life is rather more picturesque here than
with us, and I find that I am accumulating a certain kind of wealth which may be useful to me
hereafter. The condition and character of the
people also interest me much, and I think that
my understanding of European politics will be much
clearer than before my visit to Europe. To understand properly, however, requires time and thought
and the power of dissociating real from accidental
causes. I wish to see well what I see at all — and,
if possible, would like to visit Germany, France,
and England before coming home."

The social life of Rome in the English and
American circles engaged the travellers, and Lowell made his début as an actor. "Private theatricals," he writes his father, 1 February, 1852,
" are all the rage now in Rome. There are three
companies. I have an engagement in one of them
under the management of Mr. Black, who has
erected a pretty enough little theatre in the Pa-
lazzo Cini, where he has apartments, — or an apartment, as they would say here. We gave our first
representation last Thursday night to a select
audience of English and Americans. Our play
was a portion of Midsummer Night's Dream, including part of the fairy scenes, and the whole of
the interlude of the clowns. In this interlude, I
was the star, having the part of Bottom assigned
to me. On the morning of Thursday, I wrote a
prologue of some thirty lines which I recited to
open the performances. This, to me, was the
plum of the evening's entertainment. In the first

place, I do not think that the audience had any idea that I was a prologue at all, till I had got nearly through; for I was obliged to speak it in the costume of Bottom, not having time to dress in the interval between the prologue and my first appearance in character. But even if they guessed what I was about, it never entered their heads that it was intended to be funny till about the middle, when a particularly well-defined pun touched off a series of laughter-explosions which kept going off at intervals during the rest of my recitation, as the train ran along from one mind to another. It was exceedingly diverting to me, for, knowing the requisitions of a prologue, I had written it down to the meanest capacity, and all the jokes were *a-b-abs*. I was very much struck with the difference between an English and an American audience. The minds of our countrymen are infinitely quicker both in perception and conception, and I am certain my prologue would have set a room full of them in roars of laughter."

The list of persons who engaged in these private theatricals is an interesting one. Mr. Charles C. Black, to whom Lowell refers, was the begetter of the entertainment, and with him were W. W. Story, Charles Hemans, Shakespeare Wood, W. Temple, J. Hayllar, and T. Crawford. There were two different representations of "A Midsummer Night's Dream," and Lowell wrote two separate prologues. The first began : —

> " When Thespis rode upon his one-horse cart,
> The first exponent of the Drama's art,

> Earliest of managers, and happiest too,
> Having a theatre which always drew."

Then followed a comparison of the stationary theatre with the vagrant one, and the brief prologue ended with some jests on the actors, as on himself:

> "If Pyramus be short, restrain your ire,
> Remember none of us appear for hire; "

and on Crawford : —

> "Forgive our Thisbe the moustache she wears,
> Ladies, you know, *will* put on little 'airs."

Story, who was to play Snug, hunted through Rome for a lion's skin, and finally had to content himself with the skin of a tiger.

> "But now comes one fact I proclaim with glory,
> Snug is enacted by our attic Story,
> Who sought a lion's hide through Rome, a week,
> Quite a new way of playing hide and seek."

In the first representation Lowell had the part of Pyramus, in the second he was Bottom, and as he intimates made his new prologue more comprehensible by his audience. He pretended to have received a request from Mr. Black to write the prologue, and so begins : —

> "'Dear Bottom, if you can, I wish you 'd write
> A prologue for our comedy to-night;
> Just tap that comic vein of yours which runs
> Discharging a continuous stream of puns.' "

And that is what the second prologue consists of, with some repetition even of the jokes of the first, ending : —

> "Now who plays Pyramus! no, that won't go well,
> I cannot get a good thing out of Lowell.
> Faith, that 's too near the truth, it 's past my power,

For I 've been trying at it half an hour.
At all events I can proclaim with glory
Snug is enacted by our Attic Story ;
Who sought a lion's skin through Rome a week,
Quite a nice way of playing hide and seek.
But the last lion that was seen in Rome
Was Dickens, — and he carried his skin home.
Thisbe's moustache. The Greek girls never had any ?
I 'll just remind them of Miss Hairyadne.
But I can't do it. Dite al Signore, —
What 's more I won't — che sono fuori." [1]

An undercurrent of anxiety and affection for his father runs through the correspondence at this time, and a month later he seeks to gratify a grandfather's feelings by devoting a whole letter, written as clearly as possible that his father might read it himself, about the sayings and doings of the two children. "Some theologic questions are beginning," he writes, "to vex her [Mabel's] mind somewhat. She inquired of me very gravely the other day, when I said something to her about her Heavenly Father, 'Papa, have I got a Heavenly Grandfather?' The pictures in the churches make a great impression (and not always a pleasant one) upon her. She said to me one day : 'O my dear papa, I love you so very much, because you take care of me; and I love mamma very much because

---

[1] Mr. Black's daughter, Mrs. Hayllar, kindly sends the two prologues, which are in a way wholly from memory. Lowell afterwards, she writes, "tore up his notes, saying the lines were too insignificant for preservation, when to his astonishment, my father, who had a quite remarkable memory, repeated them both to him." From her own memory Mrs. Hayllar recalled the bits of the first prologue, and afterward found amongst her father's papers the whole of the second.

she takes care of me; and I love Mary very much because she takes care of me; and I love Heavenly Father because he takes care of me; and I love the Madonna very much because she takes care of me; and I love the angels because they take care of me; and I love that one with the swords stuck into her, and that other one with the stick.' These last were no doubt pictures she had seen somewhere. During Carnival, we did not let her go to the Corso much, because there was so much throwing of *confetti*, which are small seeds or pellets of clay about as large as peas, coated with plaster of Paris. However, she saw the edges of the great stream, here and there, as it overflowed into the side streets, and talked a great deal to Faustina about *Pulcinelli* and *Pagliacci*. She threatened rather sharply to pay back ' Mister *Pulcinello* ' (as she always respectfully called him when she spoke of him in English) in his own coin, if he threw any *confetti*, or oftener, *nasty confetti*, at her. One day she was walking with me through the Piazza di Spagna, with half a roll in her hand, when she saw one of the lacqueys of the S. P. Q. R. in his queer costume. She instantly set him down for a *Pulcinello*, and I had much ado to hinder her from hurling the fragment of her roll at him, much as she once threw a dry bun at somebody else who shall be nameless. She is making great progress in Italian under the tuition of Dinda and Amelia, two nice little girls, daughters of our Padrone. One of the great events in her day is always the pudding — in *trattoria* Italian *il budino*.

As soon as the great tin *stufa* has safely made its
descent from the head of the *facchino* to the floor,
she begins a dance around it, shouting in a voice
loud enough to be heard as far as the Trinità dei
Monti, ' *O Faustina, ditemi! C'è un puddino
oggi?* ' And if it turn out that there be only a
pie, which is a forbidden *dolce* to her, she forthwith drops her voice to its lowest key and growls
— ' *Mi dispiace molto, mŏ-o-lto, Faustina; pu-
dino non c'è: ce sono solamente pasticcie.*' Sometimes I have heard her add with a good deal of
dignity, ' *Dite al cuoco che mi dispiace molto.*' A
day or two ago, when she saw a plum-pudding
come upon the table, she could not contain herself,
but, springing up into her chair (for she can never
express satisfaction without using her legs — her
intoxications seeming to take direction the reverse
of common), she began dancing and waving her
arms quite like a Bacchanal, at the same time singing —

> ' Oh, quanto mi piace, roba dolce, il puddino!
> Quando lo mangio, sono felice, padrino ! '

I offer this to Jemmy to translate, as an Italian
exercise, for his paper. If it be not equal to
Dante, upon my word I think it quite up to a good
deal of Tasso, and much more to the point than
nine tenths of Petrarca. Improvisations are seldom put to the test of being written down, but
this bears it very well. The tender *padrino* —
Dear little Father — was an adroit bribe, which
got her a third piece of pudding by the unanimous
vote of our household senate. Ask Charlie to

read over the muddy stuff which Byron thought it
necessary to pump up about St. Peter's, etc., in
'Childe Harold,' and say if he do not agree with me
that his lordship would have made a better hand
of it if he had devoted himself to sincerities like
this? . . .

"As for Walter, he grows and thrives finely.
He can say A, B, C, D, or something considerably
like it — nearer, in fact, a good deal, than the first
four letters of the Chinese alphabet would be. He
has done, during the last week, what I have chal-
lenged many older persons to do, namely, cut a
double tooth. I doubt if a cabinet minister in
Europe can say the same of himself. He has
grown very fond of his papa, and sometimes crawls
to my door of a morning before I am out of bed,
and then, getting upon his feet, knocks and calls
'Papa! papa!' laying the accent very strongly on
the first syllable. If he hears my voice, he immediately springs up in Mary's lap, and begins shouting lustily for me. He is the fairest boy that ever
was seen, and has the bluest eyes, and is the bald-
est person in Rome except two middle-aged Englishmen, who, you know, have a great knack that
way. . . . In a word, he is one of that countless
number of extraordinary boys out of which the
world contrives afterward to make such ordinary
men. I think him rather intelligent — but, as the
picture dealers say, *chi sa?* As he is mine, I shall
do rather as the picture-buyers, and call what I
have got by any name I please. One cannot say
definitely so early. It is hard to tell of a green

shoot just worming out of the ground whether it
will be an oak or an onion — they all look much
alike at first."

Not an oak, but a plant and flower of light,
Lowell might shortly have said, for this is the last
reference in life to the child suddenly stricken
down and left behind in a Roman grave by the
mourning parents, when, on the 29th of April,
they went away from Rome to Naples with the
one child of their four who lived to them.   On
the 13th of the month Lowell wrote to his eldest
sister: " We are now within a fortnight of bidding farewell to what I am now forced to call dear
old Rome.   In spite of its occupation by an army
of ten thousand French soldiers, in spite of its
invasion by that more terrible force, the column of
English travellers, in spite of the eternal drum-
ming and bugling and sentinelling in the streets,
and the crowding of that insular Bull — *qui sem-
per habet fœnum in cornu* — there is an insensible
charm about the place which grows upon you from
hour to hour.   There must be few cities where one
can command such absolute solitude as here.   One
cannot expect it, to be sure, in the Colosseum by
moonlight, for thither the English go by carriage
loads to be lonely with a footman in livery behind
them, and to quote Byron's stuff out of Murray's
Guide; there perch the French in voluble flocks,
under the necessity (more painful to them than to
any other people) of being poetical — chattering
Mon Dieu! qu'un joli effet!   But an hour's walk
will take one out into the Campagna, where you will

look across the motionless heave of the solitude dotted here and there with lazy cattle to the double wall
of mountain, the nearest opaline with change of
light and shadow, the farther Parian with snow that
only grows whiter when the cloud shadows melt
across it — the air overhead rippling with larks too
countless to be watched, and the turf around you
glowing with strange flowers, each a wonder, yet so
numberless that you would as soon think of gathering a nosegay of grass blades.   On Easter Sunday
I spent an incomparable day at the Fountain of
Egeria, stared at sullenly, now and then, by one of
those great gray Campagna bulls, but totally safe
from the English variety which had gone to get
broken ribs at St. Peter's.   The show-box unholi-
ness of Holy Week is at last well over.   The best
part of it was that on Holy Thursday all the Vati-
can was open at once — fifteen miles of incomparable art.   For me the Pope washed perfumed feet,
and the Cardinal Penitentiary wielded his long rod
in vain.   I dislike such spectacles naturally, and
saw no reason why I should undergo every con-
ceivable sort of discomfort and annoyance for the
sake of another discomfort or annoyance at the
end. . . .

"The finest *show* I have seen in Rome is the
illumination of St. Peter's.   Just after sunset I
saw from the head of the *scalinata*, the little points
of light creeping down from the cross and lantern
(trickling, as it were) over the dome.   Then I
walked over to the Piazza di San Pietro, and the
first glimpse I caught of it again was from the

Ponte Sant' Angelo. I could not have believed it would have been so beautiful. There was no time or space to pause here. Foot passengers crowding hither and thither as they heard the shout of *Avanti!* from the coachmen behind — dragoon-horses getting unmanageable just where there were most women to be run over — and all the while the dome drawing all eyes and thoughts the wrong way, made a hubbub to be got out of as soon as possible. Five minutes more of starting and dodging, and we were in the piazza. You have seen it and know how it seems, as if the setting sun had lodged upon the horizon and then burnt out, the fire still clinging to its golden ribs as they stand out against the evening sky. You know how, as you come nearer, you can see the soft travertine of the façade suffused with a tremulous golden gloom like the innermost shrine of a water-lily. And then the change comes as if the wind had suddenly fanned what was embers before into flame. If you could see *one* sunset in a lifetime and were obliged to travel four thousand miles to see it, it would give you a similar sensation; but an everyday sunset does not, for we take the gifts of God as a matter of course.

" After wondering long enough in the piazza, I went back to the Pincio (or rather the Trinità dei Monti) and watched it for an hour longer. I did not wish to see it go out. To me it seemed better to go home with the consciousness that it was still throbbing, as if I could make myself believe that there was a kind of permanence in it, and that I should see it there again some happy evening. Before leaving it, I went away and came back several times, and at every return it was a new miracle — the more miraculous for being a human piece of fairy work.

" Last night there was another wonder, the Girandola, which we saw excellently well from the windows of the American legation. Close behind me, by the way, stood Silvio Pellico (a Jesuit now), a little withered old man in spectacles, looking so very dry that I could scarce believe he had ever been shut up in a *damp* dungeon in his life. This was (I mean the Girandola) the most brilliant and at the same time tasteful display of fireworks I ever saw. I had no idea that so much powder could be burned to so good purpose. For the first time in my life I saw rockets that seemed endowed with life and intelligence. They might have been thought filled with the same vivacity and enjoyment so characteristic of the people. Our rockets at home seem business-like in comparison. They accomplish immense heights in a steady straightforward way, explode as a matter of course, and then the stick hurries back to go about its terrestrial affairs again. And yet why should I malign those beautiful slow curves of fire, that I have watched with Charlie and Jemmie from Simonds's Hill, and which I would rather see again than twenty Girandolas? If Michelangelo had designed our fireworks, and if it did not by some fatal coincidence always rain on the evening of 4th July, doubtless they would be better."

Something of the total impression made upon
Lowell in this first visit to Rome may be seen in
the fragment of a letter to Mr. John Holmes, written near the end of his stay : —

" After all, this is a wonderful place. One feels
disappointed at first, everything looks so modern.
But as the mind, taking in ruin after ruin, gradually reconstructs for itself the grandeur and the
glory, of which these city-like masses are but the
splinters sprinkled here and there by the fall of
the enormous fabric, and conceives the spiritual
which has outlived that temporal domination, and
even surpassed it, laying its foundations deeper
than the reach of earthquake or Gaul, and con-
quering worlds beyond the ken of the Roman
eagles in their proudest flight, a feeling of the
sublime, vague and vast, takes the place of the first
hurried curiosity and interest. Surely the American (and I feel myself more intensely American
every day) is last of all at home among ruins —
but he is at home in Rome. I cannot help believing that in some respects we represent more truly
the old Roman Power and sentiment than any
other people. Our art, our literature, are, as
theirs, in some sort exotics ; but our genius for
politics, for law, and, above all, for colonization,
our instinct for aggrandizement and for trade, are
all Roman. I believe we are laying the basis of a
more enduring power and prosperity, and that we
shall not pass away till we have stamped ourselves
upon the whole western hemisphere so deeply, so
nobly, that if, in the far-away future, some Gibbon

shall muse among our ruins, the history of our
Decline and Fall shall be more mournful and more
epic than that of the huge Empire amid the dust
of whose once world-shaking heart these feelings
so often come upon me."

The last week before leaving Rome was spent
in an excursion with Story to Subiaco, as related
at length in "Leaves from my Journal in Italy."
On their way to Naples the Lowells made a halt
at Terracina, from which place Lowell wrote to
Robert Carter: "Here I am, with a magnificent
cliff opposite my window crowned by twelve arches
of what is called the Palace of Theodoric. I have
just come in from seeing the Cathedral, the dirtiest
church I have seen in Italy (with a very picturesque old Campanile, however), and the remains of
the old Roman port, which astonished me by their
size even after all I had seen of Roman hugeness.
The port is now filled with soil, and there is a fine
orange garden where vessels used to lie. Terracina is nothing like what I expected to see. The
inn (or 'Grand' Albergo, as it is called) is one of
the least cutthroat looking places I ever saw. It is
quite out of the town, between the great cliff and
the sea. Behind it, on the beach, the scene is quite
Neapolitan — forty or fifty bare-legged fishermen
are drawing a great seine out of the water, and
forty or fifty dirty, laughing, ragged, happily-
wretched children gather round you and beg for
caccose or *cecco*, by which they mean *qualche cosa*.
The women sit round the doors, nasty and contented, urging on their offspring in their profes-

sional career. They are the most obstinate beggars
I have seen yet. In Rome the waving of the two
first fingers of the hand and a decided *non c'è* is
generally sufficient, but here I tried every expedi-
ent in vain. The prickly pear grows bloatedly in
all the ledges of the cliff, an olive orchard climbs
half-way up the back of it where the hill is less
steep, and farther to the left there are tall palms
in a convent garden, but I cannot see them.

"The drive over the Pontine marshes is for more
than twenty miles a perfectly straight, smooth
avenue, between double rows of elms. I had been
told it was very dull, but did not find it so; for
there were mountains on one side of us, cultivated,
or cattle and horse-covered fields or woods on the
other, and the birds sang and the sun shone all
the way. It seemed like the approach to some
prince's pleasure-house. . . . On the whole, the result of my experience thus far is that I am glad
that I came abroad, though the knowledge one
acquires must rust for want of use in a great measure at home. To be sure, one's political ideas
are also somewhat modified — I don't mean retro-
graded."

The progress of the travellers is but briefly recorded after this. They were in Naples early in
May, and thence they appear to have made their
way to Venice, and to have spent the summer in
leisurely travel through the Italian lakes, Switzerland, Germany, Provence, and France, reaching
England in the early autumn. Here they saw
London, Oxford, and Cambridge. "We have

been also," Lowell wrote to his father, " at Ely, where the cathedral is one of the most interesting I have seen. I know nothing for which I am more thankful than the opportunity I have had of seeing fine buildings. I think they give me a more absolute pleasure than anything except fine natural scenery. Perhaps I should not except even this, for the sense that it is a triumph of the brain and hand of man certainly heightens the delight we feel in them. I think that Ely, more than anything else, turned the scale and induced us to stay a month longer." From London, Lowell made an excursion with Kenyon to Bath to see Landor, and thirty-six years later he jotted down some of the impressions he then received of the man, whose writings he had long admired.[1]

A trip followed through England and into Scotland and Wales, which took in Peterborough, Lincoln, York, Ripon, Fountains Abbey, Durham, Edinburgh, and the haunts of Scott, the Scottish and English lakes, and then the Lowells took steamer from Liverpool, 30 October, 1852.

[1] See " Walter Savage Landor," in *Latest Literary Essays and Addresses*, p. 51.

CHAPTER VIII

AN END AND A BEGINNING

1852–1857

LOWELL had the good fortune to have for a companion at sea Thackeray, who was on his way to America to give his lectures on the English Humourists; he liked the man very much, and his occasional references to the author in his letters and critical papers intimate the high regard he had for his work. Another congenial companion on shipboard was Arthur Hugh Clough, with whom he formed a warm and enduring friendship. It was a thirteen days' passage, and on the 12th of November the Lowells were again at home in Elmwood. The coming of the two Englishmen gave occasion for many little festivities in Boston and Cambridge. A glimpse is given of them in Mr. Longfellow's printed journal, when the poet summoned Clough, Lowell, Felton, and C. E. Norton to feast on some English grouse and pheasant sent him from Liverpool by Mr. Henry Bright, and in the evening at the Nortons' there were private theatricals with a " nice little epilogue written by Mr. Clough," who shortly established himself indefinitely in Cambridge.

Clough has left a little picture of the interior

of Elmwood : " Yesterday I had a walk with James Lowell to a very pretty spot, Beaver Brook. Then I dined with him, his wife, and his father, a fine old minister who is stone deaf, but talks to you. He began by saying that he was born an Englishman, i. e. before the end of the Revolution. Then he went on to say, ' I have stood as near to George III. as to you now ; ' ' I saw Napoleon crowned Emperor ; ' then, ' Old men are apt to be garrulous, especially about themselves ; ' ' I saw the present Sultan ride through Constantinople on assuming the throne ; ' and so on, — all in a strong clear voice, and in perfect sentences, which you saw him making beforehand. And all one could do was to bow and look expressive, for he could only just hear when his son got up and shouted in his ear." [1] Lowell gave briefly his estimate of Clough's genius when he wrote a few weeks later to Mr. Briggs : " I wish to write a review of his ' Bothie,' to serve him in event of a new edition. It is one of the most charming books ever written, — to my thinking quite as much by itself as the ' Vicar of Wakefield.' "

With his European experience behind him Lowell was eager to plunge into literature, and his intention at first was to try his hand at fiction, possibly turning his experience to account somewhat after the manner of his neighbor's " Hyperion."   At any rate, Longfellow notes in his diary under date of 29 November, 1852 : " Met Lowell in the street and brought him home to smoke a

[1] *The Poems and Prose Remains of Arthur Hugh Clough*, i. 188.

pipe. He had been to the bookseller's to buy a
blank book to begin a Novel, on the writing of
which his mind is bent. He seems rather sad and
says he does not take an interest in anything.
This is the reaction after the excitement of foreign
travel. Lowell will write a capital novel, and when
he gets warm in the harness will feel happier ; "
and a fortnight later he makes the entry : "Lowell
came in. He has begun his novel."

It is to be suspected that he never went far in
the attempt. A dozen years later, when Mr. Fields
wanted him to write a novel for the *Atlantic
Monthly*, he made the summary answer : "I can't
write one nor conceive how any one else can." Yet
he could not have abandoned the trial immediately,
for in June he was writing to Briggs: "I have got
so far as to have written the first chapter of a prose
book, — a sort of New England autobiography,
which may turn out well." [1]

Meanwhile, he was met on his arrival in America
with a piece of literary news which was welcome
for its own sake and because it promised an outlet for his productions. His friend Briggs as
editor-in-chief, with G. W. Curtis and Parke God-
win for assistants, was just about launching a new
magazine in New York, which was likely to come
nearer fulfilling the ideal Lowell had long cher-

[1] Perhaps his partial friend Briggs was referring to this when
he wrote, 18 March, 1860 : "If you bring out that long promised
volume of fireside travels, I hope you will not omit that racy chapter of the novel you read to me, but which you will never write.
I think it was much better than anything of the Autocrat's that I
have read."

ished than anything thus far issued in America.
Putnam's Monthly had behind it an active publishing house, whose head, Mr. G. P. Putnam, had
that indefinable quality which makes a publisher,
if not an author himself, a genuine appreciator of
good literature, and a man whose friendship with
authors rested on a basis which was social as well
as commercial. He had shown his sagacity and
business insight by taking up the writings of
Washington Irving when that author was in neglect, and winning a substantial success with them.
He cared for the books he published and listened
willingly to Mr. Briggs when that gentleman, who
had been engaged in many editorial enterprises,
argued that the time was ripe for a literary
monthly which should stand for American literature of the best sort, and should at the same time
concern itself with public affairs and furnish also
that miscellaneous entertainment of narrative and
description for which the American public showed
a liking. *Harper's New Monthly Magazine* had
been started a couple of years before, but it was
almost wholly a reprint of English current literature, and even its cover was a copy of *Bentley's*.
It had, however, struck a popular taste, and its
success made other publishers jealous, while its easy
use of foreign matter made the men of letters
angry.

The prospectus of *Putnam's Monthly*, in which
the fact that it was to be " an entirely original
work " was emphasized, announced that it was " intended to combine the more various and amusing

characteristics of a popular magazine with the
higher and graver qualities of a quarterly review,"
and that when a subject needed illustrations or pic-
torial examples, such illustrations would occasionally be given. The rate of payment was fair for
the time: poetry had no fixed rates, but Lowell
received fifty dollars for a poem of two hundred
and fifty lines or so, and prose was paid at the rate
of three dollars a page. Hawthorne and Emerson
were among those who promised their work, though
neither seems to have contributed, but Longfellow printed several poems. The articles and
poems were all unsigned. The early numbers gave
good promise, and Curtis, with his " Prue and I "
papers gave a distinction of lightness and added
the flavor which every literary magazine covets but
can rarely command. The first number, Briggs
declared with elation, had run up to twenty thousand copies, and the second number had one of
those articles, " Have we a Bourbon among us ? "
which are the joy of the magazine editor for the
buzz which they create in the reading community.
But the high hopes with which *Putnam's* started
out somehow faded. There were exceptionally
good poems and the general average of writing
was high, but the magazine soon satisfied curiosity
without creating a demand, and the financial embarrassment of the publisher after two years compelled a transfer of the publishing interest which
was followed by a steady decline in quality.

Meanwhile, Mr. Briggs looked eagerly to Lowell
for help, and for his first number received the

poem " The Fountain of Youth," which had been
lying in the poet's portfolio for three years. He
suggested that Lowell should publish " The Nooning " as a serial. This was not to be, but whether
from this suggestion or not, Lowell suddenly took
it into his head to start a serio-comic poem in
Alexandrines, under the heading " Our Own, his
Wanderings and Personal Adventures," in which
he intended to personate a correspondent of the
magazine, who should travel in Europe, and em-
ploy his nonsense and satire on men and things.
He began leisurely enough, heading his page with
a Greek, a Latin, and an English motto, each cleverly hinting at the plan and the name of the piece.
The Latin " *Quæ regio in terris Nostri non plena
laboris?* " was Englished in

> " Full many cities he hath seen and many great men known;
>   What place on earth but testifies the labors of *our own*? "

Then he makes a doggerel verse under Digression
A which slyly imitates Spenser's verse table-of-
contents, and so with Digressions, Invocation, and
Progression he saunters carelessly along. "The
last few days," he writes to Briggs, 17 February,
1853, "I have worked in earnest. I wrote one
hundred and fifty lines yesterday, and it is thought
funny by the constituency in my little Buncombe
here. I have hopes that it will be the best thing
I have done in the satiric way after I once get
fairly agoing. I am thus far taking the run back
for the jump. I have enlarged my plan and, if
you like it, can make it run through several numbers. It is cruel, impudent, — sassy, I meant to

write. Some parts of it I have flavored slightly with Yankee, — but not in dialect. I wish to make it something more than ephemeral, and shall put more thinking into it as I go along. My idea for it is a glass of punch, sweetness, sourness, spirit, and a dash of that Chinese herb favorable to meditation."

There were three numbers only published of "Our Own," though the last carried the legend "To be continued" at its foot. The perplexed editor hardly knew how to answer Lowell's demand for criticism. He himself was immensely entertained, he averred, but nobody else was; although he had heard of one or two, and Lowell added the names of two or three more, it was clear to Mr. Briggs that the verses did not take, and he grew petulant over the stupidity of the public. Lowell's own ardor cooled. The style of composition was indeed to real writing what the pun is to real wit. In the heat of firing off these fire-crackers, ever so much execution seems to be done, but the laugh that follows is not repeated, and the cleverness and point seem dulled when the bristling jests crowd each other, giving no relief to each.

Lowell could not quite agree with Briggs in the deference which the latter was disposed to pay to the expressions of the public upon the contents of his magazine: "I doubt if your magazine," he writes, "will become really popular if you edit it for the mob. Nothing is more certain than that popularity goes downward and not up (I mean per-

manent popularity), and it is what the few like now
that the many have got to like by and by. Now
don't turn the tables on me and say that, — not the
very few. I have pretty much given up the notion
that I can be popular either upward or downward,
and what I say has no reference to myself. I wish
I could be. But it strikes me that you want as
much variety as possible. It is not merely necessary that the matter should be good, but that it
should be individual."

A good many years afterward when Lowell was
making up a volume of poems, he looked again at
"Our Own" to see if it was worth preserving, and
out of the whole six hundred lines he saved only
the verses now headed "Fragments of an Unfinished Poem" and the two charming stanzas "Aladdin." [1] The insertion of this little poem in the
midst of his nonsense indicates that if Lowell had
found sufficient encouragement he might, especially
after reaching Europe in his plan, have worked off
the surplusage of high spirits and thrown into his
rambling discourse both caustic satire and genial
humor.

A more satisfactory and successful contribution
which was enthusiastically received by the editor
was "A Moosehead Journal," which was in effect
a journal, sent home to his wife, of an excursion
made by Lowell in the summer of 1853 with his
nephew Charles; and in the spring of 1854 ap-

[1] The lines on pp. 80, 81, of "Cambridge Thirty Years Ago"
are also saved from the same poem, but from the unprinted portion.

peared in two parts the well-known sketch of
" Cambridge Thirty Years Ago," under the title,
" Fireside Travels." The paper seems to have
grown out of an unused sketch of Allston which
Lowell had begun for *Putnam's* in September,
1853. " What I have written (or part of it)," he
says to the editor, " would make a unique article
for your magazine, if the other thing is given up.
It is a sketch of Cambridge as it was twenty-five
years ago, and is done as nobody but I could do it,
for nobody knows the old town so well. I mean
one of these days to draw a Commencement as it
used to be." Lowell does not appear to have contributed to *Putnam's* after December, 1854, when
his portrait, an engraving by Hall after Page's
painting, served as frontispiece to the number,
being one of a series of portraits of contributors
to the magazine.

Meanwhile, when *Putnam's* was at the top of its
brief tide, another attempt at a good literary magazine was made in Boston. The extraordinary success of " Uncle Tom's Cabin " had emboldened its
publisher, Mr. John P. Jewett, to undertake what
its projector, Mr. F. H. Underwood, called a " Literary and Anti-Slavery Magazine." It was the intention to issue the first number in January, 1854,
and to use the great reputation of Mrs. Stowe to
float it by printing a new novel by her. Mr. Underwood[1] was particularly desirous of securing Lowell's aid, especially as he esteemed his poetry quite

[1] See his two letters to T. W. Higginson, outlining his plan, and
published by the latter in his *Old Cambridge*.

the best to be had in America, and he was elated
at receiving from him the poem "The Oriole's
Nest," afterward called simply "The Nest." But
the design which had been germinating for two
or three years was suddenly brought to naught
by the failure of the luckless publishers, whose
success with "Uncle Tom's Cabin" seems to have
been thrust upon them, rather than to have been
due to their business ability. So a fortnight after
sending his poem, Lowell was forced to write the
disconcerted editor: "I cannot help writing a
word to say how truly sorry I was to hear of the
blowing up of your magazine. But it is not so
irreparable as if it had been a powder-magazine,
though perhaps all the harder to be borne because
it was only *in posse* and not *in esse*. The explo-
sion of one of those Castles in Spain sometimes
sprinkles dust on all the rest of our lives, but I
hope you are of better heart, and will rather look
upon the affair as a burning of your ships which
makes victory the more imperative. Although I
could prove by a syllogism in *barbara* that you are
no worse off than you were before, I know very
well that you *are*, for if it be bad to lose mere
coin, it is still worse to lose hope, which is the mint
in which most gold is manufactured.

"But, after all, is it a hopeless case? Consider
yourself to be in the position of all the world before the Mansion of our Uncle Thomas (as I suppose we must call it now, it has grown so respectable) was published, and never to have heard of
this Mr. Jew-wit. I think he ought to be — that

something ought to be done for him : but for that matter nearly all booksellers stand in the same condemnation. There are as good fish in that buccaneering sea of Bibliopoly as ever were caught, and if one of them has broken away from your harpoon, I hope the next may prove a downright kraaken, on whom, if needful, you can pitch your tent and live.

" Don't think that I am trifling with you. God knows any jests of mine would be of a bitter sort just now ; but I know that it is a good thing for a man to be made to look at his misfortune till it assumes its true relations to things about it. So don't think me intrusive if I nudge your elbow among the rest."

A few weeks after the return of the Lowells to America, Longfellow took Clough on a walk to Elmwood. " Lowell," he says, " we found musing before his fire in his study. His wife came in, slender and pale as a lily." In reading " A Year's Life " one is struck by the frequency with which the shadow of death falls across the page. It is true that when he wrote the poems, when indeed he fell in with Maria White, Lowell was struggling out of an atmosphere which was full of damp mist, and the image of death naturally rose constantly before him. Yet it remains that from the beginning of his passion he associated this love with the idea of death. So frail, so almost ethereal was the woman who came thus into his life, that from the first he was constantly sheltering her from the cold blast. The solicitude deepened his passion; it accustomed him at the same time to the idea of transitoriness in the life he led. It is entirely possible, nay, very probable, that this spiritually-bodied girl was permitted to develop into a gracious womanhood through the very fact of her marriage and her motherhood: Lowell's own mood during the nine years of married life was, as we have seen, often irrepressibly gay and sanguine, and after the death of each of their children the two seemed to spring back into a wholesome delight in life. Still, the fear could never have long been out of their minds, and, after Walter died in Rome, the mother seems steadily to have drooped. When Lowell sent "The Nest" to Underwood, he speaks of it as an old poem: "Perhaps," he says, "it seems better to me than it deserves, for an intense meaning has been added to it." The meaning had then indeed been deepened, but when it was written, there was more than remote prophecy in the lines —

"When springs of life that gleamed and gushed
Run chilled, and slower, and are hushed."

The year that passed after the return from Europe saw Mrs. Lowell declining in strength, though it was not till September, 1853, that his letters betray Lowell's deepening anxiety, and it was not till the end of the month that he fully realized the progress disease had made. Mrs. Lowell died 27 October, and Lowell was left alone with his little daughter. The visionary faculty, which all his life had been what might almost be

called another sense, came now to his help and for
awhile he lived as if the companion of thirteen
years, though shut out from his daily sight, visited
him in the solitude and silence of the night. " I
have the most beautiful dreams," he writes, " and
never as if any change had come to us. Once I
saw her sitting with Walter on her knee, and she
said to me, ' See what a fine strong boy he is
grown.' And one night as I was lying awake and
straining my eyes through the gloom, and the palpable darkness was surging and gathering and
dispersing as it will, I suddenly saw far, far off a
crescent of angels standing and shining silently.
But oh ! it is a million times better to have had
her and lost her, than to have had and kept any
other woman I ever saw."

It had given both husband and wife a great
pleasure to see one and another of Mrs. Lowell's
poems printed during the last year in *Putnam's
Monthly*. Mr. Briggs, with his affectionate regard
for both, was eager to print the verses as they were
sent him, and reported all the agreeable words that
came to him respecting the poems. The latest to
be printed was one on Avignon, in which the poet
kept turning back from the historic and spectac-
ular sights to some oleanders which stood by her
window. " How beautiful it was," Lowell wrote
to Briggs, " and how fitting for the last. I am
going to print them all — but not publish them yet
— she did not wish it.   I shall give a copy, with a
calotype from a drawing which Cheney is to make
from Page's picture, to all her friends."

It was a year and more before the volume was printed, bearing the title "The Poems of Maria Lowell," and inscribed to Mrs. Story, Mrs. Putnam, and Mrs. Shaw, three friends of whose loving appreciation Lowell had had many assurances. There are only twenty poems in the volume. Most had been printed before, one, "The Morning-Glory," in Lowell's own collection. None of her translations were included. One looks naturally in such a volume rather for intimations of the writer's character, and for touches of personal feeling, than for poetic art. Mrs. Lowell herself plainly had but a humble conceit of her poetic gift, and it does not appear that poetry was an abundant resource with her. But art there is of no mean order in this little book. It is a delicate instrument on which she plays; there are not many stops, but there is a vibrant tone which thrills the ear. Tenderness indeed is the prevailing note, but in one poem, "Africa," there is a massiveness of structure, and a sonorous dignity of measure which appeal powerfully to the imagination. The poems have, here and there, an autobiographic value. One written in Rome, shortly after the travellers had reached that city and the dream of childhood had come true, ended with the verses : —

> " And Rome lay all before us in its glory,
>   Its glory and its beautiful decay,
>   But, like the student in the oft-read story,
>   I could have turned away,

> " To the still chamber with its half-closed shutter
>   Where the beloved father lay in pain,

> To sit beside him in contentment utter,
>   Never to part again."

There are four sonnets in which her love for her
husband glows with a deep, steady passion, one of
them written doubtless in the solemn days near
the end, in the spirit recorded by Lowell when he
wrote to Briggs after her death : " She promised
to be with me if that were possible."

> " In the deep flushing of the Western sky
>   The new moon stands as she would fain be gone,
>   And, dropping earthward, greet Endymion :
>   If Death uplift me, even thus should I,
>   Companioned by the silver spirits high,
>   And stationed on the sunset's crimson towers,
>   Bend longing over earth's broad stretch of bowers,
>   To where my love beneath their shades might lie :
>   For I should weary of the endless blue,
>   Should weary of my ever-growing light,
>   If that one soul, so beautiful and true,
>   Were hidden by earth's vapors from my sight,
>   Should wane and wane as changeful planets do,
>   And move on slowly, wrapt in mine own night."

What most impresses the reader who takes all
these poems at a sitting is the reserve, the just
balance of sentiment which controls them. Passion is here, but it is not stormy, and love and
tenderness, but they are not feeble and tearful.
Depth of feeling and strength of character lie open
to view in the firm lines, and the fine light and
shade of the verse come incontrovertibly from a
nature evenly poised, whose companionship must
have been to Lowell that of a kindred spirit, capable indeed of guiding and not merely of seconding
his resolves.

Mrs. Maria White Lowell

The frontispiece to the volume, which is here reproduced, was a crystallotype of a drawing by Cheney after Page's portrait. "It is like," Lowell wrote at the time, "as far as there can be any likeness made of a face so full of spiritual beauty, and in which so much of the charm was subterficial." He tried to convey to a friend, with whom his association was purely literary, some notion of her when he wrote: "All that was written of Lady Digby, all that Taylor said of the Countess of Carbery and Donne of Elizabeth Drury — belongs as well to her, she was so beautiful and good. She was born 8th July, 1821, married 26th December, 1844, and went home 27th October, 1853. 'The Pilgrim they laid in a large upper chamber whose windows opened toward the sunrising: and the name of the chamber was Peace.'"

This was written more than a year after the event. He made use of the same allusion just after his wife's death, when writing to his friend Briggs, but added mournfully that he himself was not in that chamber. Indeed, in the first months of his desolation he was in a most unhappy state, and endured a loneliness from which now and then an uncontrollably passionate cry would be uttered. His father was perfectly deaf and often alarmingly excitable, and his sister Rebecca eccentric to a degree which made her preserve for days an absolute silence. He would rush out into the world, and there showed an artificial gayety which bewildered his friends, only to come back to despise himself. "I know perfectly well," he wrote to his most inti-

mate friend, "that my nature is naturally joyous
and susceptible of all happy impressions; but that
is the very reason I am wretched. I am afraid of
myself. I dread the world and its temptations,
for I do long to keep myself pure enough to satisfy
her who was better than all I can say of her. I
often troubled her while she was here, but I cannot bear to now that she is in entire felicity." He
was, as he afterward said of himself, in great agony
of mind, and he had to force himself into those
laborious hours which one instinctively feels contain a wise restorative.

He was, in a measure, undergoing solitary con-
finement. He sat in his lonely study, or walked
up and down, pencilling sentences on the wall as
if he were really a prisoner, and finding a strange
consolation in repeating the Service for the Dead,
which he had learned by heart. "I remember,"
he wrote long after,[1] "the ugly fancy I had sometimes that I was another person, and used to hesitate at the door when I came back from my late
night walks, lest I should find the real owner of
the room sitting in my chair before the fire. A
well-nigh hermit life I had led till then." There
were but few who could approach his real self in
those days, but there came from Longfellow a
gentle word of consolation in his poem "The Two
Angels," written on the coincidence of the birth of
his own daughter and the death of Mrs. Lowell.

Meanwhile, his letters, even when disclosing his
misery, contained happy references to his sturdy,

[1] See letter to Mr. Norton, 13 April, 1884, *Letters*, ii. 279.

affectionate child. True, all the losses he had suffered seemed now to be but the messengers of a
final disaster. " I have only one lamb left of
four," he wrote to an occasional correspondent,
" and think I hear the foot of the inexorable wolf
if a leaf rustle; " but as the days went by this sensitiveness subsided. He was fortunate in having
for her a most admirable governess, and he found
the child's companionship an unfailing joy. " I
said as I sat down to dinner," he writes in one of
his letters; " ' This is a rare day, I have positively
had an idea.' Not knowing the meaning of ' idea,'
and I being in the habit of telling her (when she
is *hypt*, no rare thing) that she has some disease to
which I give a very hard name, — she thought I was
joking, and said, ' Nonsense, papa, you have n't
got an idea,' — evidently thinking it some terrible complaint. ' Why, should n't you like a papa
that had ideas ? ' She threw her arms round my
neck and said : ' You dear papa ! you 're just the
kind of papa that I love ! ' " " Mabel," he writes
again, " has just begun to have ' Robinson Crusoe '
read to her. Think of that and burst with envy !
What have you and I left in life like that ? She
has already arranged a coronet of feathers, and
proposes to play Indian Chief in future. Her
great part lately has been the Great Wild Goat of
the Parlor, — produced every evening with unbounded applause, especially from the chief actor.
With a pair of newspaper horns she chases her
father (who knows what it is to be tossed on the
horns of the newspapers), qualifying his too exces-

sive terrors with a kiss at last to show that it is
really not *real*, but only play. . . . She has been in
the habit of hearing her grandfather always say,
'If Providence permit,' of course not knowing what
it meant. But one day, having made an uncommonly successful slide, she turned triumphantly to
her aunt and cried, ' There, *that* time I went like
Providence permit.' The doctor ordered her a
blanket bath. She had already tried one and said,
' If you please, papa, I had rather not.' ' But, darling, most people like them very much.' ' Well,
papa, *I* don't; people have different tastes you
know. I 've often noticed that everybody has a
different mind.' "

Added to the need of wresting his mind from
the despondency of grief was the pecuniary pressure. He had an income at this time from such
little property as he possessed of six hundred dollars a year, and that plainly would not suffice. So
he shook his portfolio, and even began writing new
poems which he sent to his friend Briggs for *Putnam's*, and he set about working over the letters he
had written in Italy, publishing them in *Graham's
Magazine*, under the title " Leaves from my Italian Journal." It was easier to do such mechanical
work as this, and he began to speculate on the possibility of editing Shakespeare, and meditated a
life of Dean Swift. He did during 1854 edit
Marvell for the series of *British Poets* which his
friend Professor Child was preparing for Little,
Brown & Co., expending a good deal of loving care
on the text, and editing Henry Rogers's brief me-

moir by omissions, illustrations from Marvell's writings, and a slight addition. He wrote also at this time, for use in the same series, the brief sketch of Keats which afterward he placed with his collected essays. As an introduction to Keats's poems, it was designedly more biographical than critical, and did little more than set forth in a lively fashion the facts gathered by Milnes. When one considers Lowell's early appreciation of Keats, it seems a little singular that he should have contented himself with so slight an expression.

Lowell spent the last week of June, 1854, at Newport, R. I., on a visit to the Nortons, and then went for the summer to Beverly, chiefly to be near his sister, Mrs. Charles Lowell. At this time the north shore of Massachusetts Bay had all the charm of rock and beach which it now has, with a pristine simplicity of life which it has lost. To-day the visitor drives through the woods near Beverly by well-kept roads, meeting at every turn other carriages and pleasure parties. Then, the woods were as beautiful, but had unbroken solitude. "At Newport," Lowell wrote to Miss Norton, "you have no woods, and ours are so grand and deep and unconverted! They have those long pauses of conscious silence that are so fine, as if the spirit that inhabits them were hiding from you and holding its breath, — and then all the leaves stir again, and the pines cheat the rocks with their mock surf, and that invisible bird that haunts such solitudes calls once and is answered, and then silence again."

A letter to Mr. Norton, dated 14 August, 1854, hints at the restful character of this seaside sojourn. "This is an outlying dependency of the Castle of Indolence, and even more lazy, — in proportion as the circulation is more languid at the extremities. By dint of counting on my fingers, and with the aid of an old newspaper and an almanac, I have approximated, I believe, to the true date of your world out there, and that seems to me quite a sufficient mental achievement for one morning. The chief food of the people here is Lotus. It is cunning to take various shapes, — sometimes fish, sometimes flesh, fowl, eggs, or what not, — but is always Lotus. It does not make us forget, only Memory is no longer recollection, it is passive, not active, and mixes real with feigned things, just as in perfectly still pools the images of clouds filter down through the transparent water and make one perspective with the matter-of-fact weeds at the bottom. I feel as if I had sunk in a diving-bell provisioned and aired for three months, and knew not of storm or calm, or of the great keels, loaded, perhaps, with fate, that sigh hoarsely overhead toward their appointed haven. . . .

"What do I do? Tarry at Jericho chiefly. Also I row and fish, and have learned to understand the life of a shore fisherman thoroughly. Sometimes I get my dinner with my lines, — a rare fate for a poet. Sometimes I watch the *net* result when the tritons draw their seine. Also I grow brown, and have twice lost and renewed the skin of my hands and, alas, my nose. Also I know what hunger is and, reversing the Wordsworthian sheep, am one feeding like forty."

He went on one or two short cruises and enjoyed the genuine country life with its salt flavor, but was back at Elmwood in the fall. The year had found some intimate expression in his verse, as well as the more objective poems like "Pictures from Appledore," suggested in part it may be by one of his summer cruises, though the last section was written four years before. Mr. Stillman, who made his acquaintance at this time, when he was foraging for *The Crayon*, the new literary and art journal which his enthusiasm had projected, speaks warmly of the princely courtesy with which Lowell received him. "Out of the depth of the shadow over his life," he writes,[1] "in the solitude of his study, with nothing but associations of his wrecked happiness permitted around him, the kindly sympathy with a new aspiration wakened him to a momentary gaiety, his humor flashed out irrepressible, and his large heart turned its warmest side to the new friend, who came only to make new calls on his benevolence; that is, to give him another opportunity to bestow himself on others." On his part, Lowell welcomed heartily this ingenuous lover of art and letters. They took long walks together over the country Lowell knew so well, to Beaver Brook, the Waverley Oaks, and the Waltham hills. "You made me fifteen years younger," he wrote, "while you stayed. When a man gets to my age,

---

[1] "A Few of Lowell's Letters" in *The Old Rome and the New and other Studies*, p. 134.

enthusiasms don't often knock at the door of his garret. I am all the more charmed with them when they come. A youth full of such pure intensity of hope and faith and purpose, what is he but the breath of a resurrection-trumpet to stiffened old fellows, bidding us up out of our clay and earth if we would not be too late ? "

The poems which register the tranquillity of a return to common life, like " The Windharp " and " Auf Wiedersehen," are tremulous with the emotion which he could bear to express. Indeed, when Lowell came to print the former of these poems he omitted one stanza, possibly as going farther than he cared to with his contemporaneous public. In the letter last quoted, he sent it to Mr. Stillman.

> " O tress that so oft on my heart hath lain,
>   Rocked to rest within rest by its thankful beating,
>   Say, which is harder, — to bear the pain
>   Of laughter and light, or to wait in vain,
>   'Neath the unleaved tree, the impossible meeting ?
>   If Death's lips be icy, Life gives, iwis,
>   Some kisses more clay-cold and darkening than his ! "

But as a comprehensive record of this whole experience, the " Ode to Happiness " written at this time may be taken as most conclusive. The very form of the ode, a form to which Lowell was wont to resort in the great passages of his life, aided the expression, for its gravity, its classic reserve, even its labored lines served best to hold that sustained mood which impelled the poet to stand as it were before an altar and make his sacrificial hymn. Tranquillity, he avers, is the elder sister of Happiness. " She is not that," he says : —

" She is not that for which youth hoped,
    But she hath blessings all her own,
Thoughts pure as lilies newly oped,
    And faith to sorrow given alone :

    .   .   .   .   .   .

                       ' I am she
Whom the gods love, Tranquillity :
    That other whom you seek forlorn
    Half earthly was : but I am born
Of the immortals, and our race
Wears still some sadness on its face :
    He wins me late, but keeps me long,
Who, dowered with every gift of passion,
In that fierce flame can forge and fashion
    Of sin and self the anchor strong ;
Can thence compèl the driving force
Of daily life's mechanic course,
Nor less the nobler energies
Of needful toil and culture wise ;
Whose soul is worth the tempter's lure,
Who can renounce, and yet endure,
To him I come, not lightly wooed,
But won by silent fortitude.' " [1]

From this time forward, however he might be
subject to transient moods, as one with so much
sensibility would inevitably be, Lowell was yet
free from the violent and tempestuous fluctuations
of mood which heretofore had marked his course.
The first desolation over, that influence which during Mrs. Lowell's lifetime had always been accompanied by the dark shadow of a threatened
loss, now became, paradoxical as the phrase may
be, peramanent and profound.   No human accident
could affect it, and as Lowell's own powers had
passed through the experimental stage, there came

[1] The poem was not printed till April, 1858, when it appeared
in *The Atlantic Monthly.*

a steadiness of aim and a maturity of expression which thenceforth were registered in successive sure and firm-footed performances. It may truly be said that Lowell had now found himself, and that from this period dates the full orbit of a course which had heretofore been more or less eccentric, but now could be reasonably calculated. Surprises there were to be, but surprises of excellent achievement, rather than of new ventures.

It is therefore with special interest that one notes the character of the work which occupied Lowell in this eventful season of 1854–1855. Some time before he had been asked by his kinsman who directed the Lowell Institute to give a course of lectures before it, and had been paid in advance; he had made some movement toward preparation, but now he set about it in earnest, and began the delivery 9 January, 1855. There were to be twelve lectures, and he was to discourse on poetry in general and English poetry in particular. Something of the exhilaration with which he entered upon the engagement may be seen in a note written to Mr. Norton three days before the first lecture, and inclosing a ticket to the course.

"This will admit you to one of the *posti distinti* to witness the celebrated *tableau vivant* of the sacrifice of Iphigenia (Iphigenia, by particular request, Mr. J. R. Lowell). It is well known that this interesting ceremony was originally performed for the sake of raising the wind, and Mr. L. will communicate a spirit of classic reality to the performance by going through it with the same end in view.

"I write this by the hand of an amanuensis whom I have had in my employment for some time, and who has learned how to catch my ideas without my being obliged to speak — a great gain.

"(A great gain indeed! the greatest bore in the world! He thinks I am writing what he dictates at this moment because he hears the pen scratch. He pretends to be a good-natured fellow — but if you only knew him as I do! He has no more feeling than a horseradish.)

"I should have come last Saturday to Shady Hill — but you may guess how busy I have been. (It is *I* who have had all the work, and only my board and tobacco for wages : *he* pretend to hate slavery!)

"I have only just got the flood on, and feel as if I might deliver a course that will not disgrace me.

"(I almost hope they will, for what right has he to keep me shut up here ? I get no walks, and he begins to keep me awake at nights with his cursed ideas as he calls them. What *is* an idea, I should like to know ?)

"I have only one *private* entrance ticket to spare — but I suppose you do not want any more.

"Give my best regards and happy New Years and all kinds of things at Shady Hill (and mine, too ; how mad he 'd be if he knew I put that in).

"Always yours,
"The Amanuensis of J. R. Lowell, esquire."

Two days after giving the first lecture, Lowell wrote to Stillman : —

" I have been so fearfully busy with my lectures! and so nervous about them, too! I had
never spoken in public, there was a great rush for
tickets (the lectures are gratis), only one in five
of the applicants being supplied — and altogether
I was taken quite aback. I had no idea there
would be such a desire to hear me. I delivered
my first lecture to a crowded hall on Tuesday
night, and I believe I have succeeded. The lecture was somewhat abstract, but I kept the audience perfectly still for an hour and a quarter.
(They are in the habit of going out at the end
of the hour.) I delivered it again yesterday afternoon to another crowd,[1] and was equally successful
— so I think I am safe now. But I have six yet to
write, and am consequently very busy and pressed
for time. I felt anxious, of course, for I had a
double responsibility. The lectures were founded
by a cousin of mine, and the trustee is another
cousin — so I wished not only to do credit to myself and my name, but to justify my relative in
appointing me to lecture. It is all over now —
and, as far as the public are concerned, I have succeeded ; but the lectures keep me awake and make
me lean."

[1] It was the custom when there was an unusual demand for
tickets, for the lecturer, besides his Tuesday and Friday evening
discourses, to repeat them on Wednesday and Saturday after-
noons. In those days also, applicants for tickets registered their
names during a certain number of days in advance, and at the
close of the registry notification was made that persons holding
numbers divisible by two, three, four, or five, as the case might
be (in the ratio of applicants to the number of seats in the hall),
might call and receive tickets.

Mr. Longfellow was a very interested auditor, and his diary bears witness to the attention which he gave to the course : —

"January 8, 1855. Lowell came in the evening and we talked about his lectures on poetry which begin to-morrow.

"January 9. Mr. Richard Grant White, of New York, author of 'Shakespeare's Scholar,' came to tea. He drove in with us to hear Lowell's first lecture : an admirable performance, and a crowded audience. After it, we drove out to Norton's, where, with T. and the lecturer, we had a pleasant supper.

"January 20. Lowell's lecture, on the old English ballads, one of the best of the course."

Charles Sumner appears also to have been one of the auditors. At any rate, he wrote to Longfellow from Washington, 6 February, 1855 : "Lowell's lecture on Milton lifted me for a whole day. It was the utterance of genius in honor of genius."

Mr. Fields asked Lowell for the lectures for publication, but he put him off "till they were better," and never published them. They were reported at the time by Lowell's old friend, Robert Carter, in the *Boston Daily Advertiser*, and some time after Lowell's death these reports were gathered into a volume and printed privately for the Rowfant Club of Cleveland, Ohio.

The form in which the lectures were reported, sometimes direct, sometimes indirect, undoubtedly robs them of some of the charm which the hearers acknowledged, but enough remains to give one a

tolerably clear impression of Lowell's mode of
treatment. The first lecture was occupied with
definitions, and in a familiar way Lowell set about
distinguishing poetry from prose, and by a variety
of illustrations gave some notion of the great op-
erations of the imagination. Having cleared the
way, he took up the consideration of English poetry
in the historical order, dealing with the forerunners, Piers Ploughman's Vision, the Metrical Ro-
mances, and the Ballads; and then devoting one
lecture each to Chaucer, Spenser, Milton, Butler,
and Pope. The discussion of Pope led him to inter-
rupt himself, and in the next lecture take up the
subject of Poetic Diction, for after expressing his
admiration of the consummate art of Pope's arti-
ficiality, he wished to inquire whether there might
not be a real, vital distinction between the language of prose raised to a high degree of metrical
efficiency and the language of poetry. His readers
will recall the amusing passage in an article on
" Swinburne's Tragedies," in which, when wishing
to illustrate the Greek battledoor and shuttlecock
style of dialogue, he finds it easier to make a burlesque imitation than to hunt up some passage in
Sophocles. In like manner he invents a piece of
descriptive verse — a Lapland sketch — as an instance of the artificial manner brought in by Pope,
but lacking his wonderful manipulation of language. It is a felicitous example of Lowell's imitative faculty, which led him, when he began to
write, to throw off lines in Burns's manner, but
which never betrayed him when he was in earnest

in poetry. The imitation was in itself a criticism. He liked to emphasize the essential element of poetry by instancing the empty form. Mr. Dante Rossetti once overpowered me by producing a thin volume of verse by T. H. Chivers, M. D., and reading aloud from it and demanding information about the author. When I applied to Lowell afterward, he said that Dr. Chivers had been wont to send him his books, and he read them aloud to his classes as illustrations of the shell of Shelley. A lecture followed on Wordsworth, and then the twelfth was devoted to the Function of the Poet, which in its brief report intimates that Lowell was thinking less of himself than of the country with its need of a seer.

The delivery of the lectures had one immediate and important result. Mr. Longfellow had been Smith Professor of the French and Spanish Languages and Literatures and Professor of Belles Lettres in Harvard College since 1836, having come to the work when Lowell was midway through his course, but he made up his mind in 1854 that he must give up the post, not from ill-health, but because he wished to try the effect of change on his mind, and of freedom from routine. " Household occupations," he wrote to Freiligrath, " children, relatives, friends, strangers, and college lectures, so completely fill up my days that I have no time for poetry, and, consequently, the last two years have been very unproductive with me." Freiligrath had heard rumors of Longfellow's resignation, and had put in an application to be his successor. Longfellow could not give him any encouragement, since, though foreigners were employed to teach the several languages, the professor himself must be an American. There were, he said, six candidates for the position, all friends of his. Lowell was not one of these, but his lectures had marked him as the fit successor, and so Longfellow wrote with satisfaction in his diary, 31 January, 1855 : "Lowell is to be my successor ! Dr. Walker talked with me about it this morning, and I have been to see Lowell about the preliminaries, and the matter is as good as settled. I am sorry for some of my friends who want the place. But for lectures, I think Lowell the best of the candidates. He has won his spurs and will give the college just what it needs." Lowell himself told the news to his friend Briggs in the following letter, dated 9 February, 1855 : —

"I have been silent ever so long because I could not help it. I have been lecturing four times a week (and am now), and, with my usual discretion, put off writing my lectures till the last moment, so that for five weeks I have been with the bayonet pricking me on close behind, and have hardly dared to *think* even of anything else. But I have not forgotten you, my dear old friend, nor my love of you, and I have felt a kind of pang now and then because I said in my last note that I would soon write to you — as, indeed, I am always intending to do.

"I write now because I have something pleasant to tell, and did not wish you to hear it first from any one but me — though you always seem to live at one end of an ear of Dionysius that brings you all the news of itself. The news is this: The Corporation of the college have asked me to take Longfellow's place, and my nomination will go to the Overseers next Thursday.

"The thing has come about in the pleasantest way, and the place has sought me, not I, it. There were seven applicants for the place, but I was not one of them. On the contrary, I had refused to be a candidate when it was proposed to me.

"I have accepted the offer, and am to go abroad for a year to prepare myself. *That* is the hardest part, but I did not feel competent without it.

"And the duties are pleasant. I am not to have anything to do with teaching, as Longfellow had, but only to deliver two courses of lectures in the year — on pretty much any subject I choose, and my salary is to be $1200.00.

"Everybody seems pleased. My first thought was a sad one, for the heart that would have beat warmest is still. Then I thought of my father, and then of you. I think it will be all the better for Mabel that I should have enough to live on, without being forced to write, and I shall have time enough after the first year to do pretty much what I like. . . .

"My lectures have succeeded quite beyond my expectation. One or two have been pretty good, but I have felt sad in writing them, and somehow feel as if I had not got *myself* into them very much. However, folks are pleased."

Very likely the fame of his lectures brought him

invitations to go elsewhere; at any rate, when his course in Boston was finished, he made a tour in the West, and became so desperately out of conceit with the business before a week had passed that he tried to escape the remaining lectures, but he was not released and had at least the satisfaction of carrying home six hundred dollars as the proceeds. " I hate this business of lecturing," he wrote from Madison, Wisconsin, to Miss Norton. " To be received at a bad inn by a solemn committee, in a room with a stove that smokes but not exhilarates, to have three cold fish-tails laid in your hand to shake, to be carried to a cold lecture-room, to read a cold lecture to a cold audience, to be carried back to your smoke-side, paid, and the three fish-tails again — well, it is not delightful exactly."

Lowell does not seem to have written anything in the short time that elapsed after the close of his lecture tour before he sailed for Europe, though he showed a lively interest in Mr. Stillman's paper *The Crayon*, and sent it his poem " Invita Minerva," in which Longfellow discovered a reminder of Emerson's " Forerunners." The fact that Lowell was to be the elder poet's successor naturally drew them together much at this time. " A beautiful morning," wrote Longfellow on the 17th of May. " Went and sat an hour with Lowell in his upper chamber among the treetops. He sails for Havre the first of June;" and on the 29th he records: " Lowell's friends gave him a farewell dinner at the Revere, whereat I had the honor of presiding. A joyous banquet: one of the pleasantest I ever attended, — a meeting of friends to take leave of a friend whom we all love." Lowell himself refers briefly to the occasion in a note written the next day: "Everything went off finely after you left. Holmes sang another song and repeated some very charming verses,[1] and Rölker to his own intense delight got through two stanzas of 'a helf to ve nortward boun',' William White having incautiously supplied him with the initial line. He gave it with so much sentiment that we were all entirely overcome and laughed so immoderately that the brave Rölker at length sat down. We sang 'Auld lang syne' in true college style and so parted. On the whole I renewed my youth last night — and my recollections of '1790' this morning, for I only had four hours' sleep. However, aboard ship I shall have leisure enough to emulate Chaucer's Morpheus

'That slept and did no other work.'"

That day Longfellow drove into town with Lowell and saw him off for New York, whence he was to sail.

But the weeks before Lowell's departure brought other things to mind than leaving home and affectionate friends. He had been asked to pronounce a poem before the senior class of Hamilton College at the coming commencement. The invitation reached him on the memorable day when the runaway slave Burns was captured in the streets

[1] Probably the verses beginning, —

"Farewell, for the bark has her breast to the tide."

of Boston, and he wrote in reply to the invitation:
"In six months I shall be in Switzerland; an ocean
between me and a slave hunt, thank God!"

Lowell again took passage in a sailing vessel,
the St. Nicholas, Bragdon, master, which left New
York 4 June, 1855, bound for Havre.   Among his
companions was Dr. Elliott, under whose care he
had been a dozen years before, when his eyes were
in a bad way.   It was a four weeks' voyage, and
Lowell amused himself with Lever's novels from
beginning to end, as he lay stretched in a ham-
mock on the quarter-deck.   Reaching France, he
spent three weeks in Paris among the pictures
chiefly, and made an excursion to Chartres, apparently his first visit, but one which left so deep an
impression on his mind that fourteen years later,
when he wrote "The Cathedral," which he wished
at first to call "A Day at Chartres," the same
images which sprang to his mind when he wrote of
his visit directly after in a letter to Mr. Norton,
recurred and found poetic expression.   "It is the
home now," he wrote, "of innumerable swallows
and sparrows, who build upon the shoulders of
those old great ones (the stone angels and saints)
— as we little folks do too, I am afraid.   Even
here I found the Norman — for when I mounted
to the spire, I saw numbers of hawks who dwell in
the higher parts, as in their castles, and prey on
the poor Saxons below."   So in the poem he takes
a parting look

"At those old weather-pitted images
Of by-gone struggle, now so sternly calm.

About their shoulders sparrows had built nests,
And fluttered, chirping, from gray perch to perch,
Now on a mitre poising, now a crown,
Irreverently happy.   While I thought
How confident they were, what careless hearts
Flew on those lightsome wings and shared the sun,
A larger shadow crossed ; and looking up
I saw where, nesting in the hoary towers,
The sparrow-hawk slid forth on noiseless air,
With sidelong head that watched the joy below,
Grim Norman baron o'er this clan of Kelts."

From Paris Lowell ran over to London, chiefly
to see the Storys, who were there, and renewed his
acquaintance with Thackeray and the Brownings,
and fell in with Leigh Hunt. But his main business was to make himself proficient in German, and
so having taken his academic vacation in advance,
he journeyed through the Low Countries, and settled himself in Dresden for the autumn and winter.
The quiet Saxon city was a favorite resort for
Americans then even more than now, and for the
first few weeks his sister, Mrs. Putnam, was there
with her family. It was with a dull, heavy feeling
that he gave himself to his tasks, seeing very little
of society. " I confess frankly," he wrote, shortly
after his establishment there, " that I am good for
nothing, and have been for some time, and that
there are times almost every day when I wish to
die, be out of the world once for all. . . . I fear
I shall come back with my eremitical tendencies
more developed than ever." But dogged persistence in work was something better than an ano-
dyne, and work hard he did. " A man of my age,"
he wrote to his father, " has to study very hard in

acquiring a new language, and I cannot be satisfied without knowing thoroughly all I undertake to know. I am very well and constantly busy."

Mr. Norton with his sisters crossed the Atlantic in the autumn, and Lowell wrote to him at Paris : " Did I tell you that I had a room on the ground floor, with a glass door giving upon a large garden ? that I have a flock of sparrows that come to breakfast with me every morning, and eat loaf sugar to the detriment of my coffee? That I go to hear lectures on the Natural Sciences and have even assisted at the anatomical class, — beginning with horror and ending with interest? That we have the best theatre here I ever saw ? And by the way, if Bouffé acts the *Abbé Galant* while you are in Paris, go and see it by all means. It is a truly artistic piece of representation. If it be not too cold, go down to Chartres. It is simply the best thing in France, and must have come out of some fine old Norman brain, — I am sure no Frenchman could ever have conceived it. After all, there are no such facts as the elements. Leave a thing to them, and they redress all imperfections and expunge all prose."

He had planned spending a portion of his time in Spain, and took lessons in Spanish in Dresden, but finally abandoned the notion. His host and hostess, with whom he talked, assured him that he made astonishing progress in German. " What a language it is to be sure ! " he wrote ; " with nominatives sending out as many roots as that witch-grass which is the pest of all child-gardens, and

sentences in which one sets sail like an admiral
with sealed orders, not knowing where the devil he
is going to till he is in mid-ocean ! " To his friend
Stillman he wrote, as the winter wore away : " To
say all in one word, I have been passing a very
wretched winter. I have been out of health and
out of spirits, gnawed a great part of the time by
an insatiable homesickness, and deprived of my
usual means of ridding myself of bad thoughts by
putting them into verse, for I have always felt that
I was here for the specific end of learning German,
and not of pleasing myself." Fifteen years later,
looking back, he wrote : " I once spent a winter in
Dresden, a southern climate compared with England, and really almost lost my respect for the sun
when I saw him groping among the chimney-pots
opposite my windows as he described his impov-
erished arc in the sky." [1]

As spring drew on he was possessed with a longing for Italy, especially for the near friends who
were there, his sister Mary who had left Dresden
for Rome, the Storys, the Nortons, and others. He
turned his face thitherward the first of March,
meaning to be absent for two or three weeks only,
but he was not back in Dresden till the beginning
of June. " My journey in Italy," he wrote to his
father on his return, " was of much benefit to me.
I spent a fortnight with Mary in Rome, went with
her to Naples and spent another fortnight with her
there. At Naples we parted. I went to Sicily
and made the tour of the island, hoping to find

[1] " A Good Word for Winter," in *Literary Essays*, iii. 267.

Mary still in Naples when I returned. But Sicily required much more time than I had expected, and when I came back I found Mary gone back to Rome. I could not follow her thither, but took the steamer to Genoa, and so over the Alps back to Germany. I found Sicily very interesting in scenery and associations, and very saddening in its political aspect. I believe it is the worst governed country in Europe. With every advantage of climate and soil, it is miserably poor, — there are no roads, and vexatious restrictions repress trade in every direction. The people struck me as looking more depressed than any I have seen."

His itinerary, to be a little more detailed, was to Venice, then by rail to Verona, and to Mantua. There he hired a vettura to take him to Parma, and in the same mode he went to Bologna, sleeping at Modena on the way. From Bologna he went to Ravenna and thence to Florence. He went to Siena by the slow, roundabout rail, and then was driven to Orvieto by Chiusi. At Orvieto he was greeted by Mr. Norton, Mr. Page, and Mr. John W. Field, who had come out to meet him and to escort him to Rome. On his return from Genoa he made a stop at Nuremberg. He lingered in Dresden a few weeks, made another brief stay in Paris, and was once more in Cambridge, in August, 1856.

On his return from Europe Lowell did not resume life at Elmwood, but took up his quarters with his brother-in-law, Dr. Estes Howe, on Kirk-

House of Dr. Estes Howe

land Street, in Cambridge.   Longfellow was in his
summer home at Nahant, and Lowell ran down to
see him, looking, as the elder poet notes in his diary,
"as if he had not been gone a week."   He took
renewed delight in his country walks, and tingled
afresh at contact with nature.   "How I do love
the earth!" he writes to Mr. Norton, who was still
in Europe.   "I feel it thrill under my feet.   I feel
somehow as if it were conscious of my love, as if
something passed into my dancing blood from it,
and I get rid of that duty-feeling, — 'What right
have I to be?' — and not a goldenrod of them all
soaks in the sunshine or feels the blue currents of
the air eddy about him more thoughtlessly than I."

The college year opened a few weeks after his
return, and he began his duties by repeating the
course of lectures which he had delivered before
the Lowell Institute the winter of 1855, before
taking up his more specific work in German literature and Dante.

It was in the teaching of Dante that Lowell
made the strongest impression on the students who
gathered about him, if we may judge by the reminiscences which more than one has printed; and
the methods he adopted in his teaching never
greatly varied, for he came to the work of teaching
without any specific training, when he had been
nearly twenty years out of college, and when the
kind of interest in literature, which in his college
days had disputed for supremacy with the docile
habit of the schoolboy, had now become confirmed
by study, by travel, and by his own productions.

In an address which he gave in 1889 before the
Modern Language Association of America, he recorded his judgment on the vexed question of the
distribution of emphasis upon the philological and
the æsthetic pursuit of the study of literature. It
was twelve years since he had discontinued the
practice of teaching, and it is reasonable to infer
that he was distilling in a few sentences the experience which his method of study and his method
of teaching recalled to him.

" In reading such books," he says, " as chiefly
deserve to be read in any foreign language, it is
wise to translate consciously and in words as we
read. There is no such help to a fuller mastery of
our vernacular. It compels us to such a choosing
and testing, to so nice a discrimination of sound,
propriety, position, and shade of meaning, that we
now first learn the secret of the words we have
been using or misusing all our lives, and are gradually made aware that to set forth even the plainest
matter as it should be set forth is not only a very
difficult thing, calling for thought and practice,
but an affair of conscience as well. Translating
teaches us as nothing else can, not only that there
is a best way, but that it is the only way."

Again, in the same address, thinking no doubt
of the expansion of the curriculum at Harvard,
even since he laid aside the teacher's gown: " We
have every reason to congratulate ourselves on the
progress the modern languages have made as well
in academic as in popular consideration. They are
now taught (as they could not formerly be taught)

in a way that demands toil and thought of the student, as Greek and Latin, and they only, used to be taught, and they also open the way to higher intellectual joys, to pastures new, and not the worse for being so, as Greek and Latin, and they only, used to do. . . . If I did not rejoice in the wonderful advance made in the comparative philology of the modern languages, I should not have the face to be standing here. But neither should I if I shrank from saying what I believed to be the truth, whether here or elsewhere. I think that the purely linguistic side in the teaching of them seems in the way to get more than its fitting share. I insist only that in our college courses this should be a separate study, and that, good as it is in itself, it should, in the scheme of general instruction, be restrained to its own function as the guide to something better, and that something better is Literature. The blossoms of language have certainly as much value as its roots, for if the roots secrete food and thereby transmit life to the plant, yet the joyous consummation of that life is in the blossoms, which alone bear the seeds that distribute and renew it in other growths. Exercise is good for the muscles of mind and to keep it well in hand for work, but the true end of Culture is to give it play, a thing quite as needful. What I would urge, therefore, is that no invidious distinction should be made between the Old Learning and the New, but that students, due regard being had to their temperaments and faculties, should be encouraged to take the course in modern languages as being quite as good in point of mental discipline as any other, if pursued with the same thoroughness and to the same end. And that end is Literature, for there language first attains to a full consciousness of its powers and to the delighted exercise of them. Literature has escaped that doom of Shinar which made our Association possible, and still everywhere speaks in the universal tongue of civilized man."

Lowell's office did not require of him elementary instruction in modern languages, nor indeed was it expected that he should do drill work in linguistics. There were competent instructors then in the several languages, some of whom afterward came to be eminent professors, as the department was divided. He was not indifferent in the choice of assistants, but once they were at work he left them to their own devices, and exercised the slightest sort of supervision of them. There was no very nice division of labor, except that, as I have said, these assistants took the more exact grammatical details, yet they all included more or less of literature in their work with students. It can hardly be said that Lowell did more than flavor his instruction of literature with a pinch of grammar. Words in their origin and changing meanings he did comment on, but inflections, paradigms, and all the apparatus of grammar formed no part of his interest in his work.

In his essay on "Shakespeare Once More" he has said : "There would be no dispute about the advantages of that Greek culture which Schiller

advocated with such generous eloquence, if the
great authors of antiquity had not been degraded
from teachers of thinking to drillers in grammar,
and made the ruthless pedagogues of root and in-
flection, instead of companions for whose society
the mind must put on her highest mood. . . .
There is much that is deciduous in books, but all
that gives them a title to rank as literature, in the
highest sense, is perennial. Their vitality is the
vitality not of one or another blood or tongue, but
of human nature; their truth is not topical and
transitory, but of universal acceptation; and thus
all great authors seem the coevals not only of each
other, but of whoever reads them, growing wiser
with him as he grows wise, and unlocking to him
one secret after another as his own life and experience give him the key, but on no other condition."

Now Lowell's own interest in literature had been
direct. It would be idle to say that literature was
interesting or valuable to him only so far as it was
a criticism of life. It would be equally idle to say
that his pleasure in it was derived only from his
perception of it as great art. He carried to it the
same kind of interest which he carried into his own
production of literature. He was at once full of
that human sense which made him delight in a fine
expression of humanity, and he had the craftsman's
pleasure in excellent work, so that on the one
hand, though in his youth he raged against Pope,
in his more mature judgment he rejoiced in the
patience in careful finish which characterized him;

and, on the other hand, he gave himself with the fullest abandonment to an admiration of Dante as "the highest spiritual nature that has expressed itself in rhythmical form." He thought him "the first great poet who ever made a poem wholly out of himself." In one of his unpublished lectures Lowell uses Dante as a text for a discourse on the pursuit of literature, and mingles with it a slight element of autobiography, which makes it specially fitting to repeat the passage here : —

"One is sometimes asked by young men to recommend to them a course of reading. My advice would always be to confine yourself to the supreme books in whatever literature ; still better, to choose some one great author and grow thoroughly familiar with him. For as all roads lead to Rome, so they all likewise lead thence ; and you will find that in order to understand perfectly and weigh exactly any really vital piece of literature, you will be gradually and pleasantly persuaded to studies and explorations of which you little dreamed when you began, and will find yourselves scholars before you are aware. If I may be allowed a personal illustration, it was my own profound admiration for the 'Divina Commedia' of Dante that lured me into what little learning I possess. For remember that there is nothing less fruitful than scholarship for the sake of mere scholarship, nor anything more wearisome in the attainment. But the moment you have an object and a centre, attention is quickened, the mother of memory ; and whatever you acquire groups and arranges itself in an order which is lucid because it is everywhere in intelligent relation to an object of constant and growing interest. Thus, as respects Dante, I asked myself, What are his points of likeness or unlikeness with the authors of classical antiquity? in how far is either of these an advantage or defect? What and how much modern literature had preceded him? How much was he indebted to it? How far had the Italian language been subdued and suppled to the uses of poetry or prose before his time? How much did he color the style or thought of the authors who followed him? Is it a fault or a merit that he is so thoroughly impregnated with the opinions, passions, and even prejudices not only of his age but his country? Was he right or wrong in being a Ghibelline? To what extent is a certain freedom of opinion which he shows sometimes on points of religious doctrine to be attributed to the humanizing influences of the Crusades in enlarging the horizon of the Western mind by bringing it in contact with other races, religions, and social arrangements? These and a hundred other such questions were constant stimulants to thought and inquiry, stimulants such as no merely objectless and, so to speak, impersonal study could have supplied."

When, therefore, Lowell was brought face to face with a company of young men, in the relation of teacher, he appears not to have cast about to see how he could adjust his powers to some prevailing method of teaching, but to have used the material of literature as an instrument of association, and

naturally, untrammelled by pedagogic theory, to
have tried to communicate to the minds about him
the kind of interest which the literature he was
handling inspired in him. So far was he from a
professional teacher that it is doubtful if he indi-
vidualized his students much, or made any attempt
to find entrance into this or that mind by first trying to detect what opening the mind offered. Undoubtedly, one or another with special aptitude or
appreciation may have stimulated him and quickened his faculty of instruction, but for the most
part these young men gave him the occasion for
utterance, and the text before him gave the theme
of discourse. Mr. Barrett Wendell, in his illumi-
nating paper on Lowell as a teacher, confesses
with a generous chagrin, that though he had been
an enthusiastic pupil and had used Lowell's hospitality fully, the acquaintance was very one-sided.
He came to know Lowell well, but Lowell when he
met him again after no great interval of time, had
quite forgotten his face, and almost forgotten his
name.[1]

Though he could scarcely be said to have re-
sorted to any set or customary methods of a professional sort, he was not without recourse to simple
aids in his teaching. "Thirty odd years ago," he
wrote in 1889,[2] "I brought home with me from
Nuremberg photographs of Peter Fischer's statu-

[1] "Mr. Lowell as a Teacher : " Scribner's Magazine, November,
1891. Included in his volume Stelligeri : Charles Scribner's Sons.
[2] "Address before the Modern Language Association of America."

ettes of the twelve apostles. These I used to show to my pupils and ask for a guess at their size. The invariable answer was 'larger than life.' They were really about eighteen inches high, and this grandiose effect was wrought by simplicity of treatment, dignity of pose, a large unfretted sweep of drapery. This object lesson I found more telling than much argument and exhortation." He made also some attempt, when the method was much more of a novelty than it is to-day, to bring in the aid of illustration from art. He interested himself to rid his class-room in University Hall of some dismal charts that hung on the walls, and brought down from Elmwood a number of engravings and photographs which he had collected in his travels abroad, especially illustrations of Florence and Rome; one year he presented each of his class who had persevered with a copy of the recently discovered portrait of Dante by Giotto; and again he gave to each of his small class in Dante a copy of Mr. Norton's privately printed volume on the "New Life."

The actual exercise in the class-room was simple enough and unconventional. The classes were not large, and the relation of the teacher to his students was that of an older friend who knew in a large way the author they were studying, and drew upon his own knowledge and familiarity with the text for comment and suggestion, rather than troubled himself much to find out how much his pupils knew. A student would trudge blunderingly along some passage, and Lowell would break in, taking up the translation himself very likely, and quickly find some suggestion for criticism, for elaboration or incidental and remote comment. Toward the close of the hour, question and answer, or free discussion yielded to the stream of personal reminiscence or abundant reflection upon which Lowell would by this time be launched. Especially would he recall scenes in Florence, sketch in words the effects of the Arno, Giotto's Tower, the church in which Dante was baptized, where he himself had seen children held at the same font; and so Lowell gave out of his treasures, using that form of literature which was perhaps the most perfectly fitted to his mind, free, unconstrained talk. Suddenly, glancing at his watch before him, — a time-piece which was as idly whimsical as its owner, — he would stop, bow and walk quickly out of the room, the men rising respectfully as he left.

And the listeners? They went away, a few carelessly amused at the loose scholastic exercise and complacent over the evasion of work, but some stirred, quickened in their thought, and full of admiration for this brilliant interpreter of life as seen through the verse of Dante. One charm was in the unexpectedness of it all. There was no predicting what direction his talk would take. " Now and again," says Mr. Wendell, " some word or some passage would suggest to him a line of thought — sometimes very earnest, sometimes paradoxically comical — that it never would have suggested to any one else; and he would lean back in his chair, and talk away across country till he felt like stopping ; or he would thrust his hands into the pockets of his rather shabby sack-coat, and pace the end of the room with his heavy laced boots, and look at nothing in particular, and discourse of things in general."

The formalities of academic work were of little concern to Lowell. To be sure, after the first year of neglect he yielded to Dr. Walker's persuasion, and attended Faculty meetings with commendable regularity, and took his share in the little details of discipline which were gravely discussed. It must have brought a smile to his mind, if not to his face, when he found himself called upon to join in a public admonition of ——, junior, " for wearing an illegal coat after repeated warnings." And examinations of his classes were wearisome functions. " Perhaps," says Mr. Wendell, "from unwillingness to degrade the text of Dante to such use, Mr. Lowell set us, when we had read the Inferno and part of the Purgatorio, a paper consisting of nothing but a long passage from Massimo d'Azeglio, which we had three hours to translate. This task we performed as best we might. Weeks passed, and no news came of our marks. At last one of the class, who was not quite at ease concerning his academic standing, ventured at the close of a recitation to ask if Mr. Lowell had assigned him a mark. Mr. Lowell looked at the youth very gravely, and inquired what he really thought his work deserved. The student rather diffidently said that he hoped it was worth sixty per cent. 'You may take it,' said Mr. Lowell, 'I don't want the bother of reading your book.'"

Nevertheless, indifferent as he may have been to the customary details of academic work, and not a little impatient of dry formalities, Lowell gave to the college liberally of the best he had to give. Not merely did he go through with his appointed tasks; he was always ready to take additional labor on himself and to perform works of supererogation. He had men come to read with him in his house, and one season at least offered to conduct a group of divinity students through the Inferno. It must be remembered, moreover, that Lowell's instruction was of two sorts, one in a special author or group, to small select classes, the other general lectures upon literature to large classes. Something of the character of his free handling of subjects may be seen in the extracts from these lectures preserved in *The Harvard Crimson* in 1894; and the attitude which he took toward this side of his work is recorded in the introductory passage to a lecture on the Study of Literature.

"I confess," he says, "it is with more and more diffidence that I rise every year to have my little talk with you about books and the men that have written them. If I remember my terrestrial globe rightly, one gets into his temperate zone after passing the parallel of forty, and arrives at that, shall I call it, Sheltered Haven of Middle Age, when, in proportion as one is more careful of the conclusions he arrives at, he is less zealous in his desire that all mankind should agree with him. Moreover, the longer one studies, the more thoroughly does one persuade himself that till he knows everything, he knows nothing — that after twenty years of criticism, one is still a mere weigher and gauger : skilled only to judge what he may chance to have been in the habit of inspecting at his own little provincial custom-house. And as one gets older he is apt to allow more for personal idiosyncrasy, and to have less certainty that the truth he had reached is not a one-sided one, and that there are not fifty others equally important, and (perhaps) equally unsatisfactory. Every bait is not for every fish. We begin by admitting the old doctor's apothegm that Art is long ; we gradually become persuaded that it is like the Irishman's rope, the other end of which was cut off. So different is Art, whose concern is with the ideal and potential, from Science, which is limited by the actual and positive. Life is so short that it may be fairly doubted whether any man has a right to talk an hour, and I have learned at least so much, — that I hope less to teach than to suggest."

The tone of distrustfulness which is an undercurrent in this passage is familiar enough to the conscientious teacher, and Lowell, measuring the vastness of literature and his own inadequacy to press it home to his students, was fearful that the outcome was slight in proportion to the cost to himself. Yet he did not therefore spare himself. During the years of his teaching, he was more than ever the scholar, taking generous draughts of the literature he was to teach, for long stretches

of time even engaged with his books twelve hours
out of the twenty-four. And so quickening was
his imagination that he went to his classes not to
decant the wine of learning from bottles just filled,
but to give them of his own rare essence distilled
from the hours of study. Hence he was a strong
and vivifying influence to the best men under him,
and to all he communicated something of that rich
culture which is not easily measured by lessons
learned and recited. No one could listen to his
teaching, as has been well said, without becoming
conscious that he was listening to a man not less
wise than accomplished and gifted.

In this matter of teaching, as in all the other
undertakings of his life, Lowell kept no strict
debit and credit account. He gave his measure
not according to the stipulated return, but freely,
generously. Especially did he overflow in friendli-
ness. As he turned the lecture and recitation hour
into a *causerie*, and was careless in his exactions,
so he not only suffered but encouraged encroach-
ment on his unprofessional hours. At first in Kirk-
land Street, afterward at Elmwood, he made his
students welcome, and the only difference it may
be between an hour in University Hall and an
hour by the wood fire at Elmwood, was in the
wider range of talk. It was here that his students
came nearest to him, for it was the men he quickened in the class-room who were avid of more just
such talk, and sought him in the greater intimacy
of his study. Yet, nearer as they came to him as
he sat with his pipe in slippered ease, and much as

they drew from him, it is doubtful if there was much reciprocity in the intercourse. As a comparative stranger might draw from Lowell one of his most delightful letters, if some question he sent him happened to catch him at a favorable moment, when he needed only an occasion for the letter that was on tap, so these students, one or more, offered an easy audience, and Lowell, rarely out of the mood for talk, would spin his gossamer or weave his strong fabric for them as well as for any one else, without paying very close heed to them personally. In fine, the twenty years of college work made little inroad on Lowell himself. He was furnished with occupation, he was made comparatively easy in his simple need of a livelihood, and for the rest his class-room work offered a natural outlet for his abundant intellectual activity. He grumbled sometimes over its demands on his time, but it is doubtful if the reading world would have had very much more from him had he never been subject to this demand. It is even quite possible that the work kept him very much more alive than he might otherwise have been, saving him from a species of intellectual luxury of an unproductive sort ; it is certain that the hours added thus to his other productive time were a stimulus and inspiration to many men, and that as a practical matter the work done for his classes in the way of direct preparation was the foundation of a good deal of his published criticism.

And yet it is not so certain that his mood for poetry was helped by his academic life. He wrote

to Mr. Stillman 14 May, 1857 : " While my lectures are on my mind I am not myself, and I seem
to see all the poetry drying out of me.   I droop on
my rocks and hear the surge of the living waters,
but they will not reach me till some extraordinary
springtide, and maybe not then." It is true, this
expression must not be pressed too hardly — it may
have been only the mood of the moment ; but it is
evident that the time of freedom in poetic composition had largely passed for him ; it returned once
and again, as for instance in " Agassiz " and the
" Commemoration Ode," it was compelled for him
by the occasion which drew out the second series
of the " Biglow Papers," but for the most part his
poetry after this date bears rather more the touch
of deliberation and less the abandon of his early
enthusiasm.   How far this is to be referred to the
circumstance of the constraint of academic work,
and how far to the change which came over his
life in the passage from ebullient youth to chas-
tened manhood one would not care to say.   But
the period of his next twenty years was the period
of prose in his production.

The regular, punctual life which the daily college exercise demands came as a steadying influence after the vagrancy and informality of the previous years, and now there was added the gracious
and helpful presence of a self-contained, sympathetic, congenial woman.   Mrs. Lowell, before her
death, had wished her daughter to be under the
oversight of an intimate friend, Miss Elizabeth
Dunlap, but before the arrangements could be com-

pleted, Miss Dunlap died, and her sister Frances took the place and had had charge of Mabel Lowell ever since her father had left America for his year of study in Germany. He had thought himself most fortunate in making the arrangement, and the friendly intercourse which naturally sprang from this relation ripened steadily into affection. In September, 1857, they were married, and now he was enabled to resume the old life at Elmwood.

One or two passages from letters written at this time by Lowell to Mr. Norton give a glimpse of this new relation : " I have told you once or twice that I should not be married again if I could help it. The time has come when I cannot. A great many things (which I cannot write about) have conspired to bring me to this resolution, and I rejoice in it, for I feel already stronger and better, with an equability of mind that I have not felt for years." [1] " I was glad as I could be to get your heartily sympathizing letter. I had taken a step of great import to my life and character, and though I am careless of Mrs. Grundy's sentiments on the occasion, I do care intensely for the opinion of the few friends whom I value. With its personal results to myself I am more than satisfied, and I was convinced of the wisdom of what I was about to do before I did it. I already begin to feel like my old self again in health and spirits, and feel secure now, if I die, of leaving Mabel to wise and loving government. So intimate an acquaintance as mine has been with Miss Dunlap for

[1] 21 August, 1857.

nearly four years has made me know and love her, and she certainly must know me well enough to be safe in committing her happiness to my hands. . . . I went down last week to Portland to make the acquaintance of her family, and like them, especially her mother, who is a person of great character. They live in a little bit of a house in a little bit of a street, behind the great house (the biggest in town) in which they were brought up, and not one of them seemed conscious that they were not welcoming me to a palace. There were no apologies for want of room, no Dogberry hints at losses, nor anything of that kind, but all was simple, ladylike, and hearty. A family of girls who expected to be rich, and have had to support themselves and (I suspect) their mother in part, are not likely to have any nonsense in them. I find Miss Dunlap's education very complete in having had the two great teachers, Wealth and Poverty — one has taught not to value money, the other to be independent of it." [1] " I am more and more in love with Fanny, whose nature is so delightfully cheerful that it is impossible for me to get into the dumps even if I wished." [2]

Mr. Stillman, a keen observer, has given a good estimate of Mrs. Lowell's nature in these words: " She was one of the rarest and most sympathetic creatures I have ever known. She was the governess of Lowell's daughter, when I first went to stay at Elmwood, and I then felt the charm of her character. She was a sincere Swedenborgian, with

[1] 31 August, 1857.   [2] 31 December, 1857.

the serene faith and spiritual outlook I have generally found to be characteristic of that sect; with a warmth of spiritual sympathy of which I have known few so remarkable instances; a fine and subtle faculty of appreciation, serious and tender, which was to Lowell like an enfolding of the Divine Spirit. The only particular in which the sympathy failed was in the feeling that she had in regard to his humorous poems. She disliked the vein. It was not that she lacked humor or the appreciation of his, but she thought that kind of literature unworthy of him. This she said to me more than once. But, aside from this, she fitted him like the air around him. He had felt the charm of her character before he went to Europe, and had begun to bend to it; but as he said to me after his marriage, he would make no sign till he had tested by a prolonged absence the solidity of the feeling he had felt growing up. He waited, therefore, till his visit to Germany had satisfied him that it was sympathy, and not propinquity, that lay at the root of his inclination for her, before declaring himself. No married life could be more fortunate in all respects except one — they had no children. But for all that his life required she was to him healing from sorrow and a defence against all trouble, a very spring of life and hope." [1]

Mr. Howells also, who first knew her a decade later, has sketched her in these lines: " She was

---

[1] " A Few of Lowell's Letters," in *The Old Rome and the New, and Other Studies,* by W. J. Stillman.

a woman perfectly of the New England type and tradition : almost repellently shy at first, and almost glacially cold with new acquaintance, but afterward very sweet and cordial. She was of a dark beauty, with a regular face of the Spanish outline ; Lowell was of an ideal manner toward her, and of an admiration which delicately travestied itself and which she knew how to receive with smiling irony." [1] Mrs. Herrick, in an unpublished reminiscence, speaks of her in similar terms : " She was a noble and beautiful woman eminently practical in all the affairs of life. Commanding in presence, gracious in her hospitality, highly cultured, and full of a keen appreciation of every word of Mr. Lowell, and always charming and womanly."

Stillman's tender sketch of Mrs. Lowell brings to mind that it was in the summer of his marriage that Lowell joined this friend in a reconnaissance of the Adirondacks which was followed by the formation of the Adirondack Club, and the successive sojourns in the wilderness which Emerson has enshrined in his poem "The Adirondacs," and Stillman himself has recorded delightfully in his Autobiography as well as in magazine articles.[2]

"Ten men, ten guides, our company all told,"

says Emerson, but his chronicle was of the next

[1] *Literary Friends and Acquaintance*, p. 242.

[2] See especially " The Subjective of It," first printed in the *Atlantic Monthly*, and " The Philosophers' Camp," printed in *The Century*, and both included in *The Old Rome and the New, and Other Studies*. And more particularly see the first volume of *The Autobiography of a Journalist*.

year when the club was fully organized, and Stillman, Emerson, Lowell, Jeffries Wyman, E. R. Hoar, Dr. Howe, Binney, Woodman, Agassiz, and John Holmes, went into the wilderness. In 1857, the tentative exploring party, led by Stillman, consisted of John Holmes, Dr. Estes Howe, Lowell, and his two nephews, Charles and James Lowell, forever immortalized in the passionate verse of the second " Biglow Papers." Lowell, who had known the near charms of nature in the Waverley Oaks and Beaver Brook, and had tasted the wild wood in his Maine excursion, entered with frolic delight into this forest picnic. The conditions were such as to bring out the best that was in him, for he had the freedom of the woods and the satisfaction of congenial society. " He was the soul," says Stillman, " of the merriment of the company, fullest of witticisms, keenest in appreciation of the liberty of the occasion and the *genius loci*. . . . Not even Emerson, with all his indifference to the mere form of things, took to unimproved and uncivilized nature as Lowell did, and his free delight in the Wilderness was a thing to remember." To these companions, quick to appreciate and respond, Lowell, light-hearted with the new promise of happiness and set free in his mind by the large privacy of the woods, brought the treasures of his fancy, his wit, his imagination. He revelled especially in recounting those visionary experiences which seemed all the more real under the starry skies and in the companionship of trees and silent forest creatures. Yet with it all, his in-

quisitive, searching mind, quickened too by the
presence of scientific and philosophic comrades, was
forever probing these phenomena to discover what
was their ultimate rationale.

There can be little doubt that at this period of
his life Lowell was poised for flight, as it were,
having reached a stage when all the conditions
were most favorable for the full expression of his
powers. It is true that his academic work, as I
have said, did in a measure supplant a freer poetic
movement. But it may not unfairly be affirmed
that Lowell's attitude toward poetry was always
that of expectation of some greater gift to come.
His poems " Fancy's Casuistry," " In the Twilight," " To the Muse," all written about this time,
record with iteration his restless pursuit of the elusive dream. His academic work afforded indeed a
daily outlet, but it could not satisfy the demand
for expression. Best of all, there was a pleasure-
house in which he dwelt with his wife and daughter, perfectly fitted to the contentment of his spirit,
and to furnishing that ease of mind which gives
health of nature. Stillman has in another passage
drawn a picture which may well be given here in
evidence.

" Lowell was indeed very happy in his married
life, and amongst the pictures Memory will keep on
her tablet for me, till Death passes his sponge over
it once for all, is one of his wife lying in a long
chair under the trees at Dr. Howe's, when the sun
was getting cool, and laughing with her low, musical laugh at a contest in punning between Lowell

and myself, *haud passibus æquis*, but in which he found enough to provoke his wit to activity; her almost Oriental eyes twinkling with fun, half-closed and flashing from one to the other of us; her low, sweet forehead, wide between the temples; mouth wreathing with humor; and the whole frame, lithe and fragile, laughing with her eyes at his extravagant and rollicking word-play. One would hardly have said that she was a beautiful woman, but fascinating she was in the happiest sense of the word, with all the fascination of pure and perfect womanhood and perfect happiness."

CHAPTER IX

THE ATLANTIC MONTHLY

1857–1861

LOWELL had not been a year in his professor's chair when he was invited to take another position more closely identified with literature and having its own cares and drudgery. Under the present conditions of magazine editorship and of college professorship as well, the union of the two offices would be quite out of the question.[1] But the condition in 1857 was different, and to install a professor in Harvard College as editor of a new magazine was both natural and in a measure traditional. I have already called attention to the effort made in 1853 to establish a literary magazine, and to Lowell's interest in the venture. The person most concerned in that effort did not lose sight of his project, and now pushed the matter through to a fortunate conclusion.

Mr. Francis Henry Underwood was in 1857 the literary adviser and reader for the firm of Phillips & Sampson in Boston, and he was an ardent admirer of Lowell. He was a strong advocate of anti-slavery doctrines, and in his first proposals for

[1] It is worth noting that the year in which this sentence was written, the *Atlantic Monthly* was, in a special contingency, edited by the Professor of English Literature at Princeton.

a magazine in 1853 was working in conjunction
with the firm of John P. Jewett & Co., that had
just sprung into notice as publishers of "Uncle
Tom's Cabin." The firm with which he was now
connected was active chiefly in the publication of
cheap editions of standard works in literature. It
had a large Southern constituency, and when
"Uncle Tom's Cabin" was offered to it in the
form of a scrap-book of clippings from *The National Era*, commercial prudence dictated a polite
refusal. When, however, Mrs. Stowe's name had
become one of great value, it was easy for Phillips, Sampson & Co. to publish, as they did, her
"Sunny Memories" in 1854 and "Dred" in 1856.

Mr. Moses Dresser Phillips had been brought
up in the book trade and knew it first as a bookseller. He was a man who had large business
energy and laid his plans for wide connections and
not merely a local trade. Mr. Charles Sampson,
with whom he had formed his partnership, had died
about five years before, and his only partner at this
time was Mr. William Lee, well known for many
years as the senior partner in the publishing house
of Lee & Shepard. He was nearer Mr. Underwood's age and it was chiefly with him that Mr.
Underwood talked over his cherished plan. It was
through him, indeed, that Mr. Underwood expected
to gain over Mr. Phillips, who had the practical
man's distrust of new enterprises suggested by
authors, and a temperament which was calculated
to chill enthusiasm. Mr. Underwood had already
won consent to engage in the work from Lowell,

Longfellow, Holmes, and others, and he represented strongly to Mr. Lee the possibilities of a
magazine which should have at once a staff of
writers of a character so eminent. I suspect he
kept in the background any purpose he might have
of making the magazine play a part in politics.
Mr. Lee in turn at his daily lunch with Mr. Phillips kept that gentleman in mind of the project,
though he was himself neither an advocate nor
an opponent. He simply used Mr. Underwood's
arguments, the most effective of which may have
been the prospect held up before Mr. Phillips of
the association he should thus form with a distinguished group.

Mr. Phillips having been won over, the plans for
the new magazine were rapidly pushed forward.
In all this Mr. Underwood was the active manager,
but Mr. Phillips as the head of the business now
took the leading place. At an early date, Tuesday,
5 May, 1857, he called together the men on whom
he most relied to give the enterprise distinction,
and gave them a dinner at the Parker House.
Fortunately an account of this meeting is in his
own words in a letter to a niece : —

" I must tell you about a little dinner party I
gave about two weeks ago. It would be proper,
perhaps, to state that the origin of it was a desire
to confer with my literary friends on a somewhat
extensive literary project, the particulars of which
I shall reserve until you come. But to the party :
my invitations included only R. W. Emerson,[1] H.

[1] Mr. Phillips was by marriage connected with Mr. Emerson's
family.

W. Longfellow, J. R. Lowell, Mr. Motley (the 'Dutch Republic' man), O. W. Holmes, Mr. Cabot,[1] and Mr. Underwood, our literary man. Imagine your uncle as the head of such a table, with such guests. The above named were the only ones invited, and they were all present. We sat down at three P. M., and rose at eight. The time occupied was longer by about four hours and thirty minutes than I am in the habit of consuming in that kind of occupation, but it was the richest time intellectually by all odds that I have ever had. Leaving myself and 'literary man' out of the group, I think you will agree with me that it would be difficult to duplicate that number of such conceded scholarship in the whole country beside.

"Mr. Emerson took the first post of honor at my right, and Mr. Longfellow the second at my left. The exact arrangement of the table was as follows : —

Mr. Underwood

Cabot	Lowell
Motley	Holmes
Longfellow	Emerson

Phillips

"They seemed so well pleased that they adjourned, and invited me *to meet them* again tomorrow (the 20th), when I shall again meet the same persons, with one other (Whipple, the essayist) added to that brilliant constellation of philosophical, poetic, and historical talent. Each one is known alike on both sides of the Atlantic, and

---

[1] Mr. J. Elliot Cabot.

is read beyond the limits of the English language. Though all this is known to you, you will pardon me for intruding it upon you. But still I have the vanity to believe that you will think them the most natural thoughts in the world to me. Though I say it that should not, it was the proudest day of my life." [1]

There was another writer not at the dinner whose coöperation it was important to secure. Mrs. Stowe returned in June to America from England, whither she had gone to secure copyright for " Dred," and Mr. Phillips at once laid his plan before her. She approved it most heartily and promised to give it her cordial support. It is not impossible that she made a definite promise of a serial novel to begin with the first number, but the sudden death a month later of her son Henry brought such a mental strain upon her that it was nearly a year before she could undertake any continued writing. The first number of the *Atlantic Monthly* contained a brief allegory by her, " The Minister's Mourning Veil," and she contributed later an essay, but " The Minister's Wooing " was not begun in the magazine till December, 1858.

As a result of these preliminary plans, Mr. Underwood was dispatched in June to England to secure the aid of English authors, and Mr. Lowell was asked to take the position of editor. Lowell had already taken an active part in creating an interest in the venture among writers. Underwood had turned to him as his most important ally, and

[1] E. E. Hale's *James Russell Lowell and his Friends.*

Longfellow records in his diary, 29 April, 1857:
" Lowell was here last evening to interest me in a
new Magazine to be started in Boston by Phillips and Sampson. I told him I would write for
it if I wrote for any Magazine." Dr. Holmes
christened the magazine, and Lowell, from the
first, reckoned upon him for contributions. In
1885, when Dr. Holmes was resuming his regular
prose contributions after a long intermission, he
wrote in the introductory paper : [1] " He (Mr.
Lowell) thought there might be something in my
old portfolio which would be not unacceptable in
the new magazine. I . . . wondered somewhat
when Mr. Lowell urged me with such earnestness
to become a contributor, and so, yielding to a pressure which I could not understand, and yet found
myself unable to resist, I promised to take a part
in the new venture, as an occasional writer in the
columns of the magazine." Lowell, reading this
number of the *Atlantic* in London, wrote to Dr.
Holmes : " The first number of your New Portfolio whets my appetite. Let me make one historical correction. When I accepted the editorship of
the *Atlantic*, I made it a condition precedent that
you were the first contributor to be engaged. Said
I not well ? " [2]

Emerson apparently had asked if the contribu-

---

[1] " The New Portfolio," January, 1885.

[2] In publishing in book form *The Mortal Antipathy*, of which
the first paper of " The New Portfolio " was made the Introduction, Dr. Holmes so far corrected his statement as to make it read :
" I wondered somewhat when Mr. Lowell insisted upon my becoming a contributor."

tions were to be signed, for Lowell wrote him, 14 September, 1857: " All the articles will be anonymous, but you will be quite helpless, for your name is written in all kinds of self-betraying anagrams over yours. But as far as we are concerned there shall be as strict honor as the XIXth century allows of. Your wishes shall govern the position of the article ['Illusions,' in the first number], though I should have preferred to give it the precedence. I am afraid that where that is will be the head of the table, whether or no."

In the same first number appeared four of Emerson's poems, printed in a group: " The Romany Girl," " The Chartist's Complaint," " Days," and " Brahma." Emerson seems to have raised some question about this, for in the same letter Lowell writes: " About the poems I ought to say that when I spoke of printing all four I was perhaps greedy, and Mr. Underwood says we can't afford it, reckoning each as a separate poem — which means giving $50 apiece for them. Forgive me for coming down into the kitchen thus, but as I got the magazine into the scrape I must get it out. My notion was that all the poems would be published at once in a volume, and that therefore it would be alike to you. I ought to have thought that you sent them for selection, — and I will never be so rapacious again till I have another so good chance. If I am to have only one, give me 'Days.' That is as limpid and complete as a Greek epigram. I quarrel, though, with one word 'hypocritic,' which I doubt does not give the very shade of meaning you intended. I think you did wish to imply *intentional* taking-in? I will take the liberty to draw your notice to one or two things in the proofs (of the poems), leaving them to your own judgment entirely. . . . It is not often that a magazine carries such freight as your ' Illusions.' . . . How about Mr. Thoreau? "

It was not "Days" so much as "Brahma" that seized upon the imagination. Mr. Trowbridge, in his article on "The Author of Quabbin," says it was "more talked about and puzzled over and parodied than any other poem of sixteen lines published within my recollection. ' What does it mean?' was the question readers everywhere asked; and if one had the reputation of seeing a little way into the Concord philosophy, he was liable at any time to be stopped on the street by some perplexed inquirer, who would draw him into the nearest doorway, produce a crumpled newspaper clipping from the recesses of a waistcoat pocket, and, with knitted brows, exclaim, ' Here! you think you understand Emerson; now tell me what all this is about, — *If the red slayer think he slays,*' and so forth."

The magazine appeared about the first of November, and on the 19th Lowell wrote to Emerson: "You have seen, no doubt, how the Philistines have been parodying your ' Brahma,' and showing how they still believe in their special god Baal, and are unable to arrive at a conception of an omnipresent Deity. I have not yet met with a single clever one or I would have sent it to you for your amusement.   Meanwhile, they are advertising the *Atlantic* in the very best way, and Mr. Underwood tells me that the orders for the second number are doubling on those for the first.   I think you will find the second an improvement. . . . Your poem ["Two Rivers"] is to go into No. 3, simply as a matter of housewifery, because we had already three articles at $50.   I think I told you which I chose — 'Musketaquit.'   The 'Solitude and Society' [published in No. 2] has only one fault, that it is not longer, but had it been only a page, there would have been enough in it.   Did you use the word *daysman*[1] deliberately?   It has a technical meaning, and I suppose you used it in that sense. Mr. Nichols (the vermilion pencil) was outraged, and appealed to me.   I answered that you had a right to use any word you liked till we found some one who wrote better English to correct you.   Or did you mean the word to be merely the English of *journeyman*?

"I hope you will be able to give us something more for No. 3 before you go off to lecture.   The number promises well thus far, but I wish to make it a decided advance.   You have no notion how hard bestead we are.   Out of 297 manuscripts only at most six accepted.   I begin to believe in the total depravity of contributions.

"Let me thank you in especial for one line in

[1] "He envied every daysman and drover in the tavern their manly speech."   In reprinting the paper in his volume *Society and Solitude*, Emerson corrected to "He envied every drover and lumberman."

' Brahma,' which abides with me as an intimate —

'When me they fly, I am the wings.'

You have crammed meaning there with an hydrau-
lic press. Will not Thoreau give us something
from Moosehead ? "

Fourteen years earlier Lowell had welcomed
Whittier as a contributor to the *Pioneer*, and now
he renewed the old relation. He printed " Tritemius " in the first number and " Skipper Ireson's
Ride " in the second. Indeed, the *Atlantic* came
into existence most fortunately for Whittier, whose
fortunes it helped distinctly, as it gave him a medium for the publication of his purely literary
poems, and thus not only filled his pocket but
helped materially to place him before the public in
another guise than that of an ardent reformer.
Lowell's letter upon receipt of " Skipper Ireson's
Ride " is interesting both for its cordiality and for
the contrast in tone to his manner of addressing
Emerson. It may not unfairly be said that Emerson was the only one of his contemporaries whom
Lowell addressed as if he were profoundly conscious of his relation to him as a pupil to his master. Lowell's letter to Whittier is dated 4 November, 1857.[1]

" I thank you heartily for the ballad, which will
go into the next number. I like it all the better
for its provincialism, — in all fine pears, you know,
we can taste the old *puckers*. I know the story

[1] Most of this letter is given in Mr. Pickard's *Life and Letters
of John Greenleaf Whittier.*

well.   I am familiar with Marblehead and its dialect, and as the burthen is intentionally provincial
I have taken the liberty to print it in such a way
as shall give the peculiar accent, thus : —

> ' Cap'n Ireson for his horrd horrt
> Was torred and feathered and corried in a corrt.'

That 's the way I 've always ' horrd it,' — only it
began ' Old Flud Ireson.'   What a good name Ireson (son of wrath) is for the hero of such a history !

"You see that ' Tritemius ' is going the rounds !
I meant to have sent you the proofs, and to have
asked you to make a change in it where these four
rhymes come together (assonances I mean), —
' door,' ' poor,' ' store,' ' more.'   It annoyed me, but
I do not find that any one else has been troubled
by it, and everybody likes the poem.   I am glad
that the Philistines have chosen some verses of
mine [1] for their target, not being able to compre-
hend the bearing of them.   I mean I am glad that
they did it rather than pick out those of any one
else for their scapegoat.   I shall not let you rest
till I have got a New England pastoral out of you.
This last is cater-cousin to it, at least, being a pis-
catorial.

"Will you be good enough to let me know how
much Mr. Underwood shall send you ?   He will
remit at once.

"The sale of Maga has been very good considering the times, and I think you will find the second

---

[1] " The Origin of Didactic Poetry."

number better than the first. If you do not wish
the burthen so spelt, will you write me ? "

The year 1857 was one of great financial dis-
tress, and the magazine felt something of this
influence even before it was published, for it was
intended to bring it out earlier than its first number actually appeared. It was in May that the
preliminary arrangements were made and Lowell
secured as editor. As late, however, as the end
of that month, he was writing to a foreign correspondent that the editorship was a dead secret.
But as we have seen he had interested himself
in the venture from the outset. From time to
time after his attempt with the *Pioneer* he had
revolved in his mind plans for magazines. It is
safe to say that few prominent writers in America, Longfellow and Cooper being the chief exceptions, failed to dream of launching some vessel of
this sort that should be freighted with the best
of literature, and the initiative in almost all the
cases of important magazines has been taken by
the author rather than by the publisher. We have
perhaps come to the close of the period when a
new monthly magazine seems essential for the carrying of American thought and letters, and enterprise of this sort is more likely to seek an outlet
in weekly journalism; but the men of letters who
were at the front in the middle of the century not
only had strong intellectual sympathy with the
brilliant *Blackwood* of that day, — Lowell in his
correspondence repeatedly uses the familiar form
Maga when referring to the *Atlantic*, — and had

been brought up on *Tait*, *The London Journal*,
Fraser, and other vehicles of contemporaneous
English and Scottish letters, but they demanded
some direct, open means of reaching readers, for
they had a great deal to say, which was ill-adapted
to daily journalism and for which they could not
wait till it should cool for book publication.

The conditions were favorable also from the
point of view of the publisher, and Phillips &
Sampson were in a good position to know this.
They were aware that the leading writers were in
their neighborhood. Washington Irving was an
old man, and Mr. Bryant by his associations was
rather of New England than of New York. Excepting these two the men of national distinction,
Emerson, Hawthorne, Longfellow, Prescott, Motley, Lowell, were New Englanders, and men known
by these to have large gifts, Holmes, Higginson,
Thoreau, Cabot, Norton, who were chiefly relied on
to make the early numbers, were their neighbors
and friends, while the commanding reputation of
Mrs. Stowe could at once be counted on to give
éclat to any magazine with which she was connected. Besides, the business of this house, which
was largely that of a jobbing house, so called, that
is, a house which sold miscellaneous books from
whatever publishers all over the country, was of
such a nature as to create a confidence in the
existence of a widespread audience of intelligent
readers.

Thus the publishers were prepared to undertake the venture upon a somewhat liberal scale for

those days. They chose the best printer near by,
Mr. Houghton, who had already given distinction
to the name " Riverside," and they proposed to
make a handsome magazine, not wholly unlike in
its appearance the Edinburgh *Blackwood*. They
paid their editor a salary of $2500, and they ex-
pected to pay contributors on a scale not to be
sure much in advance of what the best writers
could secure in other periodicals in Philadelphia
and New York, but more generous as regards the
average contributor. I think the mean rate of
prose was six dollars a page, though it may occasionally in the case of a tyro have dropped to five
dollars, and for poems they paid usually fifty dollars apiece. In a letter to a contributor who took
exception to the price paid him, Lowell wrote,
when the magazine had been running three or
four months, " You must be content. Six dollars a
page is more than can be got elsewhere, and we
only pay ten to folks whose *names* are worth the
other four dollars. *Capite?* What we may be
able to do hereafter, I know not. *I* shall always
be for liberal pay."

It might seem as though the distinction thus referred to would hardly exist when all the articles
were unsigned, but the authorship for the most
part was an open secret. In those days the *North
American Review*, as well as other like periodicals,
used to print a little slip with the authorship of
the separate articles set against the successive
numbers of the articles, and this slip, though not
inserted in all the copies sold or sent to subscrib-

ers, was at the service of newspapers and the inner
circle of contributors and near friends.   In like
manner the authorship of the principal articles and
poems in the *Atlantic* leaked out, and for some,
like Emerson's poems and Holmes's "Autocrat,"
there could be no concealment.

The authors themselves sometimes were glad of
the privacy, as they thought it secured them more
independence and possibility of frankness.   Lowell
thus wrote in September, 1859, to one of his contributors, who complained of what he thought want
of care: "I am very sorry indeed for the mis-
chance, but am quite sure it was no fault of mine.
Where the 'copy' passes through four or five
hands, all of whose owners know the handwriting,
the chances of leakage are great.   I confess that
in the worry of the last week or two, I did not
remember to give any new caution just before the
publication of the October number.   I am the more
sorry if it is to deprive us of your contributions.
For myself, I have always been opposed to the
publication of the authors' names at all.   I do as
well as I can with so many things to think of at
once."   The practice of withholding names publicly continued till 1862, when the index at the end
of the volume disclosed the authorship of the articles in the body of the magazine, and in 1870, the
practice was begun of signing contributions.   The
anonymous character of the early volumes served,
however, to bury the authorship in some cases past
resurrection, as I found when I undertook to prepare a General Index in 1877, and again in 1889.

The ideal which Lowell formed for the magazine may best be inferred from the character of the numbers issued under his control, but in a few passages in his letters to contributors and friends he gives some glimpses of what was going on in his mind as he faced the very practical questions which arose in the conduct of the magazine. When I became editor of the *Atlantic*, in the spring of 1890, he contrasted my position with his own, and remarked on the very much larger number of writers on whom I could call for contributions, and the higher average of training in literary work. " Your task," he wrote me, " will be in one respect at least easier than mine was thirty odd years ago, for there are now twenty people who can write English where there was one then. Indeed, there are so many, and they do it so well, that it looks as if literature as a profession or guild were near its end, and as if every man (and woman) would do his or her own on the principle of Every man his own washerwoman." I thought and said, however, that it was not general average but distinction which gave a stamp to the magazine, and that in that respect he certainly had the advantage. In one of his letters to Mr. Richard Grant White, who feared a Shakespeare article he had furnished might be the one paper too much, he wrote: " I don't care whether the public are tired of the Divine Villiams or not — a *part* of the magazine, as long as I have anything to do with it, shall be expressly *not* for the Mob (of well-dressed gentlemen who read with ease)."

At the outset, before any number had been published, he wrote to a friend from whom he solicited a contribution : " The magazine is going to be free without being fanatical, and we hope to unite in it all available talent of all shades of opinion. The magazine is to have opinions of its own, and not be afraid to speak them, but I think we shall be scholarly and gentlemanlike." " This reading endless manuscripts," he wrote to the same friend, when he was in full tide of preparation for the first number, "is hard work, and takes a great deal of time, but I am resolved that nothing shall go in which I have not first read. I wish to have nothing go in that will merely *do*,[1] but I fear I can't keep so high a standard. It is astonishing how much there is that keeps just short of the line of good and drops into the limbo of indifferent."

" There is a constant pressure on me," he writes again, " to ' popularize ' the magazine, which I resist without clamor." It is easy to understand this attitude. Lowell cared greatly for the success of the *Atlantic*, and he was governed in his conduct of it by prudential considerations. In the letter just quoted he had occasion to refer to a controversy which was then hot. " I am urged," he says, " to take ground in the Albany controversy, but do not feel that there is any *ought* in the matter, and am sure the Trustees will beat in the end. I think it would be unwise to let the magazine take

---

[1] I recall the sententious principle which another editor announced to me as the rule by which he was governed. " The only question I ask myself is, *must* I take this ? "

a losing side unless clear justice required it. Am
I not right?" But though he was not indifferent
to the commercial prosperity of the *Atlantic*, and
knew well that its opportunity for serving letters
was largely conditioned on its subscription list, he
did not make the fatal mistake of subordinating
his own judgment to a supposititious judgment of
the mysterious public which buys and reads magazines. It was his business to keep his own judgment free from the partisan bias of idiosyncrasy,
but he perceived well the more subtle danger to
which he was exposed of abdicating his authority
while keeping his title in the supposed interest of
the magazine. It was just because he was Lowell,
a man whom the public was ready to follow in
literary judgments, that he was in this place, and
it was in the application of a well-seasoned taste
that he demonstrated his fitness for the position.
He cared greatly to be the instrument of organiz-
ing a body of first-rate literature, and the tone
which he gave the *Atlantic* during the few months
of his editorship became a tradition which powerfully affected its character after he retired from it.
He put his own stamp on it emphatically.

The public, meanwhile, began at once to exercise
that censorship which is a somewhat whimsical but
very substantial witness to the value of an enterprise which is only technically private. The Lowell
Institute, for example, is on a foundation so exclusively personal that there is not even a nominal
board of trustees to be consulted in its management: the courses of lectures which it offers are

absolutely free ; yet ever since its establishment it has been subjected to criticism, good or ill natured, which would seem to imply some indefeasible right on the part of the public that criticises. Really, the criticism is simply an ingenuous expression of the profound interest which the public takes in a noble trust. Somewhat in the same way when the *Atlantic* was established, the public refused to regard it as offering wares which people might buy or not as they liked. It recognized it as a literary organon, as a power for good or ill ; it was immensely interested in it, and showed its interest by attacking it severely on occasions.

Such an occasion, especially, was the appearance of Dr. Holmes's "Professor at the Breakfast-Table," in which this writer, who had leaped into popularity through the "Autocrat," delivered himself of opinions and judgments which were regarded by a good many as dangerous and subversive, all the more dangerous by reason of their wit and entertaining qualities. If one could believe many of the newspapers, Dr. Holmes was a sort of reincarnation of Voltaire, who stood for the most audacious enemy of Christianity in modern times.

Some intimation of what Lowell was to encounter as editor may be gathered from a few words in a letter to T. W. Higginson, written at the end of his first year, when "The Autocrat" had already drawn the fire of one class of critics.

"I only look upon my duty," he says, "as a vicarious one for Phillips and Sampson, that nothing may go in (before we are firm on our feet)

that helps the 'religious' press in their warfare
on us.   Presently we shall be even with them, and
have a *free* magazine in its true sense.   I never
allow any personal notion of mine to interfere,
except in cases of obvious obscurity, bad taste, or
bad grammar."   And Mr. Norton prints [1] a letter
written shortly after to Dr. Holmes, which shows
clearly the cordial support which the editor gave
his contributor.

   In one respect Lowell held a somewhat different
position from that occupied by later editors.   The
Atlantic was so little troubled by competitors, and
its company of contributors was so determined by
a sort of natural selection, that Lowell's editorial
function was mainly discharged by the exercise of
discrimination in the choice of articles, and the
distribution of material through successive numbers; he had little to do in the way of foraging
for matter.   It must not be supposed, however,
that there was anything perfunctory in his editorship.   He was in love with literature, and his fine
taste stood him in good stead, not only in the rejection of the commonplace, but in the perception
of qualities which might redeem an otherwise undistinguished poem or paper.   He had, too, that
enthusiasm in the discovery of excellence which
made him call his friends and neighbors together
when he had found some pearl of great price; an
enthusiasm which he was very sure to share with
the author.   He gave thus to the magazine that
character of *distinction* which conscientiousness

[1] *Letters*, i. 288, 289.

alone on the part of the editor, or even careful
study of conditions, cannot give.

He was, to be sure, a trifle negligent of the
business of writing to his contributors. He left as
much of the correspondence as he could to Mr.
Underwood, but in his somewhat capricious fashion
he might make an article an excuse for a long and
friendly letter. To one of his contributors who
pursued him for his opinion upon some accepted
manuscripts, he wrote a little testily : "You have
a right to frankness and shall have it. I *did* like
the article on —— better than the other, and I
should like the —— one particularly. But what of
that ? other folks may have liked the other better,
for aught I know. The fault of our tastes is in
our stars, not in ourselves. My wife can't endure
'The Biglow Papers,' and somehow or other her
dislike of them is a great refreshment to me and
makes me like her all the better. But I think it
is rather hard on an editor to expect him to give
his opinion about everything he prints — I mean
as to whether it is specially to his taste or not.
How long would my contributors put up with me
if I made Archbishops of Granada of them all? I
tell you again, as I have told you before, that I
am always glad of an article from you, let it be
what it will, but (don't you see ?) I am gladdest
when it is such a one as only you can write. If I
could only print one number made of altogether
such, I could sing my *nunc dimittis* with a joyful
heart." A little of the fret of his life in this particular appears in a whimsical tirade which he sent

to Mr. Norton on the eve of a flight to the Adirondacks in the summer of 1859: —

"To-day is Sunday; at least the bells have been
shouting it, but 'the Sabbath dawns no Sabbath-
day for me.' I have been reading proof and picking out manuscripts all the morning. Do you ever
get desperate? I feel so now that I have got all
my manuscript-household in order. They appal me
by their mass. I look first at one box, and then at
another, and — fill my pipe. 'It is dreadful!' as
Clough's heroine says in the Bothie. And 128
pages which it would take one so long to fill with
his own stuff eats up that of other folks — no, I
don't mean that and would not allow such a meta-
phor to a contributor — is satiated so soon with
that of other folks — that is, uses it up so slowly.
Mille-dam! Have not two articles of —— been on
hand now for a year? He seems to spin out his
brains as tenuously and uselessly as those creatures
that streak the air with gossamer — no chance of
catching even a stray fly of thought. Nay, his object is, I fancy, precisely what that of the aforesaid
creatures may be — merely to swing himself over
a gap. He is my ink — my pen-and-ink-ubus. I
could scalp him the rather as he wears a wig and
is deaf, and so would not be likely to hear of it.
Then there is —— who can't express himself in
less than sixteen pages on any imaginable topic.
It it a terrible thing this writing for the press, by
which a man's pen learns gradually to go by itself
as those Chinese servants are said to fan and sleep
at the same time. 'No, no, by heaven I am not

ma-a-d !' but I expect to be.   I believe I have so
far settled matters that everybody will think me a
monster.   But never mind, I get out of ear-shot
to-morrow."

How fully and carefully he could and would
write under special urgency may be seen by the
long letter which he addressed to Mrs. Stowe when
"The Minister's Wooing" had been running three
or four months in the *Atlantic*.   The letter was
published in C. E. Stowe's life of his mother, and
is quoted also in Mrs. Fields's "Life and Letters
of Harriet Beecher Stowe."

The criticism for which this letter was an excuse
illustrates one very important element in Lowell's
editorial mind.   However little he might exert
himself to go afield for articles in the body of the
magazine, he did not trust to luck for the critical
notices.   In that department he took great pains
to secure competent workmen.   To Lowell and his
contemporaries this matter of book reviews was
one of great consequence.   In the evolution of literary periodical literature the article of the old
Quarterly type, which was part a summary of a
book, part a further contribution to the subject,
and part a judgment on the author, had shed the
first constituent, had lost much of the second, but
preserved the third in a more condensed and, to a
certain degree, in a more impersonal spirit.   But
criticism in its finest form was highly valued, and
the form of the book review was accepted as recognized and permanent.   When the *Atlantic*, therefore, was set up emphasis was laid on this serious

side of literary study, and the causerie, the light
persiflage which serves as a relief in most magazines of a literary type — the *Atlantic* itself has
now its Contributors' Club — was disregarded. To
be sure, in the first number, Lowell printed what
seemed to promise a gay side to the magazine, a
leaf entitled " The Round Table," the purpose of
which, in this instance, was to introduce an occasional poem by Dr. Holmes, but I suspect he was
either a little alarmed at the prospect of setting
his table monthly with a dessert, or was satisfied
that the " Autocrat " would serve the same end.
At any rate, no second number of " The Round
Table" appeared. But each month the last few
pages of each number were given up, after the
well-accepted tradition, to notices of new books
with occasional surveys of current music and pictures.

Lowell's estimate of the value of literary criticism is expressed in a letter to Mr. Richard Grant
White, 10 June, 1858, apropos of a purpose Mr.
White then had of starting a weekly literary journal in New York. " There is no one opprobrium
of American scholarship and letters so great," he
says, " as the general laxity and debasement of
criticism. With few exceptions our criticisms are
venial (whether the pay be money or friendship)
or partisan. An invitation to dinner may make a
Milton out of the sorriest Flecknoe, and a difference in politics turn a creditable poet into a
dunce." Lowell relied on White for a certain
amount of criticism and wrote him, 8 March, 1859,

" There is nothing I so especially desire as to have
' experts ' make the *Atlantic* their pulpit. As long
as I continue editor, I wish you to understand that
your contributions will always be welcome, on no
ground of personal friendship, but because I know
they will be of value.   I particularly wish to have
the department of ' Lit. Notices ' made more full.
I find so few people whom I can trust to write a
review ! Personal motives of one kind or other are
always sure to peep out. I think I have gained
one good from the fearful bore of reading manuscripts ; it is gradually making me as impartial
as a chemical test — as insensible, too, perhaps ?
That is the only fear."

As a result partly of his difficulty in securing
satisfactory criticism and partly of his own aptitude
for work of this kind, Lowell wrote more than
forty reviews in the department during his editorship, besides several articles in the body of the
magazine which were really reviews, like his careful study in two numbers of White's Shakespeare.
He was in such friendly communication with Mr.
White regarding his work that it would have been
idle to wear any mask in his presence, and Mr.
White wrote him in great excitement over the first
of the two articles.   " I am very much obliged to
you for your kind letter," Lowell replied ; " I
never saw a man who did not think himself indifferent to praise, nor one who did not like it.   In
this country, where praise (or blame) is so cheap,
one can't think much of the old *laudari ab lau-*
dato, for the *laudatus* himself may be the cele-

brated Snooks, but I think I know how to value it
from a man of discernment. I hope you will like
the last half of my article as well as the first. It
is honest, anyhow, and kindly meant, and I endeavored to avoid all picking of flaws. Years ago
I laid to heart the saying of an old lady — 'that
the eleventh commandment was — Don't twit.' . . .

"I don't like reviewing, especially where the
author is an acquaintance. I find it so hard to be
impartial, but in your case I think my commendation would lose half its force were it not qualified
with some adverse criticism. Please believe that I
wrote all with the kindest feelings."

Lowell certainly had nothing of that superficial
habit of reviewing which is at the bottom of most
of the unsatisfactory work of this kind. In reviewing White's Shakespeare, for example, he read
over twice every word of the commentary and notes
and then laid the book aside that his impression
might settle and clarify before he wrote his criticism. Swift as he was in writing, there was, for
the most part, a long period of brooding over his
creative work and in study over his criticism. He
wrote an article, for instance, on "Wedgwood's
Dictionary," and complained regarding it to Mr.
Norton: "You know my unfortunate weakness for
doing things not quite superficially. So I have
been a week about it — press waiting — devil at
my elbow (I mean the printer's) — every dictionary and vocabulary I own gradually gathering in a
semicircle round my chair, — and three of the days
of twelve solid hours each. And with what result?

at most six pages, which not six men will care
anything about. And now it is done I feel as if I
had taken hold of the book the wrong way, and
that I should have devoted myself to his theory
more and to particulars less; or, rather, that I
ought to have had more space. But I had a gap
to fill up, — just so much and no more. There is
one passage [1] in it that I wager will make all of
you laugh, and heavens! what fun I could have
made of the book if I had been unscrupulous!
But I soon learned to respect Wedgwood's attainments, and resisted all temptation."

Just as Lowell's fun could find its way even
into an index, so in his sober criticisms he would
sometimes hide a jest for the delectation of especially discerning readers, as when in his article
on White's Shakespeare, he remarks incidentally:
"To every commentator who has wantonly tam-
pered with the text, or obscured it with his inky
cloud of paraphrase, we feel inclined to apply the
quadrisyllabic name of the brother of Agis, king
of Sparta." Felton, Longfellow tells us in a letter to Sumner, was the first to unearth the joke
and to remember or discover that this name was
Eudamidas.

Apart from his considerable criticism Lowell
contributed to the volumes which he edited chiefly
poems and political articles. He printed the "Ode
to Happiness" already referred to, the notable
verses on "Italy, 1859," and the striking poem,

[1] There are three or four witty passages, to which this is appli-
cable.

" The Dead House," which has an autobiographic
interest, not from its being the record of an incident or even from the mood which it reflects, but
from the fact that Lowell could write it at all and
disclaim any personal connection with the theme.
Mr. Norton has printed an interesting comment on
the poem by Lowell,[1] and in another letter written
a few days later Lowell adds : " I have touched
here and there the poem I sent, and think of putting it in the *Atlantic*.   Did you like it ?   It is
pure fancy, though founded on a feeling I have
often had, — but for æsthetic reasons I put an
' inexpressive she ' into it."   In how healthy a
mind must he have been, and how graciously
healed in his new life to write thus without having
his own great grief thrust itself between him and
his poem.

Yet there was a poem entitled " The Home,"
written at the same time which was rather a record of personal experience than a universal mood
caught in terms of common life, and he cast it
aside therefore and never printed it.   It has its
place in a memoir of his life.

> " Here once my step was quickened,
>   Here beckoned the opening door,
>   And *welcome !* thrilled from the threshold
>   To the foot it had felt before.
>
> " A glow came forth to meet me,
>   The blithe flame laughed in the grate,
>   And shadows that danced on the ceiling
>   Danced faster with mine for a mate.

[1] See *Letters*, i. 283, 284.

" ' Glad to see you, old friend,' yawned the armchair,
 ' This corner, you know, is your seat ; '
' Rest your slippers on me,' beamed the fender,
 ' I brighten at touch of your feet.'

" ' We know the practised finger,'
 Said the books, ' that seems all brain,'
And the shy page rustled the secret
 It had kept till I came again.

" Hummed the pillow, ' My down once trembled
 On nightingales' throats that flew
Through the twilight gardens of Hafiz
 To gather quaint dreams for you.'

" Ah me ! if the Past have heartsease,
 It hath also rue for men : —
I come back : those unhealed ridges
 Were not in the churchyard then !

" But (I think) the house is unaltered —
 I will go and ask to look
At the rooms that were once familiar
 To my life as its bed to the brook.

" Unaltered ! alas for the sameness
 That makes the change but more !
How estranged seems the look of the windows,
 How grates my foot on the floor !

" To learn this simple lesson
 Need I go to Paris or Rome,
That the many make a household,
 But only one the Home ?

" 'T was a smile, 't was a garment's rustle,
 'T was nothing that you could phrase,
But the whole dumb dwelling grew conscious
 And put on her looks and ways.

" Were it mine, I would close the shutters
 As you smooth the lids of the dead,

And the funeral fire should wind it,
This corpse of a Home that is dead!

" For it died that summer morning
When she, its soul, was borne
To lie all dark in the hillside
That looks over woodland and corn."

" Is it anything? " he wrote to the friend to
whom he sent it, " or is it nothing? Or is it one
of those nothings that is something? I think the
last stanza should be last but one and begin ' But
it died,' if ' dwelling' will do for an antecedent.
Is the first half too special? "

There was indeed a gayer mood on him in the
midst of his work which could make him turn his
discomforts into a jest. " I cannot learn the knack
of doing six things at once," he wrote to a friend.
" I had my whole time to myself for too many
years, and the older I grow the unreadier writer I
become. What a lucky dog Methusalem was!
Nothing to know, and nine hundred years to learn
it in." He was writing to a somewhat dry-minded
correspondent, but to a more congenial friend he
wrote at the same time: " Nothing has happened
to me since I saw you except manuscripts, and my
mind is gradually becoming a blank. It is very
depleting, I find, to read stuff week in and week
out (I almost spelt week with an *a*), and does not
help one to be a lively correspondent. But I believe I could dictate five love stories at the same
time (as Napoleon the Other could despatches)
without mixing them in the least — and indeed it
would make no difference if I did. ' Julie gazed

into the eyes of her lover, which sought in vain to escape her enquiring look, while the tears trembled on her long dark lashes, but fell not (that ' fell not' is new, I think). "And is it indeed so?" she said slowly, after a pause in which her heart leaped like an imprisoned bird.' — 'Meanwhile, the elder of the two, a stern-featured man of some forty winters, played with the hilt of his dagger, half drawing and then sheathing again the Damascus blade thin as the eloquence of Everett and elastic as the conscience of Cass. "Didst mark the old man tremble?" "Cospetto! my uncle, a noted leech, was wont to say that iron was a good tonic for unsteady nerves," and still he trifled with the ominous looking weapon, etc., etc.' I think of taking a contract to write all the stories myself at so much a dozen — a good murder or a happy marriage to be paid double."

One is reminded of Lamb's famous letter to Manning when he reads a letter which Lowell wrote to his brother-in-law, Captain Parker, then in China: "A man who is eccentric enough to prefer a part of the world where folks walk with their heads down certainly deserves the commiseration of his friends, but as for letters — how to write and what to write about? I can't write upside down, and I suppose you can't read rightside up. So it is clearly a waste of time, but you will be able to read this after you get home again, when old age will have given all the news in it a kind of second-childhood, and it will have become fresh by dint of having been forgotten.

"Of course there is n't any news — when was there ever any?   For my own part, I don't regret it, looking on news as generally only a short way of saying nuisance, and believing Noah to have been the happiest man that ever lived, for all the gossips were five thousand fathoms under water, and he knew that he should not hear anything when he got into port.   The daughters must have been put to it, though, with nobody left but Shem, Ham, and Japhet to work slippers and smoking caps for, and never a new engagement to discuss.

"As for news here, — there was the College Exhibition day before yesterday, which was a good deal like other Exhibitions only that it rained.   I suppose your wife has written you of the appointment of Caihee as professor of the Chinese language and literature with a salary of ten piculs a year, which she is allowed to raise in the college grounds, the Corporation finding cucumber seed and Theodore Parker the vinegar.   A compromise has been effected in theological matters, and she is to worship Josh Bates the London banker instead of simple Josh, in consideration of which Mr. Bates will pay half the salary of a Bonze to be imported express.   The students will be allowed to let off fire-crackers during her lectures.   She begins with an exposition of the doctrine of the venerable confuse-us, which can hardly fail of being in harmony with all existing systems of philosophy and theology.   As all the Professors are obliged to do something outside for a living, she will continue to be on duty with Maggie.   This is

a great triumph for the Woman's-Rights party,
who have nominated Mrs. —— for Governess, with
a Council of old women, including, I am told, Mr.
——. You see the world moves up here. As to
other political intelligence, there is not much —
that quality is commonly wanting in such matters :
but the Charleston Convention is expected to nomi-
nate the Captain of the yacht Wanderer [1] for President, as an exponent of the views of the more
moderate wing of the party (I mean, of course, the
Southern wing) on the subject of slavery. A Red
River overseer is to adorn the ticket as candidate
for the Vice-Presidency. We shall be likely at
last to get a truly conservative administration. At
home we have a rehearsal of ' Bonnie Doon,' Banks
being the Republican man, while the *brays* are well
performed by Mr. B. F. Butler.

"Cambridge meanwhile is all agog with a wedding to come off this afternoon, Darley the artist
and Miss Jenny (I think) Colburn. There is to
be a wonderful turn-out of handsome bridesmaids,
the bride having the good luck to be beautifully
cousined. A great crush of hoops is looked for at
Christ Church, and the coopers, it is said, will take
the occasion for a strike. All the girls are crazy
to go, and many who go in with a diameter of ten
feet will come out with only two. I have sent for
a new pair of lemon-colored gloves for the wedding
visit. There will be a jam, of course, but then I
am one of the harder sex, and shan't mind it.

[1] The Wanderer was a slave-ship seized in New York harbor.
A Charleston jury refused to convict the captain.

They have my best wishes for a crop of little Dar-
leyings.

"So you are to have another war over there. I
think it a shabby piece of business. Can you
thrash a nation into friendly relations? And if
a man don't like your society, can you change his
views by giving him a black eye? The Chinese
are not a nation of savages, and with two hundred
and forty millions of people they can hold out a
great while in killed, wounded, and missing. I
think John Bull and Johnny Crapaud will have
their hands full before they are done with it.
What has a Bull to do in a China-shop?"

There was an incompatibility of temper in Lowell which stood in the way of entire pleasure in
editing the *Atlantic*. He was not averse to work
—instances enough have been shown of this—but
he chafed under methodical work. He could work
hours and even days with scarcely a respite, but
he could also help himself to large measures of
loafing. A magazine, with its incessant inflow of
letters and manuscripts, and the demand which it
makes for periodic punctuality, ill befits such a
temper, and Lowell found a good deal of irksome-
ness in his daily task. "I used to be able to answer letters in the month during which I received
them," he wrote ruefully to Mr. White, 6 April,
1859, "but now they pile up and make a jam behind the boom of my occupations, till they carry
everything before them, and after a little confused
whirling float placidly down to the ocean of Obliv-
ion. I do not know if it be so with everybody,

but with me the perpetual *chance* of interruption to which I am liable induces a kind of stolid despair. I am afraid that at this moment there are at least a hundred and fifty unanswered letters in and on and round my desk, whose blank [looks] seem to say 'how long?' Your letter came just in the midst of a bother in the *Atlantic*, which it took all my diplomacy to settle so that both sides should not bite their own noses off, to which mad meal they had violent appetites. It is all 'fixed' now, and things go smoothly again — but meanwhile the hiatus in my correspondence grew daily wider."

"I am at last even with my manuscripts," he wrote to another friend. "It is splendid. Such a heap as had gathered. It had snowed poems and tales and essays, and an eddy had drifted them into my study knee-deep. But I have shovelled myself out, and hope 't is the last great storm of the season. I even found time to go to Dresel's concert last evening, where I saw one of your cousins. The concert was nearly all Mendelssohn and seemed to me a little vague and cloudy — beautiful clouds, rose tinted and — indefinite. I longed for a good riving flash of Italian lightning. Fanny liked it, however, but I was rather bored. It seemed to me like reading manuscripts titillated with promise continually and finding no egregious and satisfying fulfilment."

"Don't come this way again," he writes to Mr. White, "without letting me know you are coming. I want a talk with you, and I can't talk by letter, for I can't write them when I am tired, and I am tired all the time. If there be any truth in the doctrine of compensations, the bobolinks in some other stage of existence will all be caged in Grub Street and made editors. They are altogether too happy here. Well, maybe we shall be bobolinks. If ever we should be, I can show you a fine meadow for building in, a kind of grassy Venice with good tussock foundations jutting everywhere from the water."

After something more than a year's experience, he wrote to Mr. Norton : " I am resolved that no motive of my own comfort or advantage shall influence me, but I hate the turmoil of such affairs, despise the notoriety they give one, and long for the day when I can be vacant to the Muses and to my books for their own sakes. I cannot stand the worry of it much longer without a lieutenant. To have questions of style, grammar, and punctuation in other people's articles to decide, while I want all my concentration for what I am writing myself — to have added to this personal appeals, from ill-mannered correspondents whose articles have been declined, to attend to — to sit at work sometimes fifteen hours a day, as I have done lately — makes me nervous, takes away my pluck, compels my neglecting my friends, and induces the old fits of the blues." [1]

" If my letters seem dry," he wrote again to Mr. White, " it is no fault of mine. I am overworked and overworried and overinterrupted. I *can't* write

[1] *Letters*, i. 286.

a genial letter, but I want you and like you all the same. If ever I get back to my old nest among the trees at Elmwood, and I am no longer professor or editor, with time enough to follow up a doubtful passage in Shakespeare or a bit of dilettante philology, — then what pleasure I should have in corresponding with you and exchanging thoughts and suggestions. But now, if anything occurs to me, I feel too tired to communicate it to anybody, for my days are so broken that I am forced sometimes to sit up till the birds sing to get any time for my own studies."

In one point of excellence Lowell was exceedingly particular. He told me once in later life, when we were discussing a proposed reissue of the British Poets, of which he was to be editor-in-chief, that I must not think he would accept any one's proof-reading but his own. " I am really a very careful proof-reader," he said, " though people fancy I am too indolent for such work." In a letter to Mr. Norton, 18 October, 1859, presaging some changes, he writes: " As to proofs, I *must* read those myself, or I don't feel safe. Yet a piece of bad grammar got into the October number in spite of Mr. Nichols and me together." He had, indeed, a most admirable aid in Mr. George Nichols, who was a vigilant officer, carrying a search warrant for any and all literary misdemeanors. The *Atlantic* at this time was printed at Riverside, and there is a charming description, in a letter which Mr. Norton prints,[1] of the morning

1 *Letters*, i. 281.

walk which Lowell was wont to take to the Press by the footpath that lay along the river bank.

The pressure upon Lowell, which his college work and his editorship brought, did, during these four years, stop, somewhat, his spontaneity. He wrote but few poems, and his letters show the ... some gayety. "...," he wrote to ... forgive him the ... silence, staying ... comes — and I ... believe that my ... her, and that I ... er than most. I ... I could give the ... deserve it best, ... either employed ...? I believe that ... good letter. I mean by idle, a man who is not under the necessity of tapping his brain on the public side, and tapping so freely that the runnings on the other cannot be sprightly for want of *head*. This is why women are such good letter-writers. Their ordinary employments do not suck them dry of all communicativeness, — I can't think of any other word, — and their writing is their play, as it should be. As for me, nowadays, taking up my pen is only the reminder of work. This that I write with is one worn to a stump with my lectures three years — four years ago. I would not write with the same one I had used for Mr. Cushing and

choose between the white and the y...
low, Germany stands by the wh...
The "Yellow Danger" is accepted ...
Germany as a substantial fact and ...
is believed that Japanese imitation h...
already resulted in injuring Gremany...
trade in the far east.

SECRETARY HAY WINS.

Belligerents Will Respect His Suggestion To Ignore China.

WASHINGTON, Feb. 13.—Secretary Hay has added another to his long list of di... matic triumphs and the United ... once more favored by diplo-... head the nations in a con-... non... effort to preserve the integrity

drudgery. So the fault is not in the quill that
I am stupid. If I had only been laid away in a
drawer these four years, as it had been! What a
fury I should be in to declare myself on all manner of topics! But this exhaustion one feels from
overwork extends itself to the receptive faculties
as well. A dry sponge floats and is long in satu-
rating. The mind, I think, goes even beyond this
— it must be *full* to take up more."

The diversions which Lowell found in this period
were not many. He made his yearly excursion
to the Adirondacks, always looking forward eagerly
to it, and working furiously just before home-leav-
ing, that he might go with some serenity of mind.
He saw scarcely anything of social life in Cambridge or Boston; [1] he went frequently to Shady
Hill, the home of the Nortons, but nowhere else to
speak of, and he found true relaxation in his whist
club. Aside from all this, he derived most entertainment from the very informal clubs, with their
dinners, which had sprung chiefly out of the establishment of the *Atlantic*. For a short time, apparently, there were two of these loose organiza-
tions, the Atlantic Club, so called, which was the
gathering of the contributors at dinner, under the
auspices of the publishers, during the first months
of strong interest, — dinners which seem to have
sprung from the little one given by Mr. Phillips

---

[1] He was elected into the American Academy of Arts and
Sciences, 14 November, 1855, and into the Massachusetts Historical Society, 14 May, 1863, but he does not appear to have been a
frequent attendant at the meetings of either of these bodies.

at the institution of the magazine; and the Saturday Club, which still survives, a dining club, made up at first chiefly of literary men naturally connected with the *Atlantic*, and of congenial spirits, some of whom never and some rarely contributed. This latter club appears, after a while, to have supplanted the former. "Dined with the *Atlantic Monthly* people," Longfellow writes in his diary, 21 December, 1857, and again, 14 May, 1859, "Dined with the Atlantic Club, at Fondarivés's. The 'Atlantic' is not the 'Saturday' club, though many members belong to both;" and on 9 July, 1859, he again notes that he dined with the Atlantic Club at the Revere House, but the references cease at this point, and the club dinners which he attends afterward are Saturday Club dinners, held on the last Saturday of the month at Parker's Hotel. Dr. Holmes also, in later years, found the flourishing Saturday Club so constant in his recollection that he was disposed to deny the existence of any Atlantic Club. Properly speaking there never was any club, but only occasional dinners to which contributors were invited by the publishers. It was of one of the Saturday Club dinners that Lowell wrote 11 October, 1858: "You were good enough to tell me I might give you an account of our dinner. There at least was a topic, but I find that when I am full of work, I do not see the men I go among, but only shadows which make no impression. It is odd that when one's mind is excited by writing so that one cannot sleep, one should see in the same way a constant succession

of figures without really seeing them. They come
and change and go without any dependence on the
will, without any relation to the preoccupying
thought.

"I remember one good thing at our last dinner.
The dinner was for Stillman, and I proposed that
Judge Hoar should propose his health in a speech.
' *Sir!* ' (a long pause) ' in what I have already
said, I believe I speak the sentiments of every
gentleman present, and lest I should fail to do so
in what I might further say ' — (another pause) ' I
sit down.' And two days before at Agassiz' — the
Autocrat giving an account of his having learned
the fiddle, his brother John who sat opposite, exclaimed, 'I can testify to it; he has often fiddled
me out of the house as Orpheus did Eurydice out of
the infernal regions.' Is n't that good? It makes
me laugh to look at it now that I have written it
down. The Autocrat relating how Simmons the
Oak Hall man had sent him the two finest pears
— 'of trowsers?' interrupted somebody. But can
one send poured-out Champagne all the way to
Newport, and hope that one bubble will burst after
it gets there to tell what it used to be? A dinner
is never a good thing the next day. For the moment, though, what is better? We dissolve our
pearls and drink them nobly — if we have them —
but bring none away. A good talk is almost as
much out of the question among clever men as
among men who think themselves clever. Creation in pairs proves the foreordained superiority of
the *tête-à-tête*. Nevertheless, we live and dine and

die." And a few months later he recorded a bit about a dinner of the Atlantic people, which has had more than one raconteur. "Our dinner the other day was very pleasant. Only Mrs. Stowe and Miss Prescott, author of 'In a Cellar.' She is very nice and bright. Mrs. Stowe would not let us have any wine, and I told her that I was sorry she should deprive herself of so many pleasant dinners in England (whither she goes 3d August) by so self-denying an ordinance. She *took* at once, colored a little, laughed, and asked me to order some champagne."

Perhaps the very necessity for constant criticism, whether unrecorded, as where he determined the grounds for acceptance and rejection of manuscripts, or in his correspondence with contributors, and his own articles in the magazine, tended to stimulate Lowell's critical faculty. At any rate, in the midst of his busy hours he would now and then yield to the impulse, created by some current publication it may be, and give expression to judgments, either publicly or in his letters to friends. Thus his interest in "The Minister's Wooing" led him not only into writing the letter to Mrs. Stowe, already noticed, but into a careful, unsigned analysis of Mrs. Stowe's power in the *New York Tribune*.[1]

In August, 1859, Mr. Phillips, the publisher, died. Lowell characterized him as a man of great energy and pluck ; but during the months previ-

[1] This criticism also is given in C. E. Stowe's *The Life of Harriet Beecher Stowe*.

ous to his death Mr. Phillips had by no means
been in sound health, and had fretted much over
complications in his affairs. He seems to have
had reason, for a few weeks after the death of
Mr. Phillips, the firm of Phillips & Sampson suspended payment, and went into the hands of an
assignee, Mr. Harvey Jewell. " What is to come,
or why they have done it," Lowell wrote to Mr.
Norton, " I cannot conjecture. I trust arrangements will be made to put the *Atlantic* in good
hands. *That* at least is a paying thing. If it
shall end in my losing the editorship, it would
cause me little regret, for it would leave me more
time to myself." The assignee brought out the
October number of the magazine, pending the settlement of affairs, and there was a lively competition among publishers to secure the publication.
The Harpers proposed to buy it, to suppress their
rival, it was said ; there were offers from Philadelphia, and some of the younger men connected with
the firm of Phillips & Sampson made an effort to
establish a new firm which should buy the whole
business of Phillips & Sampson, including the
magazine. Mr. William Lee, who had left a large
sum with the firm when he withdrew from it, was
at the time travelling in Europe, and by a series
of mischances did not even learn of the situation
till it was too late for him to have a hand in any
reorganization. There was even a plan mooted
by which Lowell and his friends should buy the
magazine, but Lowell's own judgment was against
this. " It ought," he said, " to be in the hands of

a practical publisher for we should be in danger of running aground."

In the end, Ticknor & Fields bought the magazine. "As friend to friend," Lowell wrote to Mr. Norton, "I may say that I think it just the best arrangement possible, though I did not like to say so beforehand too plainly. I did not wish in any way to stand in ——'s light, but it is much better as it is. Whether T. will want *me* or not, is another question. I suppose that he will think that Fields will make a good editor, beside saving the salary, and F. may think so too. In certain respects he would, as the dining editor for example, to look after authors when they came to Boston and the like. I shall be quite satisfied, anyhow, — though the salary is a convenience, for I have done nothing to advance my own private interest in the matter."

The break-up of the business of Phillips & Sampson naturally led to the distribution of their copyright books, and Emerson was one of the authors publishing with them, who was now considering the transfer of his books to Ticknor & Fields. "I saw Ticknor yesterday," Lowell wrote him, 21 October, 1859, "and he says he wants the magazine to go on as it has gone. I never talked so long with him before, and the impression he gave was that of a man very shrewd in business after it is once in train, but very inert of judgment. I rather think Fields is captain when at home.[1] My opinion about your book is this. The

[1] Mr. Fields was in Europe when the transaction occurred.

book is a sure one at any rate, and if Little &
Brown publish it, they will sell copies to all who
would buy anything of yours at any rate. They
are eminently respectable and trustworthy. Ticknor would have of course the same chance to start
on that L. & B. would have, but I should think it
natural that he would be able to sell more copies
because the *kind* of book he publishes is rather
less of the library-completing sort than those of L.
& B., and because (I suppose) he has correspondents who always take a certain number of his
books whether or no. In short, it seems to me
that his chances in the way of distribution and
putting the volume on many counters and under
many eyes are the best. With an author like you
this is not much, but it is something. . . .

" I have quite a prize in the December number
— the story of a real filibuster written by himself.[1]
It is well done and will interest you. I wish to
get together a few of our chief tritons at a dinner
soon to make them acquainted with the new Posei-
don. Will you come? At Porter's or Parker's,
whichever you prefer, and as early as you like so
that you may get back to Concord."

After Mr. Fields returned from Europe the
question of the editorship came up anew. The
times were lowering, every one who had ventures
was taking in sail, Mr. Fields had been the editorial member of the book firm, his relations with
authors both at home and abroad were of the most

[1] " Experience of Samuel Absalom, Filibuster," by D. Deade-
rick.

friendly nature, and it was thus most reasonable
and natural that he should take charge of the
Atlantic, and Lowell resigned the editorship in a
half-serious, half-whimsical letter which Mr. Norton has printed.[1] It is clear that he had a divided
mind. He had become so far wonted to his work
that he had less anxiety in performing it, and he
had an honest pride in maintaining the high standard which his own taste and judgment had created.
He was glad also of the greater ease in money matters which the salary gave; and yet, as his letters
show, he welcomed the freedom from the daily
exactions of the editorial life, and the return to
the more self-determined occupation which he had
known most of his days.

Yet in editing the *Atlantic*, Lowell was more or
less consciously reënforcing the love of literature
which commanded him, and the combined labor of
academic study and teaching and the organization
of literature undoubtedly enriched his life, and
made him more ready for the large enterprises
which lay before him.

It was a great reënforcement of contentment
that he had returned to his old home at Elmwood.
There had been some talk of his taking the house
which Professor Felton was to give up on getting
a new one, but arrangement was made, finally, to
go back to Elmwood, and there the new establishment was set up with Dr. Lowell and Miss Rebecca
Lowell as joint occupants. This was a few months
before Lowell retired from the editorship of the

[1] *Letters*, i. 310.   May 23, 1861.

Atlantic, and his content appears in a letter which he was writing to Mr. Richard Grant White, 15 March, 1861: " We are having," he says, " the finest snowstorm of the winter. And what a delight to me to be here in my old garret at Elmwood, no college to go to (it is Saturday), sheltered by the very wings of the storm, and shut in from all the world by this white cloud of peace let down from heaven! The great chimney stacks roar a deep bass like Harlaem organ pipes. The old lightning rod thumps and rattles with every gust, as I used to hear it so long ago when there were no colleges nor magazines, nor any world outside our belt of pines. I am at *home* again. I like everything and everybody. Presently I shall draw on my Canada leggings and wade down to the post with this. I shall come back full of snow and northwest wind and appetite. I shall sit down at my own table in the old familiar room where I hope to welcome you one of these days." [1]

In his L'Envoi, " To the Muse," which appears to have been written not far from this time, he has some bright reflections on the elusiveness of the spirit of poetry which beckoned him. In point of fact there was very little poetry written by him while he was at once professor and editor. His " Biglow Papers " had been republished in England, with an Introduction by T. Hughes. His old friend, Mr. Gay, was in England at the time and had a hand in the business. The publication natu-

---

[1] The household at Elmwood was broken in upon apparently not long after the return of the Lowells, by the death of Dr. Charles Lowell, 20 January, 1861.

rally drew fresh attention to Lowell's satiric verse, and he wrote, a trifle piqued : " I confess I am a little jealous of people who like my humorous poems best. I guess they are right ' up to date,' but I feel also as if it were a little unfair to t' other half of me, which has not fairly worked itself free so as to combine — here I was interrupted day before yesterday, and I believe I was going to say — so as to combine the results of life with those of study. However, I grow more and more persuaded that what a man *is* is of greater consequence than what he *does*, especially than what he writes. The secret is, I suppose, to work oneself out clear so that what he is may be one with what he writes."

END OF VOLUME I

The Riverside Press

Electrotyped and printed by H. O. Houghton & Co.
Cambridge, Mass., U. S. A.

DISCARD

DATE